LEO STRAUSS AND THE RECOVERY OF MEDIEVAL POLITICAL PHILOSOPHY

Rochester Studies in
Medieval Political Thought

Edited by
Douglas Kries, Gonzaga University
Joshua Parens, University of Dallas

LEO STRAUSS AND THE RECOVERY OF MEDIEVAL POLITICAL PHILOSOPHY

Joshua Parens

UNIVERSITY OF ROCHESTER PRESS

Copyright © 2016 by Joshua Parens

All Rights Reserved. Except as permitted under current legislation, no part of this work may be photocopied, stored in a retrieval system, published, performed in public, adapted, broadcast, transmitted, recorded, or reproduced in any form or by any means, without the prior permission of the copyright owner.

First published 2016
Reprinted in paperback 2019

University of Rochester Press
668 Mt. Hope Avenue, Rochester, NY 14620, USA
www.urpress.com
and Boydell & Brewer Limited
PO Box 9, Woodbridge, Suffolk IP12 3DF, UK
www.boydellandbrewer.com

ISSN: 2380-565X
Hardcover ISBN: 978-1-58046-553-3
Paperback ISBN: 978-1-58046-958-6

Library of Congress Cataloging-in-Publication Data

Names: Parens, Joshua, 1961– author.
Title: Leo Strauss and the recovery of medieval political philosophy / Joshua Parens.
Description: Rochester, NY : University of Rochester Press, 2016. | Series: Rochester studies in medieval political thought, ISSN 2380-565X ; v. 1 | Includes bibliographical references and index.
Identifiers: LCCN 2015048904 | ISBN 9781580465533 (hardcover : alk. paper)
Subjects: LCSH: Strauss, Leo. | P olitical science—Philosophy. | Political science—History—To 1500. | Philosophy, Medieval. | Fārābī. | Maimonides, Moses, 1135–1204.
Classification: LCC JC251.S8 P37 2016 | DDC 320.01—dc23 LC record available at http://lccn.loc.gov/2015048904

This publication is printed on acid-free paper.
Printed in the United States of America

CONTENTS

Foreword by Douglas Kries		vii
Acknowledgments		xiii
Abbreviations		xv
Introduction		1

PART ONE: THE PECULIAR PLATONISM OF ALFARABI AND MAIMONIDES

1	The Comprehensiveness of Political Philosophy in Alfarabi and Maimonides	11
2	Law, Prophecy, and Philosopher as King and Outcast	17
3	Vipers, Weeds, and Disorder in the Whole	27

PART TWO: STRAUSS'S DEPARTURE FROM THE CHRISTIAN SCHOLASTIC PARADIGM

4	Escaping the Scholastic Paradigm	39
5	Spinoza's Scholasticism and Alfarabi's Platonism	55
6	The Differing Places of Metaphysics in Alfarabi and Thomas Aquinas	67

PART THREE: STRAUSS ON ALFARABI AND MAIMONIDES IN THE 1930s THROUGH THE 1950s

7	From Political Philosophy to Enlightened Kalām: The 1930s and 1940s	83

8	Maimonides's Secretiveness about Political Philosophy: The 1950s	95

PART FOUR: POLITICAL PHILOSOPHY AS FIRST PHILOSOPHY

9	Theoretical Philosophy, Political Philosophy, and Happiness	113
10	Maimonides's *Guide* as a Work of Political Philosophy	119
11	Da capo: An Introduction to the *Guide*	125
	Appendix: A Critique of Pines's "Limitations" Article	137
	Notes	149
	Bibliography	179
	Index	187

FOREWORD

This volume, *Leo Strauss and the Recovery of Medieval Political Philosophy*, is the first to be published in the series Rochester Studies in Medieval Political Thought. Such titles immediately give rise to a number of questions, the answers to which may not be self-evident: Why political thought? Why medieval political thought? Why does medieval political thought need to be recovered?

To answer the first of these questions, it is necessary to be more precise about the term "political thought." Political thought could be understood simply as "thinking about governments" or "thinking about governmental structures and institutions." If we understand the term in this way, we might ask questions about democratic political thought, for example, and talk about voting patterns and behaviors. We might study the role and function of the judicial branch as well as the structures of laws and the implications of economic policies. In this sense, "political thought" would look a lot like what is known in our time as "political science."

Such a view of political thought is not entirely wrong, but it is surely incomplete, at least from the medieval point of view. The medieval view of politics is based on the ancient view, which understood political thought, especially in the form of political philosophy, as being an architectonic science that orders the pursuit of all the other sciences in a city or regime. In this more elevated sense of the term, "political thought" is political philosophy in the grand sense, as the philosophical pursuit of all the human things. Such an inquiry studies the complete panoply of human possibilities, the various ways of living, the sorts of perfections available, and the fundamental problems faced by humanity. In this second sense, political thought is "architectonic anthropology," for such a study, when conducted in the spirit of Socrates, reveals human beings to themselves in a way no other intellectual pursuit is capable of.

A third sense of the term understands political thought, or political philosophy, almost as an oxymoron. According to this understanding, one must acknowledge that political life and philosophical life are not easily reducible to a common goal. Politics is about the good for human beings, but science aims at knowledge of the whole, both human and nonhuman. Because citizens and scientists have different ends, it is possible for those ends to conflict; philosophers can therefore undermine the political community. It thus behooves philosophers to attend to the requisite buffers between themselves and the cities in which they live. Philosophers must understand that their preoccupations may damage political society and that the city may defend itself in ways that damage philosophers, as was made clear to Socrates.

Perhaps an analogy can help explain this third sense of political thought: an astrophysicist peers through a powerful telescope and encounters light emitted from distant galaxies millions of years ago; obviously, the gaze of such an observer can have no bearing on the distant stars that he or she views. If, however, a physicist attempts to see with a specialized microscope an electron or other subatomic particle, that physicist will have to use a photon of light or a gamma ray to "illuminate" the particle. But by sensing it in this way, the physicist will change the particle's position or momentum. In other words, by the very act of looking the physicist will alter the subject of study.

According to this third sense of political thought or political philosophy, philosophers who study political society are like the physicist looking through the special microscope rather than the astrophysicist looking through the telescope. In other words, scientists need to be attentive to the way in which they themselves impact the political life that they seek to understand. Political philosophers are not disengaged investigators looking at events that they cannot possibly alter. They are not looking backward in time like the astrophysicist with the telescope. Rather, they are like the physicist studying the particle—their very act of philosophizing has a profound impact on human life. They, as it were, change the subject they study by their very act of studying it.

But why *medieval* political thought? Medieval political thought surely builds on the basis of ancient political thought, so perhaps it seems we should study ancient political philosophy rather than medieval. Of course, the medievals were themselves adamant about the necessity and worthiness of ancient political philosophy, especially as it was articulated by Plato and Aristotle. Because of the rise of theistic religions based on revelations, however, the medieval situation was also novel. Indeed, the most fascinating aspect of studying medieval political philosophy is the singularly remarkable situation created by the encounter of ancient political philosophy with Judaism, Christianity, and Islam.

This encounter of two originally very different intellectual impulses occurred primarily (not exclusively) within two languages: Latin and Arabic. The Latin tradition began within the ancient period itself, when Cicero undertook the enormous task of bringing Greek political philosophy into the Latin world. Cicero himself traveled within Greek-speaking lands and studied philosophy with the finest proponents of Greek philosophy in his time. He did not himself translate the works of Plato into Latin but rather wrote his own versions of Plato's *Republic* and *Laws* for the Roman situation and in the Latin tongue. Some of his friends as well as his critics, he tells us, were not especially pleased with his writing of philosophy at all, and others were not pleased that he wrote philosophy in Latin rather than Greek.

It was primarily through Cicero's dialogues that Augustine encountered ancient political thought. He knew other ancient Latin authors, of course, such as Vergil and Sallust. The African Christian bishop developed a genuine respect for ancient philosophy and expressed that respect in his own Latin writings; at the same time, he was extremely critical of it. The Platonists, he famously states, had glimpsed the goal of human existence but were completely clueless with respect to finding the correct means for attaining that goal.

The Latin medieval tradition relied principally on Cicero and Augustine for its political thought and political philosophy until the thirteenth century, when the *Politics* of Aristotle was translated into Latin. A new, complete, and scholarly edition of the *Nicomachean Ethics* was also made about the same time, along with translations of the rest of the books of Aristotle. The medieval disciples of Augustine resisted the new advocates of Aristotle's work, and these two interpretations of ancient philosophy were hotly disputed within the Latin Christian world. That dispute was still ongoing as the medieval period drew to a close.

Like the Latin tradition, the Arabic tradition of medieval political philosophy was thoroughly rooted in and dependent on ancient Greek philosophy. In the Arabic-speaking world, however, this tradition was not filtered through Cicero and Augustine. The figure standing at the head of the Arabic-language tradition of political philosophy is Alfarabi, who taught and wrote extensively during the first half of the tenth century. Alfarabi lived and worked in the eastern part of the Islamic world, spending much of his career in Baghdad. The study of political thought, however, spread into the western part of the Arabic-speaking world as well—especially into the region known as Andalusia, located on the Iberian Peninsula. The most renowned name associated with Islamic political thought in the west was probably that of Averroës, who died in 1198.

Rabbi Moshe ben Maimon, or Moses Maimonides, was a contemporary of Averroës in Andalusia and likewise wrote in Arabic, or rather Judeo-Arabic, which can be described as Arabic written in Hebrew alphabetic characters. Judah Halevi, perhaps the most remarkable Jewish medieval political thinker prior to Maimonides, also wrote in Judeo-Arabic. Maimonides, however, recommends that his readers study Alfarabi. We can speak, then, of an illustrious tradition of medieval political philosophy written primarily in Arabic that began with Alfarabi and extended at least through the death of Maimonides in 1204. Of course, some Muslims and especially Jews continued to articulate political thought after the thirteenth century. One of the more visible of these was Isaac Abravanel (or Abarbanel), who was writing in Hebrew toward the end of the Middle Ages.

The question remains, however, as to why we should study this unique form of political philosophy written primarily in two languages and within the context of three theistic religions. Three reasons emerge to justify such study. First, many of the most important medieval thinkers understood themselves as standing in an unbroken tradition of political philosophy that began with the Greeks. The medieval readers were thus first and foremost attempting to understand the ancients on their own terms. As a result, their understanding of ancient political philosophy is in many cases not identical with contemporary interpretations. The medievals thus offer interpretations of the ancients that could turn out to be superior to our own. At the very least, the medieval interpreters often challenge contemporary interpretations and hence offer the opportunity for deepening them.

A second reason for reading medieval political thought is to look forward to our modern situation. The Christian tradition of medieval political thought is rarely consulted by leaders of regimes today, but some groups of Christians continue to find resources in the medieval tradition for how to think about current political life. Within the Catholic world, it was not that long ago that Robert Bellarmine's political thought still held sway, and Bellarmine understood himself to be, above all else, a student of Thomas Aquinas.

The importance of reading the medieval tradition for Muslims and Jews, as well as for those who think about Islamic and Jewish politics, is today obvious. Whether Jews live in the Diaspora or in the modern state of Israel, they will find insight in how to negotiate the questions of religion and politics in Maimonides and in Judah Halevi, to name only two. And nothing could be more relevant to modern Islamic political thought than reading the great medieval tradition that includes Alfarabi, Avicenna, and Ibn Tufayl—again, to name only a few.

But the most important reason for reading medieval political philosophy—just as for reading any author or group of authors—is that it helps those who study it better understand themselves and their fellow human beings. The first two reasons just mentioned—looking backward and looking forward—are rather extrinsic and somewhat instrumental. This third and ultimate reason is intrinsic. Maimonides, Alfarabi, and Augustine all enable thoughtful human beings to know themselves better, and of course "know thyself" was the dictate with which Socrates himself began to philosophize.

But why did medieval political philosophy need to be *recovered*, as the title of Joshua Parens's new book suggests? In the first instance, it was not so much that the Latin tradition of political philosophy needed to be recovered, but the Arabic. The Latin tradition was primarily Christian; it tended to preserve Augustine and Thomas Aquinas, not to mention their sources, especially Cicero and Aristotle, respectively. Perhaps nineteenth- or twentieth-century Christian readers did not understand Augustine and Thomas as well as earlier scholars, but the texts were always available and there always existed pockets of readers who took them seriously.

The Islamic Arabic tradition, however, came to be almost completely forgotten. At the dawn of the twentieth century, very little was even known about Alfarabi. Many of his writings existed only in manuscript form; some of the major works were completely unknown to the world of scholarship. But Alfarabi had influenced the subsequent Islamic tradition, and so long as his work was neglected, it was harder to understand what the others had done. Indeed, Maimonides says that he was greatly indebted to Alfarabi; without understanding Alfarabi, therefore, it may not be possible to understand accurately the most towering figure in the history of Jewish political philosophy.

Joshua Parens's book explains how the work of Leo Strauss led to the recovery of Alfarabi and the rest of the Arabic tradition of political philosophy. Only the barest outline of that story may be recorded here: Strauss was a young Jewish scholar studying in the enlightened German universities in the late 1920s and early 1930s. He became increasingly disaffected with Enlightenment thought, whether in its Christian or Jewish context, and began to contemplate a return to premodern philosophy. He began to study and write on Maimonides, but Maimonides quickly pointed him back toward Alfarabi. By 1936, commenting on a then recently published edition of a work of Alfarabi, Strauss was referring to him as a "towering figure" who set the course of future developments in medieval Arabic political philosophy.

The recovery of Arabic political philosophy was not confined to the efforts of Strauss himself, of course. We cannot discuss all the important names here, but mention should especially be made of Muhsin Mahdi and Charles Butterworth. Mahdi (1926–2007) was an Iraqi who came to study with Strauss at the University of Chicago. He went on to complete a distinguished career at Harvard that was devoted to the translation and interpretation especially of Alfarabi and Ibn Khaldun. Butterworth, former student of Mahdi and professor emeritus at the University of Maryland, has taught and researched on Arabic political philosophy in France, Germany, and Egypt. His work is especially important in the English-speaking world because of his translations of Alfarabi and Averroës.

Although Islam arose after Judaism and Christianity, the emergence of political philosophy within the Islamic world can be said to have preceded the emergence of political philosophy within Judaism and Christianity, or at least to have preceded the major medieval flowerings of political philosophy in Judaism and Christianity. But if this is so, then we will not be particularly surprised to find that the recovery of Islamic political thought has had echoes for how to understand subsequent Jewish and Christian authors. Strauss himself used his discovery of Alfarabi and other Islamic writers to offer to the world a dramatically new—and still hotly contested—interpretation of Maimonides. Alfarabi did not directly enter the Latin Christian world in the Middle Ages to any great extent, but much of his thought indirectly did so, especially through the work of Averroës. Thus, the recovery of Islamic political philosophy has also renewed interest in so-called Latin Averroism in the Christian world. It is necessary to note in this context the work of Ernest Fortin, also a student of Strauss, on Dante Alighieri.

For these reasons, then, *Leo Strauss and the Recovery of Medieval Political Philosophy* is an appropriate volume with which to begin the Rochester Studies in Medieval Political Thought, and it is with great satisfaction that we begin the series in this way. We do, however, want to be clear that the series is not restricted to Straussian views of medieval political philosophy. Indeed, it would be a mistake to conclude that Strauss and his students are the only scholars working to provide the contemporary world with a clearer understanding of the insights of medieval political thinkers. Rochester Studies in Medieval Political Thought has as its goal the publication of worthy manuscripts, collections of articles, and translations and commentaries that treat medieval political thinking in all its remarkable variations.

Douglas Kries
Spokane, Washington

ACKNOWLEDGMENTS

Earlier forms of some of the material in this volume have been published previously. Chapter 1 appeared as "Showing Students the Importance of Political Philosophy in Medieval Islamic and Jewish Philosophy," *Studies in Medieval and Renaissance Teaching (SMART)* 18, no. 1 (2011): 61–68. Chapter 2 was published in French translation as "La loi divine et la prophétologie médiévale," in *Leo Strauss: À quoi sert la philosophie politique?*, ed. François Coppens, David Janssens, and Yuri Yomtov (Paris: Presses Universitaires de France, 2014), 85–103. Chapter 4 appeared as "Escaping the Scholastic Paradigm: The Dispute between Strauss and His Contemporaries about How to Approach Islamic and Jewish Medieval Philosophy," in *Encountering the Medieval in Modern Jewish Thought*, ed. Aaron Hughes and James Diamond (New York: Brill, 2012), 203–27. Chapter 7 appeared as "Leo Strauss on Farabi, Maimonides, et al. in the 1930s," in *Reorientation: Strauss in the 1930s*, ed. Martin D. Yaffe and Richard S. Ruderman (New York: Palgrave Macmillan, 2014), 157–70. Chapter 8 appeared as "Strauss on Maimonides's Secretive Political Science," in *Leo Strauss's Defense of the Philosophic Life: Reading "What Is Political Philosophy?,"* ed. Rafael Major (Chicago: University of Chicago Press, 2012), 116–36; and in *Perspectives on Political Science* 39, no. 2 (2010): 82–86. The appendix appeared as "Are Alfarabi and Maimonides Precursors to Kant?," in *Fruits of Friendship: Seven Essays in Honor of Laurence Berns*, ed. Joseph Cohen (Annapolis, MD: Free State, 2011), 77–88.

I thank the proprietors and publishers of these works for their kind permission to reprint.

ABBREVIATIONS

Alfarabi

AH	*Attainment of Happiness*
BR	*Book of Religion*

Maimonides

Guide	*Guide of the Perplexed*
Logic	*Treatise on the Art of Logic*

Strauss

CM	*The City and Man* (1964)
FP	"Farabi's *Plato*" (1945)
MSPS	"Maimonides' Statement on Political Science" (1953)
PAW	*Persecution and the Art of Writing* (1952)
PL	*Philosophy and Law* (1935)
PPr	"The Place of the Doctrine of Providence according to Maimonides" (1937)
SCR	*Spinoza's Critique of Religion* (1930)
SRMF	"Some Remarks on the Political Science of Maimonides and Farabi" (1936)
WIPP	*What Is Political Philosophy?* (1959)

INTRODUCTION

Leo Strauss identifies the theme of his thought and writings as the theologico-political problem, but he intentionally avoids defining the problem, leaving it to his readers to piece together.[1] Obviously, it is an allusion to the title of the first work he wrote a book about, namely, Spinoza's *Theologico-Political Treatise*. The closest thing to a direct indication of the problem is his presentation, in his 1965 preface to the English translation of that first book, of what he calls the "theologico-political predicament" he found himself as a Jew living in Germany in 1925–28. That predicament seems to be the result of the tension between being a Jew and being a German. As he goes on to explain, according to Nietzsche, "I have not yet met a German who was favorably disposed toward the Jews."[2] In other words, being a Jew was at odds with being a German. Being Jewish, a theological affiliation, despite the apparent success of Jewish assimilation into German life, was at odds with the basic political fact of being a German. Without sophisticated exploration of the *Theologico-Political Treatise*, it is well known to nearly all scholars how important a role Spinoza played in making Jewish assimilation possible. His attempt to facilitate this political solution of the theologico-political problem seemed to have failed, at least in 1925–28 in Germany. This gap between Jew and German, or between the minority of Jews and the majority of Christians, including largely religiously disaffected Christians at the beginning of the twentieth century, however, seems to be emblematic of a much more enduring problem. Although it is natural for us to assume that what Strauss means by the theologico-political problem must be a problem specific to monotheistic religious communities, evidence exists that that cannot be the case. To begin with, Strauss states in the 1965 preface to the reissued *Hobbes' Politische Wissenschaft* that "since then [that is, from before writing the Hobbes book, 1934–35 until 1965] the theologico-political problem has remained *the* theme of my investigations."[3] Through the 1950s and 1960s, when most of Strauss's attention had shifted from a focus on medieval and early modern authors to Platonic or Socratic political philosophy, he was still working on that problem. Strauss was less interested in the specific case of himself as a Jew than he was in the enduring and underlying problem to which this specific historical case pointed. We have little doubt that our use of "persecution" has already given away what we have in mind, that is, the specific case pointed to the ultimately more profound and enduring problem, the problem of the persecution of the philosopher. Like the Jew, the philosopher is persecuted for holding beliefs other than (or questioning) those embraced by society as a whole. The phrase "theologico-political problem" is a challenging way of indicating the theme most common in Strauss's writings, namely, the theme of the philosopher and the city or the philosopher and the Law or, put most simply, the city and man. Ultimately, Strauss is less interested in the preface to the Spinoza book in the persecution of Jews as a group by Germans as a group than he is in that phenomenon etched into the memory of educated people throughout the West, the persecution of Socrates, which he seems to have been specially attuned to as a member of such a group.

The focus of this book, however, is on Strauss's writings on the Islamic and Jewish medieval political philosophers, especially Alfarabi (ca. 870–950 CE) and Maimonides (1135–1204). In these authors the problem of the relation between the philosopher and the Law is evident throughout. Yet that problem as a problem has all too often come to be obscured by late modern tendencies to adopt syntheses of reason and faith or philosophy and revelation that were all too foreign to our medieval forbears. That tendency has been aided and abetted by the very great difficulties of interpretation posed by works such as Maimonides's *Guide of the Perplexed*.[4] The *Guide* readily appears to the modern eye to be a work of "Jewish philosophy" or "Jewish theology." Our penchant for syntheses of the components in Strauss's theologico-political problem means that we tend from the beginning to misunderstand what kind of work the *Guide* is. Although Strauss was for a short time in the late 1930s straightforward in identifying political science as either at or near the center of the *Guide*, by the beginning of the 1940s he had retreated to a kind of obscurity in identifying the genre of the *Guide* that cannot but remind us of the obscurity surrounding the theologico-political problem. He retreated in "The Literary Character of the *Guide for the Perplexed*" to the unusual claim that the *Guide* is a work of "enlightened *kalām*."[5] This movement from political science to enlightened kalām coincides with the moment, namely, *Persecution and the Art of Writing*, when Strauss makes thematic the phenomenon of persecution and the attendant development of the art of esoteric writing. Only here does Strauss begin to work out, in a systematic way, the difference between the exoteric surface and the esoteric depth of writings. As we will see, then, Strauss can maintain that the *Guide* is a work of enlightened kalām on the exoteric surface and political science or political philosophy at esoteric depth. Neither one of these coincides exactly with the widely accepted characterizations of the *Guide* as Jewish philosophy or Jewish theology. Those are instead blurring syntheses of the different levels in Maimonides's arguments.

There are perhaps two main causes of our tendency toward such syntheses: the philosophy of culture or religion that thrived in late nineteenth- and early twentieth-century Germany, which shaped significantly all contemporary study of premodern Jewish texts, and the influence of scholarship on medieval Christian Scholasticism on the study of medieval Jewish and Islamic thought. The former of these is dealt with explicitly and at length by Strauss in both *Philosophy and Law* and the preface to the Spinoza book.[6] We will touch on this only lightly in the rest of this book because Strauss deals with it at such length. For now, let it suffice to say that philosophy of culture was a reaction to the unbelief of early modern philosophy. Thinkers like Hobbes and Spinoza made it difficult to maintain belief in monotheism in the face of their mockery of traditional revealed religion. But they also seemed to make it more difficult for citizens to see their own good in the common good. Consequently, thinkers like Rousseau and the German Idealists advocated a return to religion of sorts, which led eventually to attempted syntheses of modern religious toleration with renewed faith in a religion of the heart, the conscience, and the emotions—more than a religion with clear and unambiguous doctrines. Those attempted syntheses were most widely trumpeted at the end of the nineteenth and beginning of the twentieth centuries, at about the same moment thinkers such as Nietzsche pronounced that "God is dead." A religion of religious morals without belief in God became increasingly difficult to sustain. These rough outlines of this story are more or less known to all of us.

We turn now to that other reason for finding syntheses where they may not exist, the scholarly influence of the study of Christian Scholasticism. Here, being no expert in Christian Scholasticism, I am interested only in what is obvious: Christianity presents itself, at least in the medieval period and at least in its most authoritative expression, the thought of Thomas Aquinas, as what can loosely be called a synthesis of reason and faith. The latter, or the grace that accompanies faith, is said to complete or perfect the former, much as art was said to perfect nature in Aristotle's thought. Such a synthesis, or harmony of reason and faith, then, warrants the use of phrases such as "Christian philosophy." If we are to trust Strauss, the relation of reason to faith or of philosophy and Law in Islam and Judaism is not as synthetic or harmonious. Rather than provide an extensive exploration of twentieth-century Christian Scholasticism, we will devote part 2 of this book to an exploration of Strauss's interpretation of medieval Islamic and Jewish political philosophy against the background of prevailing interpretations of these schools of thought under the profound influence of scholarship on Christian Scholasticism.

Let us return now from our digression on the syntheses that obscure a proper appreciation of the character of medieval Islamic and Jewish political philosophy to make explicit the following question: what might be the relation between the obscurity surrounding the theologico-political problem and the obscurity surrounding the genre of writings like Maimonides's *Guide*? It seems likely that there is an inner connection between these two obscurities. These syntheses claim to reconcile incompatible poles of belief and unbelief or faith and reason. The claim that faith perfects reason implies, among many other things, that no such incompatibility exists. What might the relation between reason and revelation have to do with the difference between esoteric depth and exoteric surface? If reason or philosophy or the philosophic life is incompatible with widely accepted religious beliefs or the religious way of life, would it be sensible for the philosopher to declare open battle with the faith of his community? Or might it be more sensible to question the accepted views as it were between the lines? As Strauss explains it, the express purpose of enlightened kalām is to defend religion in a manner that is "intelligent" rather than "imaginative" (*PAW*, 41). "Intelligent" here, as we will see, does not mean merely as an intelligent believer would defend religion but in a manner that does not violate the "nature of existence," which nature is identified by philosophy. Although enlightened kalām may defend religion, it does not thereby repudiate philosophy—even though earlier forms of kalām, what Strauss calls "vulgar *kalām*" had precisely that purpose. Why then cannot the surface of the text simply be "political science" or "political philosophy" rather than enlightened kalām? The obvious answer is that the Law requires defense. A less obvious answer becomes apparent when one begins to consider just how strange and unprecedented it was to declare the *Guide* was more or less centrally concerned with political science. Maimonides appears at times (*Logic*, chap. 14; *Guide*, 2.39) to argue that a community that has received a divinely revealed law or Law has no need for political science.[7] Indeed, one might well wonder what more pressing purpose the revelation at Sinai might have than to relieve man of the responsibility of developing a political philosophy. Here it should be understood that traditional Jewish interpretation of the Law is a far cry from what we mean by political philosophy. Interpreting the Law normally means taking one's lead from God and the authoritative tradition of interpretation one has inherited. Political philosophy to deserve the label "philosophy" cannot take its lead from any tradition, no matter how authoritative. How one might know what God expects or thinks outside of such a tradition is beyond the ken of any Muslim or Jewish tradition of jurisprudence or theology with which I am familiar.

The theologico-political problem is at its most basic level the tension between the authoritative opinion of one's community and the questioning of that opinion by the philosopher. That tension recurs in other sometimes essentially identical and at times somewhat different ways: city and man (that is, philosopher), philosophy and Law, Jew and German. The variety of forms contributes to the obscurity surrounding it. One expression of that tension is the opposition between exoteric surface and esoteric depth. Syntheses of the kind claimed by Christian Scholasticism seek to overcome this tension. When carried over to Islamic and Jewish political philosophy such syntheses obscure or conceal the underlying tension, the theologico-political problem.

Why did this problem become *the* theme of Strauss's inquiries? After all, in many of his writings about medieval Jewish and Islamic political philosophy, at least up to "Farabi's *Plato*" (1945), Strauss seems to undercut the centrality of political philosophy and thereby of the theologico-political problem.[8] By turns, he states that political philosophy is "the last," not the central, inquiry of medieval Islamic and Jewish philosophy (*PL*, 70). He emphasizes that because Maimonides's community has received the divine Law they need not inquire into it; they are free to "aristotelize," that is, to engage in *theoria* or contemplation (133). He even insists that political philosophy is merely the exoteric surface of philosophy (*FP*, 364–65, 382–83).[9] In other words, even though Strauss was writing a great deal about political philosophy because he was inquiring into the theologico-political problem, he seemed at least until the middle of the 1940s to undercut the centrality of his own central theme—in favor of some more purely theoretical inquiry.[10] The clearest indications that something changed in his understanding (possibly at the time identified by Heinrich Meier as Strauss's shipwreck of 1946) then became most obvious at least by the 1950s in his characterizations of political philosophy or Platonic or Socratic political philosophy in "What Is Political Philosophy?" (in *WIPP*; 1954–55), *Thoughts on Machiavelli* (1958), and "On Aristotle's Politics" (in *City and Man*; 1962).[11] In "What Is Political Philosophy?" Socratic philosophy shows up as an inquiry into the whole that is not so purely theoretical in the Aristotelian sense as, at least the received view of, metaphysics or theology. Although it remains the inquiry into the whole, it is an inquiry into the irreducible dualism of homogeneity and heterogeneity: the homogeneity of mathematics and the making of the arts and crafts, and the heterogeneity of the ends sought by the statesman and the educator.[12] What other than this dualism constitutes the theologico-political problem? The most difficult challenge we confront in this book is whether the highest and most important questions ultimately violate the conception of theoretical philosophy we've inherited from Aristotle—or from the Scholastic interpretation of Aristotle.

In *Thoughts on Machiavelli* Strauss enunciates what has been called his golden word: "The problem inherent in the surface of things, and only in the surface of things, is the heart of things" (13). And in *City and Man* he clarifies the statements made in "What Is Political Philosophy?" by not only identifying that fundamental dualism as "noetic heterogeneity" but also stating that political philosophy broadly understood is the "first philosophy" (19–21). It is significant that this is a characterization of Socratic political philosophy offered in the middle of a chapter "On Aristotle's Politics." Talk of "first philosophy" of course brings to mind Aristotle's characterization of the inquiry of his *Metaphysics* as theology as first philosophy (1026a18–33). It was Aristotle, not Plato, who established a discipline of political science in relative autonomy from metaphysics.

What significance can be attached to these characterizations of Socratic or Platonic political philosophy, the political philosophy of greatest relevance to medieval Islamic and Jewish political philosophy? Although pure theoretical philosophy had appeared to be the core of philosophy for Strauss through the middle of the 1940s, he seems late in the 1940s to have come to appreciate the extent to which his own interpretation of political philosophy may have been enthralled to the prejudice in favor of pure theory. Perhaps political philosophy, the surface of things, reveals more about the heart of things than he had thought, even as he was rediscovering the lost continent of medieval political philosophy. Although that surface *began* to appear as early as the publication of "The Literary Character of the *Guide for the Perplexed*" (1941; reprinted in *PAW* in 1952) in the play of surface and depth elaborated in that work, the subsequent characterization of surface and depth in "Farabi's *Plato*" seemed to reiterate the superficiality and purely defensive role of political philosophy. In "Farabi's *Plato*," political things appear as little more than artificial or conventional things—a far cry from the sophistication of Strauss's explorations of Socratic political philosophy in the 1950s.

Let us digress for a moment to consider the question of development in Strauss's thought. That his thought did develop is widely recognized by both his supporters and his detractors. Does not such a suggestion violate his admonitions against historicism and a corollary of historicism, the temptation to explain away conflicts between works by individual philosophers by appeal to development? Strauss's argument applies to works of philosophy as philosophic works; it does not apply to the largely scholarly effort to dig his way out of the cave beneath the cave through what he characterizes as a "most elaborate 'artificial' introduction" (*PAW*, 155) and what he describes as an "intrinsically philosophic history of philosophy" (*WIPP*, 76). Strauss's kind of scholarly inquiry into past philosophy is not something that premodern philosophy required. Scholarship (even if it can also be dubbed "philosophic") is characterized by an essential feature of scholarship, namely, that one might achieve progress in one's "interpretation" of an author (*PAW*, 143), especially when new or forgotten phenomena such as esotericism are involved.

Does all this mean then that our exploration of Strauss's writings on medieval Jewish and Islamic political philosophy, most of which were written in the 1930s and 1940s, will reveal little about the mature Strauss's understanding of political philosophy? To begin with, it should be underlined that we are not limited here to his writings of the 1930s and 1940s. We include an exploration of Strauss's crucial study of Maimonides's *Treatise on the Art of Logic* called "Maimonides' Statement on Political Science" (1953, in *WIPP*). It is not by chance that that study treats the very issue he may have misjudged in *Philosophy and Law*, namely, the misimpression that revelation had freed Maimonides of the task of having to engage with real seriousness in political philosophy. If any work leaves one with this impression, it is the *Logic*. Comparison with the similar *Guide*, 2.39, and as it is juxtaposed with the epitome of Aristotelian political science in the opening of 2.40, indicates that revelation had not relieved Maimonides of the task of engaging in political philosophy. Rather, the claims of revelation merely necessitate an apparent abstraction from political philosophy, much as those claims necessitate an apparent abstraction from prudence.[13] Although Maimonides avoids explicit reference to these terms, they are in the foreground of inquiry in these works. Strauss's initial impression at the end of the 1930s that the *Guide* is a work of political science or political philosophy is only reinforced by his discovery that the surface of the *Guide* is enlightened kalām. But Strauss seems not to have fully appreciated the significance of the interplay between surface and depth, which is the theologico-political problem, until sometime after these elements came into play. Indeed, it is difficult to appreciate the importance of that interplay before one has discovered the elements. For that reason, it is crucial for us to explore in sufficient depth the inquiries of the 1930s and 1940s, as we will especially in part 3 of this book.

Part 4 considers what Strauss's study of medieval Islamic and Jewish political philosophy, especially on Alfarabi and Maimonides, contributed to his mature view of political philosophy as more than merely a part of philosophy and more than merely the exoteric face of philosophy but what he eventually labeled as "the core of philosophy or 'the first philosophy'" (*CM*, 20).

Part 1 introduces in the broadest terms this area of inquiry, highlighting the obvious ways in which political philosophy in the medieval Islamic and Jewish setting differs from what is generally the more narrowly focused political science of medieval Christian thought. And it explores two of the most central and contradictory tropes in medieval Islamic and Jewish political philosophy, namely, the identification of the philosopher-king with the legislating prophet and the vision of the philosopher as solitary: philosopher as savior of political life versus philosopher as outcast.

PART ONE

The Peculiar Platonism of Alfarabi and Maimonides

CHAPTER ONE

The Comprehensiveness of Political Philosophy in Alfarabi and Maimonides

Medieval Islamic philosophy and medieval Jewish philosophy are, for the most part, Platonic in character. We do not mean by this that these medieval philosophers adhere slavishly to one or another metaphysical dogma widely attributed to Plato. Rather, we mean that, for the most part, they follow a Platonic approach to the relation between theoretical and practical science—that is, they tend to avoid drawing this distinction or to blur the distinction. In contrast, medieval Christian philosophy, especially medieval Christian political thought, not only embraces but even deepens the divide that Aristotle established between theoretical and practical science. Due in no small part to this divide, Christian thinkers such as Aquinas (1225–74 CE), Dante (1265–1321), and Marsilius of Padua (1275–1342) find in Aristotle an important resource for thinking about secular political powers (practice), at least to some extent, in isolation from the ecclesiastical power (theory). After all, if theoretical science can be separated from practical science, then why not separate ecclesiastical power from secular political power?[1] By rejecting Aristotle's theoretical-practical divide, at certain crucial junctures, medieval Islamic and Jewish philosophers make such a separation of politics from religion a more remote possibility. Medieval Muslims and Jews felt little need or desire to separate secular from ecclesiastical powers.[2] Leaving aside the practical issue of the relation between these two powers, the key reason for the avoidance of the theoretical-practical distinction in Muslim and Jewish philosophical circles—especially in Islamic and Jewish *political* philosophy, where one might expect it to be most in play—is that Muslim and Jewish Law are both comprehensive or total Laws, covering both actions and beliefs, the practical and the theoretical.

The suppression of this divide between theoretical and practical science has far-reaching consequences for the teaching and study of medieval Islamic and Jewish philosophy. First, one cannot assume in this setting as something of a default view, as one often might in the Christian setting, that theology provides the (theoretical) ground for (practical) human affairs. In this respect, medieval Christian thinkers tend to follow a model derived from the Bible.[3] From certain claims about God, certain claims about the political (used broadly to cover ethics as well) order can be inferred. In contrast, the relation between theoretical and practical in the Islamic and Jewish traditions tends to be far less "foundationalist" than in the Christian tradition—or, to put the matter somewhat more precisely, there is a more dialectical relationship between theoretical and practical science in these traditions.

Second, the dividing line between what belongs to theoretical philosophy and what to practical philosophy is not as neat in the Islamic and Jewish traditions as in the Christian tradition. This dividing line is often only intensified by modern scholarship, which sees (often mistakenly) precursors to modern distinctions between theoretical and applied science. To exemplify our point, let us take the Christian tradition first. On the one hand, most anthologies in medieval Christian *theoretical* philosophy—no matter how deeply informed by theology they may be—cover and are divided thematically (for example, universals and categories) in ways that are easily recognizable to the contemporary reader as theoretical. On the other hand, medieval Christian *political* philosophy or science is concerned with a more narrowly political subject matter, for example, forms of kingship and alternative regimes, than are its counterparts in Islam and Judaism. These political themes in anthologies of Christian political thought could never be confused with metaphysics or theology. As we will see shortly, matters could hardly be more different in medieval Islamic and Jewish philosophy—not that that has prevented editors from producing anthologies of Islamic and Jewish theoretical philosophy divided along similar lines as their Christian counterparts. Nonetheless, the studied avoidance of the theoretical-practical distinction—especially when philosophers inquire into the central phenomenon of these traditions, the revealed Law (*sharīʿa*)—makes it difficult and unwise to attempt to study theoretical philosophy in these traditions in apparent isolation from practical philosophy.

Third, the sciences central in Christianity are not necessarily the disciplines central in these other traditions. To take the most relevant example, the unquestioned queen of the sciences in Christianity, theology, is not matched by a comparably authoritative or central form of theology in the Muslim and Jewish traditions. Indeed, there is another science, namely, jurisprudence, which holds a position of authority in medieval Jewish and Islamic thought comparable to theology in Christianity.[4] Once again, precisely because of the interplay of the theoretical and the practical sciences, we should not be surprised to find that the queen of the sciences in these traditions is so very far from being purely theoretical.

Let us consider one exemplary author from the Islamic tradition, Alfarabi, and one from the Jewish tradition, Maimonides, to bear out the main lines of this argument. Although Alfarabi appears first, let us begin with Maimonides both because he offers a thematic discussion of the science he is engaged in and because his answer, cryptic as it is, highlights so well the challenge of attempting to understand these traditions, especially if approached from the Western or Christian point of view.[5] In his greatest and most profound work, the *Guide of the Perplexed*, Maimonides writes,

> It is not the purpose of this treatise to . . . teach those who have not engaged in any study other than the science of the Law—I mean the legalistic study of the Law. For the purpose of this treatise and of all those like it is the science of the Law in its true sense. Or rather its purpose is to give indications to a religious man . . . [who has also] studied the sciences of the philosophers and come to know what they signify (pt. 1, introd., 5).

Such a person, Maimonides continues, will have become troubled by the apparent incongruities between the "externals of the Law" and what the philosophic sciences teach. The purpose of this treatise is to point such a person toward the resolution of those troubles or perplexities. Such navigation between philosophy and Law could hardly be adequately described as purely theoretical, metaphysical, or theological.

The *Guide* concerns the Law, but more specifically what Maimonides calls the "true science of the Law," as opposed to the legalistic study of the Law (*fiqh*). The legalistic study of the Law is the genre of the Written and Oral Law (Torah and Talmud), that is, jurisprudence. In contrast, what Maimonides means by the "true science of the Law" is somehow more fundamental or deeper than the Law itself. Here is a first approximation to what is an extraordinarily elusive science: on the one hand, it seems to concern what had been called in the Islamic tradition the study of the roots of the Law (*usūl al-fiqh*).[6] On the other hand, it also comes, over the course of the *Guide*, to involve the defense of the Law or what was called kalām (usually translated "dialectical theology") in the Islamic tradition.[7] Two thoughts are likely to occur to the student of medieval thought with little experience with Islam and Judaism, as soon as matters are framed in this somewhat foreign way: the roots of the Law must be metaphysical, and defense of the Law is presumably at least a part of theology. Yet the student should be cautioned against leaping to conclusions about whether the roots of the Law are metaphysical or theological—in spite of the obvious dimension of "dialectical theology" in Maimonides's *Guide*. Not only is dialectical theology lower in rank than jurisprudence historically in these traditions, but also dialectical theology was historically engaged in almost solely for apologetic purposes. Soon the student may be tempted to wonder whether Jewish thinkers are incapable of rising to the level of a more purely theoretical form of theology—what we tend to think of as a more purely objective inquiry into theological matters. Yet we should not be surprised that theology, here, seems more tainted by practical considerations or is more apologetic than in Christianity. After all, what is at stake in Maimonides's inquiry is the Law's continuity. The Law itself is a theoretico-practical affair.[8]

At least when he announces the audience of his work, and thus the discipline to which it belongs, in the introduction to part 1, Maimonides does not make any reference to theology.[9] We have heard only about the legalistic study of law or jurisprudence (and about the mysterious "true science of the Law"). Does jurisprudence have a correlate in Christianity? Some have suggested that canon law might be a good equivalent in the Christian tradition. Yet no one would suggest that canon law has the kind of centrality that the Law has in Islam and Judaism. As a corollary to the importance of jurisprudence in these traditions, we are not surprised to find that dialectical theology, over the course of the history of both Islam and Judaism, acquired a lower status than jurisprudence. Here, we have hit upon one of the things that makes bridging the divide between Christian thought, on the one hand, and these other two, on the other, so difficult. Put very roughly, jurisprudence, or the legalistic study of the Law, is to Islam and Judaism what theology is to Christianity.[10] Unfortunately, this does not mean that one can hold up jurisprudence to theology and compare them. Rather it means that the roots of the Law, assuming that there are some theoretical ones, are going to lack the more purely theoretical character of much of Christian theology.

Our glance at Maimonides's *Guide* has so far focused on the different disciplines that play a central role in Judaism (and Islam), which was our third main point in distinguishing medieval Jewish and Islamic philosophy from their Christian counterparts. Although our example from Maimonides has enabled us to touch obliquely on the relation between theoretical and practical science in medieval Jewish (and Islamic) philosophy, let us turn now to consider some more direct evidence from Alfarabi's writings, showing how unlike the views of Christian authors are his views on the relation between theoretical and practical science. In the most popular anthologies and histories (let us take the most reputable one, Majid Fakhry's *A History of Islamic Philosophy*), Alfarabi is presented as a Neoplatonist in his metaphysics.[11] And this metaphysical theology is treated as the foundation of his thought. In other words, Alfarabi is treated on the "foundationalist" model of Christian Scholasticism.

To show how unlike the standard Christian model Alfarabi is, let us consider the role of Neoplatonism in his works.[12] Above all, Alfarabi nowhere *argues* for a Neoplatonic theology or cosmology. Rather, in two of his writings, the *Political Regime* and the *Virtuous City*, he opens with what can most accurately be described as Neoplatonic *descriptions* of the cosmos, followed by discussions of politics, which are far less descriptive and much more dialectical or philosophic treatments of politics.[13] In addition, in his *Book of Religion*, most of which is devoted to the most philosophic or scientific inquiry in his corpus into what is a virtuous religion or revealed Law, Alfarabi tacks on a similar Neoplatonic description of the cosmos, this time, to the *end* of that work (*BR*, secs. 19–27). We make two observations: Nearly everywhere we find theology or cosmology in Alfarabi we also find politics.[14] And, in what appears to be his most philosophic inquiry into the central phenomenon of Islam, virtuous religion or Law, this cosmology or metaphysics or theology appears at the end, not the beginning. The *Book of Religion* indicates, however subtly, that it, unlike works of Christian Scholasticism, is not founded on a previously established theoretical foundation. Once again, theoretical science and practical science in the medieval Islamic and Jewish traditions appear to stand in a more dialectical relation than is the norm in the Christian tradition.

In his trilogy, the *Philosophy of Plato and Aristotle*, one of his most ambitious works and certainly one with more than its share of forays into metaphysics, if not extensive quasi-theological descriptions of the cosmos, Alfarabi concludes the entirety of the work, and in particular the part on the philosophy of Aristotle, with the assertion that "we do not possess metaphysical science."[15] Although he likely does not mean by this that we know nothing about being qua being, he seems to mean that human knowledge of the whole is in some decisive respect incomplete. This provides us with the opportunity to conclude with a brief reflection on the Platonic character of his thought.

The main reason Plato did not hit upon the Aristotelian distinction between theoretical and practical philosophy may have been that he saw no need to (or possibility of) detach(ing) inquiry into the whole from inquiry into human affairs. He saw that the incompleteness of our knowledge of the whole could not help but limit and color our knowledge of human affairs. In spite of his division of theoretical from practical science, I doubt that Aristotle thought otherwise. But perhaps Aristotle thought that, as an antidote to possible misconceptions deriving from Socrates's notion of philosopher-kings, it might be better to put practical philosophy at a greater distance from theoretical science than Socrates had appeared to.[16] However things may have been with Plato and Aristotle, one thing is clear: The character of the revealed Law precludes the rigorous application of an Aristotelian wall of separation between theoretical and practical science in medieval Islamic and Jewish philosophy—especially political philosophy.

CHAPTER TWO

Law, Prophecy, and Philosopher as King and Outcast

In 1935 Strauss wrote, "Maimonides' rationalism is the true natural model, the standard to be carefully protected from any distortion, and thus the stumbling-block on which modern rationalism falls."[1] That Strauss maintained this view until the end of his life is hinted at by the appearance of three pieces on Maimonides (one more piece even than the two on Plato) in Strauss's last volume, *Studies in Platonic Political Philosophy*.[2] Although it might be more convenient if we could explain succinctly just how modern rationalism stumbles before Maimonides's rationalism, unfortunately, there are conflicting views on Strauss's interpretation of modern rationalism and especially about whether those views changed over the course of his oeuvre. Without attempting to settle those debates, we will pause to highlight some of the deficiencies of modern rationalism that Strauss identifies explicitly. One he identifies from the beginning to the end of his oeuvre, which he borrows from Lessing: modern rationalism wins out against revelation by the Napoleonic strategy of laughing revelation out of court. In other words, it does not engage in a genuine confrontation with revelation. Perhaps Maimonides does.[3]

Another deficiency of modern rationalism is indicated indirectly in Strauss's critique of Julius Guttmann, the renowned scholar of the history of Jewish thought, in chapter 1 of *Philosophy and Law*. According to Strauss, Guttmann is unable to understand Maimonides on his own terms because he understands him in light of late modern philosophy of religion. That philosophy of religion takes as its primary object of study the subjective experience of the religious believer. In modern consciousness, this subjective experience is private. The focus of Maimonides is not something private but that most public of all features of life, divine law (*PL*, 73). Here we approach more closely the focus of this chapter. It is closely related to another important deficiency of modern rationalism that Strauss identifies: modern rationalism is confident in modernity's moral progress over premodern civilization.[4] Ironically, even scholars confident in the superiority of the tools of their modern historical scholarship such as Guttmann fail to appreciate the extent to which they misread premodern thought by reading it through a modern lens. Strauss begins his critique of historicism by employing the tools of historical scholarship with greater objectivity than historicist scholars.

Lest we become sidetracked in discussions of historicism, we must return to the second of Strauss's criticisms of modern rationalism. The modern focus on the subjective religious experience of the individual believer is to be expected in the modern state with its distinction between state and civil society. At least since Spinoza, philosophers had been attempting to produce loose agreement among believers of different faiths on the rough outlines of a Judeo-Christian religion. The very superficiality of that belief was meant to cultivate the private or social character of religious experience. It is crucial not to misunderstand the significance of the social character of religion. Of course, believers continued to practice religion publicly in their respective churches and synagogues. Yet those churches were less and less directly related to the state. True, state establishment of churches continued, albeit with ever increasing toleration of nonestablished churches, but at least in this respect the United States became emblematic of the modern ideal. A variety of religions is not merely to be tolerated but to some extent encouraged. The historical background to this new approach to religion was of course the wars of religion in what was formerly known as Christendom. From its beginning Christianity had tended to distinguish secular from ecclesiastical. The medieval period was filled with failed attempts to arrive at a workable relation between these two authorities. Modernity was developed largely as a response to the previously at least apparently insoluble theologico-political problems posed by these two authorities.

Divine Law and Prophetology

Strauss's interest is less in modernity's roots, however tenuously they might be connected to Christendom, than in the neglected and misunderstood alternative posed by medieval Jewish and Islamic political philosophy. Unlike Christendom or modernity, divine law in Islam and Judaism was far less prone to distinguish secular from ecclesiastical. Indeed, divine law was, as Strauss often notes, "total" in its demands. The Law, especially in Judaism, reached into every detail of life and concerned every aspect of life (*PL*, 73). It did not lend itself to the distinction between religion and politics. Why was a phenomenon as foreign to modernity as divine law of such concern to Strauss? In the 1920s and 1930s, as he probed the limits of late modern thought and its roots in early modern thinkers such as Spinoza and Hobbes, Strauss became convinced that the Napoleonic strategy of early modern thought left philosophy in the awkward position of affirming its superiority to religion on the basis of an act of faith (*SCR*, 29–30). In these same years, he also saw that premodern political philosophy confronted revelation more profoundly because it confronted a religion that made total demands. Although philosophy had become something of a profession through the rise of the modern university, premodern philosophy was itself a total way of life—or at least it was a way of life in certain circles of medieval Jewish and Islamic thought as well as in the Greek world. The proper opponent of philosophy as a way of life was not a private religious experience but a religion or divine law as a way of life. Contrary to expectation, Strauss seems to have rediscovered the premodern meaning of philosophy by way of coming fully to terms with divine law as a phenomenon. Although divine law took on some different tasks and novel meanings in the monotheistic communities of Jews and Muslims, it was similarly totalistic in the Greek world. (For this very reason scholars often argue that the Greeks had no notion of the distinction between private and public, which is true if one means that they were disinclined to separate religion from politics but false if one means that they had no conception of interior life.)[5] It was because of this affinity between medieval Islam and Judaism, on the one hand, and the pagan Greeks, on the other, that thinkers like Alfarabi and Maimonides would pave the way back to Plato for Strauss.

Strauss often stresses the debt in the political philosophies of Alfarabi and Maimonides to Plato in contrast to Thomas Aquinas's debt in political thought to Aristotle. Here we may begin to add our second theme: prophetology. Of course, a divine law is received in one way or another by a prophet. Not only does Aristotle not say much about religion in his *Politics*, but also his emphasis is less on law in all its senses than on the regime. Consequently, for the interpretation of the meaning of divine law and the nature of the prophet, we are not surprised to find that Alfarabi and Maimonides (and their students) would turn to Plato and especially Plato's *Laws*. As we saw in the previous chapter, Aristotle establishes distinctions between theoretical and practical science that fit well with Christian distinctions between ecclesiastical and secular authority. Much as Plato is prone to ignore such distinctions between the sciences, so Alfarabi openly and Maimonides more circumspectly also violates the distinction between theoretical and practical science. Since the divine law is a total phenomenon, rigid distinctions between metaphysics and politics prove difficult to maintain. Although the total character of divine law proves to be a boon to Strauss in the confrontation between revelation and reason or religion and philosophy, the tendency to violate distinctions between theoretical and practical science lead to unexpected complications in attempting to understand a thinker such as Maimonides. Although when studying a medieval Christian thinker one usually has little difficulty saying whether one is discussing a work of revealed theology or a work of politics—even if the latter has roots in the former—Maimonides's *Guide of the Perplexed* tends to violate such distinctions. Nearly all of Alfarabi's political writings include theological elements. The significance of such elements is one of the more contested areas of scholarship on Alfarabi. Some argue that those theological elements provide the foundation of the political teaching; others argue that they do not. Be that as it may, the political is never neatly segregated from theological content in Alfarabi or Maimonides. We will return to some of these complications later. For now, we need to look more closely at the phenomenon of prophecy and the prophetologies of Alfarabi and Maimonides.

The Platonic Philosopher-King and the Prophet-Lawgiver

From his second book, *Philosophy and Law* (1935), until his penultimate book, *The Argument and Action of Plato's "Laws"* (1975), Strauss was fond of quoting a passage from Avicenna's *Division of the Rational Sciences* that identified Plato's *Laws* as containing *the* treatment of prophecy and the divine law.[6] Although Avicenna attuned Strauss to the importance of Plato for medieval Jewish and Islamic political philosophy, he was led back to this whole period and genre first by Maimonides and ultimately by Alfarabi. Indeed, Strauss focused on medieval Islamic political philosophy largely because he came to understand that he could not understand Maimonides in light of Christian Scholasticism. And he saw that interpreters like Guttmann, Wolfson, Erwin I. J. Rosenthal, and Franz Rosenthal, unbeknownst to themselves, interpreted Maimonides through Christian lenses (see chapter 3). Alfarabi enabled Strauss to see not only that divine law was the central phenomenon in the thought of Maimonides but also that the prophet was to be understood in light of the philosopher-king of Plato's *Republic*. The philosopher-king as such violates the Aristotelian distinction between theoretical and practical science. Furthermore, the philosopher-king is emblematic of the totalistic character of Platonic political philosophy. Yet we stop short of claiming that Platonic political philosophy is *totalitarian*, because the philosopher-king is meant less as the final solution of the human problem than as an emblem of that problem itself. As the third and final wave in *Republic*, book 5, the philosopher-king is said to provide the solution of all human ills (473d). Human life, however, illustrates on a daily basis the ongoing presence of such ills. In his early writings, Strauss seems to have taken the philosopher-king, especially as it appeared in medieval Islamic and Jewish philosophy, somewhat literally as the basis of the "ideal state" or the perfect law.[7] Subsequent research, especially in the thought of Alfarabi and Plato, would uncover just how remote the ideal state was. That the philosopher-king is emblematic of the human problem became readily apparent to Strauss as soon as he saw the depth of the tension between the way of life recommended by divine law (or the city) and the way of life of the philosopher (or man). Alfarabi's shocking portrait of Socrates in his *Philosophy of Plato* brought home to Strauss just how remote philosophy is from the city (see FP).

Although evidence for such tension can be found in Maimonides, it is presented far more cryptically than in Alfarabi. Such an understanding of philosophy could hardly be further from our contemporary experience of philosophy as a department within the university or from the medieval scholastic view of philosophy as a discipline subordinate to revealed theology. We should not be surprised then at how scandalized were Strauss's (and are our) contemporaries when he suggested that this tension between philosophy and city necessitated recourse to esoteric writing. It took a philosopher of the caliber and distance from university life of Nietzsche to recognize the existence of esotericism in earlier epochs.[8] When seen through the lens of scholarship on Christian Scholasticism, Alfarabi and Maimonides are thought mistakenly to engage in "Islamic philosophy" or "Jewish philosophy." According to Strauss, Maimonides and Judah Halevi indicate that philosopher and Jew, far from being coextensive, are mutually exclusive (*PAW*, 19). The basis of that exclusivity is the tension between philosopher and city retained emblematically in the prophet as philosopher-king. Prophetology then, abstruse though it appears at first, has as its key problem *the* human problem.

The Solitary Philosopher or "Weed"

A more obvious emblem of the distance between philosopher and city is the theme of the solitary, so prevalent in medieval Jewish and Islamic political philosophy. On the one hand, interpreting the prophet as philosopher-king appears to resolve the tension between city and man; on the other hand, the very same thinkers who appeal to this apparent resolution also refer more or less directly to how out of place is the philosopher. The philosopher is man as solitary. Strauss addresses this theme in medieval Jewish and Islamic political philosophy most directly not in his writings on Alfarabi or Maimonides but in one of the most difficult of all his writings, his article on Judah Halevi (ca. 1075–1141) in *Persecution*. In "The Law of Reason in the *Kuzari*," Strauss introduces the reader to one of the more enchanting of medieval writings: a conversation between a king in search of guidance in the right way of acting and a group of interlocutors including a philosopher and a Jewish scholar, as well as a Christian and a Muslim scholar. The main focus of this article is Halevi's opposition to the philosopher's intellectual *nomoi* (laws) and alliance with revelation's rational or natural law teaching. In the introductory section of the article, Strauss presents one of his most compressed but comprehensive analyses of the lines of conflict between philosophy and revelation. Halevi, Saadya Gaon, the Mu'tazilite kalām, and Thomas Aquinas as proponents of natural law appear on the side of revelation; Averroës (as well his predecessor Alfarabi), Marsilius, and Maimonides as opponents of natural or rational law appear on the side of philosophy.[9] As I have argued elsewhere, Alfarabi and Maimonides belong to the tradition of natural right derived from Plato and Aristotle—a much looser conception of right than that of natural law.[10] Strauss adumbrates the difference between the philosophic view and the view of natural law (or the city) when he explains the philosophic conception of "rational law." Here Halevi presents his stinging critique of philosophy. According to Strauss, the philosopher reveals, "if the highest perfection of man is indeed philosophy, and a life devoted to philosophy is essentially asocial, the rational *nomoi* would be the *regimen solitarii*" (*PAW*, 116). Unlike the multiplicity of other senses of rational or intellectual nomoi in the *Kuzari*, the philosopher uses it to refer to a way of life that transcends the city.

One of the ways that Strauss discovered the connection between Alfarabi and Maimonides was through one of Maimonides's letters to Samuel Ibn Tibbon, the Hebrew translator of the *Guide of the Perplexed*. In that letter Maimonides commended the writings of Alfarabi to Samuel, most notably Alfarabi's *Principles of the Beings*, known to us as the *Political Regime*. One of the most striking themes of that writing concerns the solitary, there referred to as the "weed." There are many different kinds of weeds in virtuous cities; the philosopher or potential philosopher is only one of those kinds, along with sophists and skeptics who undermine cities. Similarly, in *Guide of the Perplexed*, Maimonides touches on this sensitive topic near the end of the book in 3.34, where he states boldly that the concern of the divine law is not the rare individual or solitary but the betterment of most human beings. How can authors who identify the philosopher-king with the prophet also identify the philosopher as solitary? Are these not diametrically opposed teachings? Indeed, they appear to be. This central opposition or contradiction should give pause to those who would deny the existence of esoteric writing. Those who deny that Alfarabi and Maimonides employ esoteric writing, despite ample explicit evidence to the contrary, usually affirm that the philosopher-king teaching is the personal preference of the given philosopher.[11] They then infer that the philosopher is an advocate of totalitarianism. They would be well advised to consider the significance of this most startling and most explicitly expressed of all contradictions in the writings of Alfarabi and Maimonides, namely, that they appear to offer the perfect resolution of all human ills in the philosopher-king, and, almost in the same breath, they highlight the durability of such ills in the image of the solitary. Although the prophet as philosopher-king is the more prominent teaching in Alfarabi and Maimonides, the teaching regarding the solitary comes closer to making the truth explicit.

How Strauss Escapes Scholasticism: Maimonides, a Test Case

One of the consequences of ignoring esotericism is an inability to appreciate fully the rhetorical complexity of works as elusive as Maimonides's *Guide*. In Strauss's earliest writings on Maimonides, he declared forthrightly that it is a work of political science, along the lines we have seen so far: Maimonides employs Alfarabi's conception of the prophet as philosopher-king in his own prophetology, adapting Plato's philosopher-king from the *Republic* (see chapters 4 and 7). For at least one of a variety of possible reasons, Strauss became more reserved in stating his views: through an abundance of caution or an increased appreciation for the importance of the surface or because he saw that the scholarly consensus was that the *Guide* is a work of "Jewish philosophy" with much more of a theological focus than a focus on political science. That scholarly consensus derives at least in part from reading Maimonides in light of Christian Scholasticism. The medieval Christian view that faith supplements reason necessitates a harmonization of or subordination of philosophy to theology. The result is what is commonly called "Christian philosophy." No such harmonization or subordination is to be found in the writings of Alfarabi and Maimonides. Strauss could see that the misreading of Maimonides as a "Jewish philosopher" was the result of blending exoteric surface with esoteric depth. How could one best show the inappropriateness of such blending? To begin with, Strauss decided in the "Literary Character of the *Guide for the Perplexed*" to focus on the surface of the *Guide*. That surface is what he identified as "enlightened *kalām*." He inferred the existence of enlightened kalām from reading *Guide*, 1.71, against the backdrop of Alfarabi's discussion of vulgar kalām in his *Enumeration of the Sciences* (*PAW*, 40–41). In 1.71 Maimonides envisions a defense of Judaism that differs from prior ones because it does not violate the "nature of existence." In contrast, the vulgar kalām readily violates that nature. By avoiding that violation, Maimonides indicates his intention to offer a defense of Judaism that is not opposed to philosophy. This is no mean feat, since the very raison d'être of traditional kalām was the defense of revelation against philosophy (1.71). Already we can begin to see that Maimonides's enlightened kalām is the exoteric surface of the *Guide*. This enlightened kalām is what most interpreters have in mind when they speak of the *Guide* as a work of "Jewish philosophy." If we are to understand and credit Strauss's multilayered interpretation of the *Guide*, we will need, at least to begin, to show not only that that theology is merely the surface of the work rather than its foundation but also that the political science Strauss excavated in his earlier writings is its esoteric depth.

Before we turn to consider some of the evidence for political philosophy as the esoteric depth of the *Guide*, let us consider the precedent for Strauss's interpretation of Maimonides as a practitioner of enlightened kalām. In Alfarabi there is a foreshadowing of just such a kalām. In a book, a critical edition of which was published only well after Strauss had stopped serious work on Alfarabi, the *Book of Religion*, Alfarabi gives a parallel though revised version of the account of political science, jurisprudence, and kalām that he gives in the *Enumeration of the Sciences*.[12] Muhsin Mahdi and Charles E. Butterworth have argued persuasively that the *Enumeration* poses questions about these sciences as Alfarabi received them; the *Book of Religion* answers those questions—with answers tantamount to a reshaping of these sciences and their relation to one another. In the *Book of Religion* in lieu of kalām, Alfarabi establishes a blend of dialectic and rhetoric subordinated to philosophy that will be used to persuade adherents of virtuous religion to follow the teachings of that religion, which are themselves derived from the teachings of philosophy.[13] In effect, Alfarabi, contrary to Christian thinkers such as Thomas Aquinas, subordinates theology to philosophy. The blend of dialectic and rhetoric that Alfarabi substitutes for traditional kalām is Alfarabi's version of what Strauss calls enlightened kalām. It is a kalām most emphatically in harmony with philosophy.

At first glance, the suggestion that the *Guide* is in its esoteric depth a work of political science or philosophy seems implausible. As Strauss observes in "Literary Character," "there is practically complete agreement among the students of Maimonides that [the *Guide*] is not devoted to political science" (*PAW*, 44). Let us consider some of the reasons for this "practically complete agreement": First, even in *Philosophy and Law*, where Strauss argues that the central theme of the *Guide*, the divine law, is a political theme, he underlines the fact that thinkers like Alfarabi and Maimonides no longer felt the need to strive for the "ideal state" because they interpreted the legislative founders of their divine laws as philosopher-kings already in possession of it. Consequently, as Strauss underlines, Maimonides was able to "aristotelize" (*PL*, 133). That is, contrary to Plato's Socrates, Maimonides was freed up to spend a great deal of time discussing theoretical matters. Second, in his *Treatise on the Art of Logic*,

Maimonides seems to declare that the divine laws prevailing in his audience's communities undercut the need for political science. Third, in *Guide*, 2.39, Maimonides again seems to claim that philosophers' inquiries into nomoi have been rendered moot by the giving of divine laws (see chapter 7). In brief, all these pieces of evidence seem to suggest that revelation has made political philosophy unnecessary. What gives the lie to this suggestion is that Maimonides portrays the legislating prophet just as Alfarabi does as a *philosopher*-king. Although Moses's legislation may be the production of a philosopher-king, it has not traditionally been interpreted as such. Who could discover the philosophic foundation of the Law other than a philosopher? In other words, even if philosophy were not necessary to produce the Law, philosophy would still be needed to understand the philosophic character of the Law's foundation. Immediately following *Guide*, 2.39 in 2.40, we receive confirmation not only that political philosophy is indispensable now for Maimonides's readers but also that it is the elusive meaning of the "true science of the Law" to which Maimonides refers in the opening of the *Guide*.

Generally, the meaning of Maimonides's true science of the Law is misinterpreted because it is conflated with or even confused with the enlightened kalām surface of the *Guide*. There are two basic ways of interpreting this true science: It is either the study of the fundamental beliefs or opinions that are thought to be the foundation of the Law or it is the political, scientific study of the aims of the Law as law. In other words, it is either (largely theoretical) opinions or the ends of the Law. The former view is the "Jewish philosophy" interpretation, which holds that Maimonides's task in the *Guide* is less to defend (many scholars studying Maimonides are oblivious of the character of kalām in the medieval Muslim and Jewish communities) than to explore the roots of Judaism, much as Maimonides sets them forth in his thirteen roots or articles of faith in *Pereq Ḥeleq*, Sanhedrin 10 of his *Commentary on the Mishnah*.[14] Maimonides leaves a clue that this interpretation is mistaken: perhaps the most theoretically contentious issue in the *Guide*, namely, whether the world is created or eternal, is not among the beliefs he requires of the Jew in his thirteen articles. That is, he does not require that the Jew believe in the world's creation. Perhaps the main theoretical bone of contention in the *Guide* is missing from the beliefs Maimonides requires. The *Guide* then is not primarily concerned with exploring the thirteen roots that every Jew should believe.

Guide, 2.40—at the center of the *Guide*, the prophetology (running from 2.32 to 2.48)—is the moment that most clearly illuminates the meaning of the true science of the Law.[15] Maimonides opens with an epitome of ancient political philosophy. He follows that epitome with an account of what makes a divine law truly divine: it is that the Law should cultivate the intellect, not merely care for the well-being of the body. The simplicity of this account is deceptive. Two problems contained within it unfold throughout the rest of the *Guide*: What does it mean to cultivate the intellect in view of the fact that Maimonides claims that belief or mere opinion (even true opinion, apparently) falls far short of the intellectual perfection he envisions (3.51, 620)? (In other words, Maimonides's view of belief is very remote from more familiar Christian notions that belief on the basis of faith saves.) The other problem is, what distinguishes beliefs that exist for the sake of the body from beliefs that exist for the sake of the soul or knowledge for its own sake (3.27–28)? (In other words, some beliefs exist for the sake of communal well-being, which Maimonides treats as a form of or in the service of bodily well-being. It is unclear whether any of the beliefs in the Torah, regarding, for example, God's attributes and particular providence, are believed in for their own sake, as opposed to their beneficial communal consequences.) These two problems coalesce into the theme of the solitary, discussed earlier.

Guide, 2.40, identifies intellectual perfection as the aim of divine law, but *Guide*, 3.34, announces that the aim of the Law is the well-being of the majority, not the unique individual (Ar., *wāḥid*; cf. Gr., *idiotēs*; Plato, *Republic*, 620c; and Aristotle, *Nicomachean Ethics*, 1179a8) or solitary. This contradiction between 2.40 and 3.34 is ultimately as, or perhaps more, important than the closely related and more dramatic perplexity regarding whether the order of the heavenly bodies is rationally explicable or provided for by a particularly providential, omnipotent God (*Guide*, 2.24). Indeed, the disjunction between the individual and the city bears witness to an answer to the question of particular providence. As Strauss shows in "Place of Providence," Maimonides extracts the issue of particular providence from its usual position in Jewish dialectical theology as a part of God's justice and attaches it to the *Guide*'s prophetology, which is firmly rooted in the political science of 2.40.[16] Even though 2.40 appears to identify individual perfection as the aim of Mosaic law, closer examination reveals that only a philosophically revised divine law can combine these dissonant ends—the well-being of the city and the highest well-being of the individual.

CHAPTER THREE

Vipers, Weeds, and Disorder in the Whole

Strauss's view is that Alfarabi revived ancient, especially Platonic, political philosophy. Two obvious things seem to confirm this: that Alfarabi devoted more attention to politics than perhaps any other medieval philosopher—indeed, placing a majority of the nonlogical works that have come down to us in a political frame—and that at the end of the *Attainment of Happiness*, Alfarabi underlines that he had learned from Plato and Aristotle how to revive philosophy when it had ceased to be actively pursued. The more widely received view among scholars, however, is that Alfarabi is a Neoplatonist of some kind. Of course, Neoplatonism is hardly known for its interest in politics. Indeed, Neoplatonists prefer to focus on things that transcend earthly existence. In doing so, they highlight the way in which one thing proceeds from another in an ineluctable descent from the mysterious One or Good that is beyond Being—putatively following book 6 of the *Republic*. Now, even though Alfarabi never speaks of a One or Good beyond Being—but rather of a First Cause—he does frequently describe a hierarchy of being and of ascents and descents through such hierarchies. Indeed, many of his nonlogical works contain some form of this ascending, descending process (*Political Regime, Virtuous City, BR, AH*). As a result, Alfarabi appears to fit a premodern mold made most famous by the Neoplatonists and captured by Lovejoy's phrase, the Great Chain of Being, which is often invoked to explain why premodern thinkers were so enamored of hierarchy in politics as well as a corollary claim: theology or metaphysics as higher than politics must be its ground. The main purpose of this chapter is to show that Alfarabi, following Plato and Aristotle, highlights failures within the apparently hierarchical ordering of things, and these failures are in turn linked to and support his denial that theoretical science provides the ground of practical science.

Before turning to the evidence in Alfarabi, let us outline the parallels to the challenging of hierarchy that we find in Plato and Aristotle. We do not begin in chronological order because Aristotle's subversion of hierarchy is in some ways more obvious—even though Aristotle is often cited as maintaining that metaphysics grounds politics.

Aristotle

We have in mind both the openings of Aristotle's *Nicomachean Ethics* and *Metaphysics*, on the one hand, and *Nicomachean Ethics*, book 6, on the other. We begin with the latter because it is the more explicit and comprehensive case. At the end of book 6, Aristotle has been battling his way through the most challenging inquiry of that book, his inquiry into intellectual virtue, especially the difference between prudence (the intellectual virtue of practical affairs) and wisdom (the intellectual virtue of theoretical matters). He concludes by announcing that prudence does not have authority over wisdom; rather, it has authority for the sake of wisdom (1145a7–12). Why this should be the case was established back in *Nicomachean Ethics*, 6.7, when in the heart of the book politics or prudence was put in its rightful subordinate position vis-à-vis wisdom. The object of wisdom, the divinely ordered cosmos, is higher than the merely human. This arrangement at the end of book 6, rule by the lower for the sake of the higher, is hardly the most stable of arrangements. Must not the higher simply rule over the lower? Certainly, a Neoplatonist would uphold such a view.

Leaving aside book 6, we turn back to the opening of *Nicomachean Ethics* and of the *Metaphysics*, which both anticipate this problem. Near the opening of *Nicomachean Ethics*, Aristotle highlights the uneasy relation between politics and science and the closely related tension between practical and theoretical science. In 1.2, he is inquiring into what art or science would specify the end of human actions, and he states the following:

> One must try to grasp, in outline at least, whatever it [the end of human actions] is and to which of the sciences or capacities it belongs. But it might be held to belong to the most authoritative and most architectonic one, and such appears to be the political [art]. For it ordains what sciences there must be in the cities and what kinds each person must in turn learn and up to what point. We also see that even the most honored capacities—for example, generalship, household management, rhetoric—fall under the political [art]. Because it makes use of the remaining [political?] sciences and, further, because it legislates what ought one to do and what to abstain from, its end would encompass those of the others, with the result that this would be the human good.[1] (1094a25–b8)

The material from *Nicomachean Ethics*, book 6, that we've already considered helps explain some of the ambiguities and controversies surrounding this passage. It is ambiguous about whether what is architectonic is an art, a science, or the capacity of a ruler. In effect, might there be a political capacity of a ruler that should dictate the fate of the sciences? Or must science control the fate of the sciences? And it is somewhat ambiguous about the extent of that rule. Does it extend to all sciences or only political ones? The third sentence makes this political thing sound like the ultimate architectonic science—as if it is supposed to rule over all sciences studied in the city. The ambiguities here even lead one to wonder whether Aristotle envisions a political science that politicizes all the sciences.[2] We will return to this last concern later in this chapter.

In the second chapter of the *Metaphysics*, Aristotle reviews six reasons that wise men are considered wise. The last of the six poses challenges highly reminiscent of those we've run into in *Nicomachean Ethics*. The wise man's knowledge (1) is most universal, (2) concerns the most difficult things, (3) concerns things about which one can be most precise (about which there are the fewest principles); he (4) can teach the causes about them, (5) their objects are known for their own sake, and (6) their knowledge concerns what is *archikōtatē* (supreme or highest, 982b5)—and he knows the end for which each thing is done (*prakteon*), the good of each, and the best in the whole.[3] Whether our translator is the more adventuresome and challenging Sachs or the traditional Ross-Barnes, no one can avoid the oddity regarding things "done." Here, in the opening of the *Metaphysics* we're somewhat unexpectedly taken back to the beginning of the *Ethics*, where the relation between doing and the end(s) at which all things aim was underlined. It is unexpected here both because the present inquiry would seem to have little if anything to do with "doing" and because one would have thought that the link between the many senses of being, underlined in *Nicomachean Ethics*, 1.6, and the search for the highest good should have been severed prior to the *Metaphysics*. This odd dalliance with "doing" in the *Metaphysics* reminds us of the uneasy relation between high and low at the end of *Nicomachean Ethics*, book 6. Desirable though it might be that the high should possess unchallenged rule over the low—there is a tendency in the order of things, especially in human things, toward the inverse, the rule of the low.

Plato

Let us turn now to Plato. To some extent, Plato made this problem a, or even the, centerpiece of his corpus. There are two deeply interrelated emblems of this problem: the death of Socrates and the improbable or impossible character of philosopher-kingship. As Strauss says, regarding the accusations against Socrates, where there is smoke there must be fire (where the smoke is the public accusations against Socrates, and the fire is inquiring in a subversive fashion into the gods and the afterlife, what is above and what is below). Even if one does not take Strauss's view, everyone who has read the *Apology* senses the topsy-turvy character of the lowly Athenian *demos* putting to death that divine man, Socrates. Similarly, the ultimate source of the impossibility of the philosopher-king is the injustice of the notion that the philosopher as inquirer into the order of all things should be put in service of a band of mere human beings. That is improbable or impossible because it demands that the higher be put in the service of (that is, rule over!) the lower, which can occur only if the higher, that is, the philosophers compel *themselves* to rule! Contrary to the Neoplatonists, Plato and Aristotle argue that there is nothing necessary or even probable about the Neoplatonic expectation that the high (whether it be human wisdom or the divine itself) should rule over the low (whether it be human prudence or the city itself).

Although Neoplatonists in general are well aware of the defectiveness of humanity, their greatest departure from Plato, or at least from Alfarabi's Plato, is to emphasize the role of what is lowest in us (namely, matter) as causing disorder in the whole. This led eventually to an underlying tendency to what for lack of a better word we might call Manicheanism, or what Nietzsche has referred to as Platonism for the people, that is, it led to a tendency to denigrate this world of materiality in favor of all that is immaterial. Of course, moments in the Platonic oeuvre have seemed to sanction this view: most notably the Pythagorean drift of the *Phaedo*. One ought, however, to pay sufficient attention to the general trend of Socrates's argument (his call to remain on earth rather than to flee this putative prison of the body) and the imagery of Plato (having Socrates remark on the odd pleasure of removing the shackles and send away his wife, with a small child recently born in Socrates's old age!) to put to rest the idea that Socrates or Plato intend to support the animus against the body of his Pythagorean interlocutors, Simmias and Cebes. The radical opposition between body and mind in the *Phaedo* is surely not Socrates's last word on the relation between body and soul—as even the most casual glance at the *Republic* and *Phaedrus*, to name the obvious, would indicate. On the contrary, Plato, Aristotle, and Alfarabi all locate the most interesting and perplexing disorders not in materiality but in the strange leavening of human reason itself. For example, in the *Nicomachean Ethics*, Aristotle underscores how that indispensable power prudence in its original form, cleverness, is just as ready to serve vice as virtue. Although he implies this near the end of book 6 (1144b1–25), he shows by example in book 7 the chilling meaning of this fact: human beings are potentially ten thousand times more harmful than are the brutes (1150a9) as long as reason or intellect has not become fully what it can become, that is, prudence.

Alfarabi

Alfarabi, unlike the Neoplatonic tradition that came before him, lacked the confidence of the Neoplatonists that a neat hierarchy exists between low and high, and especially between the theological or metaphysical, on the one hand, and politics, on the other. Although he, as all or nearly all philosophers do, assents to the superiority of the theological or metaphysical, Alfarabi is just as uneasy about the confidence the Neoplatonists had in the Great Chain of Being. In the *Virtuous City*, whose full title is *The Principles of the Opinions of the Inhabitants of the Virtuous City*, he offers such hierarchy without much obvious questioning—in a manner that seems in keeping with the title of that work. That is, this work explains the opinions or the principles of the opinions of those who live in virtuous cities, which are not necessarily the opinions of the philosophers. Only when describing these opinions or their principles does Alfarabi sound like a confirmed Neoplatonist.[4]

In contrast, in the *Political Regime* he offers a far more sober account. It is not by chance that this work contains his most extended discussion of nonvirtuous political regimes—in obvious debt to *Republic*, book 8. As in the *Virtuous City*, the first half offers that Lovejoy-like account of the theological and natural order; the second half is devoted to a far more philosophical inquiry into the human things. But the insinuation that the first half somehow grounds the second half is the most widely accepted reading of both *Virtuous City* and *Political Regime*. But we are most interested in a striking parallel in the first half and the second half of the *Political Regime*: near the end of the first half as he descends toward the bottom of the natural realm, Alfarabi highlights that there are vipers that destroy things higher than they, without any apparent purpose. Similarly, near the end of the second half, after having descended to the worst kinds of regimes, he concludes with a discussion of the "weeds within virtuous cities"—nota bene, the reappearance of the term "virtuous city"—and in a most unexpected place, at the end of a descent through increasingly bad regimes. By locating these weeds in the virtuous cities, he veils their status. As misfits within the virtuous cities, they appear at first to be simply bad. Closer inspection, however, reveals that along with those enamored of falsifying things (sophists) are to be found those who are looking for the "right path" and "the truth," whose instruction is then outlined. These inquirers are nothing if not potential philosophers. At first reading, they don't appear as such because they appear in opposition to the lawgiver in the virtuous city, whom we might reflexively assume must be the philosopher-king.[5]

We could work through other interesting details in Alfarabi's account of the weeds—but we arrived here with the intention of clarifying Alfarabi's credentials as a Neoplatonic proponent of the Great Chain of Being. Several things stand out in Alfarabi's account that give the lie to that portrait: First, and most important, the chain of being is interrupted. Second, in addition to the chain, another key principle, teleology, is challenged by the existence of the viper—whether that description of vipers is correct is unimportant; here we are most interested merely in parsing what Alfarabi is trying cryptically to convey. (Please, don't misunderstand me: I do not hold that Alfarabi is wholly abandoning teleology.)[6] Third, another central theme, if not principle, is raised by these bizarre cases, the viper and the philosopher: namely, the character of evil or disorder in the whole, which, of course, is closely related to the principle of teleology (cf. *Guide*, 3.12, 3.13). Fourth, and back to the central point, the locus of the interruption of the chain of being is nearly identical in all three authors, Plato, Aristotle, and Alfarabi. The philosopher, the emblem of what is best in man, stands at the center of the failure of the chain. In other words, although the viper is an odd, quirky, and largely inconsequential example of the failure of the chain of being—obviously a mere hint—one could hardly choose a more salient case of its failure than the fate of the philosopher. Not only does the Great Chain of Being not hold in bizarre cases such as the viper; it fails in the most important instance for human affairs. Indeed, it would seem to give the lie to the most superficial reading of Alfarabi, namely, that Alfarabi is naively confident that the human order mimics a hierarchical divine order and that the former is grounded in the latter. Neoplatonism can avow such a view because it has such disdain for the human and the material that it expects little but evil in this vale of tears—in other words, it fobs off on materiality any departures from the right ordering of things, high over low. Alfarabi is not so unearthly.

Although in a number of Alfarabi's works, he outlines the character of the virtuous city or regime or religion, and although, at times, he leads his reader to expect that such virtue is not only achievable but that the philosopher-king-legislator's rule promises to bring it about; here, in the *Political Regime*, he leaves the reader crestfallen. This should lead complacent Neoplatonic readers of Alfarabi to reassess how they read Alfarabi. When he describes such ascents and descents, one must ask oneself whether he is attempting to capture the way things really are—or is merely conveying the opinions or principles of the opinions of the inhabitants of virtuous cities. At least for the most part, I believe that the latter is the case. One must resist the temptation to read such descriptions as expressing either Alfarabi's own preference or what he takes to be an accurate description of the reality of things.

We ought to consider why Alfarabi would question his own community's view but in such a roundabout way. Why wouldn't he be concerned that he is inspiring devotion to a misguided ideal? He wouldn't for the same reasons that Plato had little reason to be concerned about portraying the *kallipolis* in the *Republic* (Alfarabi is not concerned about appearing to insinuate the possibility of the rule of philosopher-king-prophets over large swaths of, if not the whole, Earth), though it might inspire the imprudent to strive to establish castles in the sky. Neither Plato nor Alfarabi were terribly concerned about this risk for two reasons: because they knew that at least some human beings will always harbor a desire to have all things, and if not all then at least the human things, conform to their own desires (*Laws* 687c) and because they knew that the best way to purge men's souls of such desires is to dramatize or perform or enact and explore them.[7]

Why the Primacy of Political Philosophy Does Not Entail the Politicization of Philosophy

Let us turn back to whether Aristotle envisions a political science that politicizes all the sciences—indeed, whether our endeavor throughout this book to show that political philosophy is the most comprehensive inquiry, according to Strauss's Alfarabi and Maimonides, is tantamount to the politicization of philosophy! When students of medieval Christian thought hear tell that political philosophy has greater primacy in medieval Jewish and Islamic philosophy, they often begin to suspect such an architectonic political philosophy of falling prey to a thorough politicization of science.[8]

No one doubts that Christian metaphysics is somehow Christianized, but that rightly doesn't raise the same kind of hackles that the suggestion that metaphysics should be politicized raises. After all, Christianity claims to have uncovered the key truth regarding the whole. Why then shouldn't that truth color metaphysics? That political philosophy should be the architectonic science, however, raises more serious questions because politics seems to be ineradicably partisan. If politics is ineradicably partisan, then the modifier "politics" in political philosophy seems to guarantee that any metaphysics developed under its auspices would be partisan. I will leave aside, at least for now, whether all politics is so deeply partisan and instead question whether "political philosophy" is political in this sense or some other.

In fact, Alfarabi and Maimonides rarely use the phrase "political philosophy." Far more frequently, they speak of "political science," but by this phrase they, of course, do not mean political science as we might think of it today. That being said, why do we use this term today? We do so because, as Strauss showed so eloquently, the term "political science" has been used and abused by modern positivistic social science. What he meant to indicate by political philosophy is often indicated by the addition of the modifier "Platonic" to the phrase. Platonic political philosophy is distinguished by having preceded Aristotle's division of the sciences—and in particular his distinction between theoretical and practical science. Although it is true that there are anticipations of such a division in Platonic works such as the *Sophist* and the *Statesman*, those divisions are championed by Plato's Eleatic Stranger rather than his Socrates. What does all this have to do with Alfarabi and Maimonides? After all, isn't Alfarabi referred to in the Muslim tradition as the "second teacher," that is, the second teacher after Aristotle? And aren't both of these authors, perhaps especially in the *Enumeration of the Sciences* and in the *Logic* under the influence of Aristotle in the divisions of the sciences they discuss?

Let us broach these questions about Alfarabi and Maimonides's view of Aristotle's division of the sciences by revisiting the striking process of reversion to Plato highlighted already in one of Alfarabi's most introductory writings, the *Enumeration of the Sciences*. In chapter 5 Alfarabi moves from an initial account of political science that sounds quite a bit like Aristotle's in the *Nicomachean Ethics* and *Politics* back to an account that sounds strikingly like Plato's approach. That is, he moves from a political science that at least appears to have little or no connection to theoretical philosophy to one that requires that the ruler possesses both theoretical and practical philosophy. In other words, Alfarabi announces that in his setting, in a community ruled by divine law, political science (or political philosophy) will take its lead from the philosopher-king conceit of the *Republic* (and to some extent the *Laws*) rather than the lead of the prudent political actor with little or no interest in theoretical knowledge of Aristotle's political writings. That the philosopher-king conceit is central to the thought of Alfarabi and Maimonides is difficult to gainsay. What needs to be added is that the philosopher-king appears variously also as prophet or legislator, depending on which work of theirs one considers. In brief, divine law somehow necessitates the reversion to Plato's philosopher-king.

Broadly speaking, it isn't difficult to say what about the divine law necessitates the reversion to Plato: the divine law is itself a theoretico-practical phenomenon or, to speak with greater precision, a theologico-political phenomenon. One cannot speak of politics and law in the Islamic and Jewish settings without also somehow talking of theology. Does this not then still imply that all theoretical inquiry (in which the truth is of paramount concern) is somehow tainted, in these traditions, by the merely useful, which plays such an important role in practical inquiry? Such a concern might be valid if it were the case that the true and the good have no bearing on each other. That they must have bearing on each other is evident from the fact that in the medieval

Christian tradition the true and the good are thought to be in harmony. If anything, Alfarabi and Maimonides are freer of the taint of the true by the useful, insofar as they do not presuppose the harmony of the good and the true. Rather, the relation of these and the relation of politics and theology is central and always in play and under scrutiny in their thought.

Let us return then to the original question about the meaning of political philosophy in the medieval Islamic and Jewish traditions. We're now able to see that what is meant by political philosophy has less to do with partisan politics than it has to do with the relation of the highest themes of theology and politics. That theology should have political implications and that politics should have theological meaning would come as no surprise to any medieval thinker. More important, though, our digression on what Strauss dubbed the "theologico-political problem" offers us another avenue to deepen our understanding of why political philosophy, in the broadly Platonic sense of the term, should be the architectonic science. Once we add to the mix of "the true" and "the good," the even more obviously political concept or idea, "the just," we begin to gain a better sense for why Alfarabi and Maimonides treat political philosophy as the architectonic science. Is the just a merely human concern or does it transcend the political by means of considerations of providence? That Christian theology (or metaphysics) bears on providence is undeniable. Indeed, providence is a very high theme of the theoretical portion of sacred doctrine. The same, however, is not true of the thought of Alfarabi and Maimonides. Matters specifically of particular providence, in Alfarabi and Maimonides, are treated not as part of a purely theoretical inquiry into providence. Rather, they are considered under the aegis of political science! Does this then mean that their inquiry into particular providence is less philosophic or scientific and more partisan than the inquiry in the Christian setting? Ultimately, we try to show in this book that the reverse is the case. Particular providence is considered under the aegis of political science in Alfarabi and Maimonides because the very notion of particular providence is itself partisan. In other words, the very conception of particular providence presupposes that the whole could take its lead from the part.

Putting the shoe on the other foot, as it were, the question could reasonably be asked whether when Christian thinkers treat matters of particular providence as part of a theoretical science, they do not presuppose the possibility of demonstrating the truth of God's particular providence for the Christian. Be that as it may, we have tried here to allay some of the fears of those who suspect that if political philosophy is first philosophy, philosophy will be tainted by a form of political partisanship. The qualifier "political" in Strauss's notion of political philosophy as first philosophy refers not to political partisanship but to the theoretico-practical comprehensiveness of the inquiry—that the highest inquiry is not limited to that which transcends the human because, as it happens, the theologico-political surface of things contains the core of things.

PART TWO

Strauss's Departure from the Christian Scholastic Paradigm

CHAPTER FOUR

Escaping the Scholastic Paradigm

At first it might appear to be a mere accident that many of the same contemporary Jewish scholars who studied medieval Jewish thought also studied medieval Islamic thought. It is not sufficient to account for the interest of the same scholars in medieval Judaism and Islam, however, by observing that so many of the towering figures of medieval Judaism, such as Saadya Gaon, Judah Halevi, and Maimonides, wrote in Arabic. The thesis of this chapter is that other special affinities between Judaism and Islam led to the special interest of Jewish scholars in Islam.[1] Yet in much of the scholarship by early twentieth-century Jewish scholars of Islamic and Jewish thought, it became tempting to ignore those affinities and lump Islamic and Jewish thought together with Christian thought under the broad rubric of monotheism. And because Christian Scholasticism had been so extensively studied, it became tempting to draw paradigms and methods of interpretation from Christian scholarship on Scholasticism.

The question then arises whether contemporary scholars should study medieval Jewish and Islamic thought under the large shadow cast by Scholasticism. In *Persecution* Strauss insisted that scholars should cease regarding Islamic and Jewish medieval philosophy "as counterparts of Christian scholasticism" (*PAW*, 8). Although he does not openly criticize specific colleagues, Strauss was engaged, however diplomatically, in a dispute with most of his contemporaries over how to read medieval Jewish and Islamic thought—contemporaries who tended to read Islamic and Jewish medieval philosophy in the light of Christian Scholasticism.[2] He was critical of contemporaries such as E. I. J. Rosenthal and Richard Walzer, and to a lesser extent Franz Rosenthal and Harry Austryn Wolfson.[3] Perhaps the most eloquent and loquacious spokesman for the view that Strauss opposed, Harry A. Wolfson argues that all three of the medieval traditions are Philonic—by which he seems to mean not only that they follow a paradigm set by Philo but also, and more important for us, that they all somehow attempt to synthesize or harmonize philosophy and religion or reason and revelation—thus, Wolfson speaks of "religious philosophy."[4] In contrast, Strauss argues that although Christian

Scholasticism engages in such synthesis, Islamic and Jewish medieval philosophy, as it was originated by Alfarabi, does not.[5]

An obvious indication that this debate between Strauss and his contemporaries is still being played out is that on occasion contemporary scholars feel the need to defend their willingness to use the concept medieval "Jewish philosophy."[6] Strauss doubts that the concept is meaningful, because, as he says repeatedly, medieval thinkers themselves, such as Maimonides and Judah Halevi, presupposed the difference between the Jew and the philosopher.[7] At least one prominent contemporary scholar has justified the continued use of the phrase not because it accurately describes the views of the medieval authors studied but because this construction of Jewish thought suits the way academic life is carved up in our own time.[8] Although this way of using medieval Jewish philosophy is undeniably open-minded, one wonders whether it will not contribute to the obscuring of the subject matter. One way in which it might is by reducing the intensity with which we desire to determine where the authors we study stand. The purpose of this chapter is to shed some light on where these medievals stand by comparing the approach that lumps Jew and philosopher together (championed by Wolfson and his colleagues) with Strauss's repudiation of that approach.

Strauss versus Wolfson

Because the approach championed by Wolfson remains, albeit in a wide array of forms, the most widely prevailing, the onus is on Strauss to explain why the leading Islamic and Jewish medieval philosophers should be contrasted with Scholasticism. According to Strauss, what then are some important features of these religions that lead to the prevailing tendency toward Scholastic or Philonic synthesis, on the one hand, and Farabian nonsynthesis, on the other? The most important feature is that Christianity is primarily a creed or dogma, and Judaism and Islam each claim to be the revealed Law (*PAW*, 9–10). As a result, the leading science in the former one and the latter two is different: in Christianity, the queen of the sciences is revealed theology or sacred doctrine; in Judaism and Islam, the queen of the (religious) sciences is jurisprudence (Heb., *talmud*, or Ar., *fiqh*) (18–19). Revealed theology is in the business of dealing with dogmas or beliefs or opinions; philosophy is also concerned with such opinions, especially about the highest things. Consequently, in Christianity, sacred doctrine is at loggerheads with philosophy. In such a battle where the prevailing conclusion is forgone, philosophy must become the handmaiden of theology. Although scholars of Scholasticism often speak of a harmonization or synthesis of reason and revelation, and I have myself used this terminology, according to Strauss, one or the other must give way. (In effect, what will be referred to as a synthesis of reason and revelation amounts to the victory of theology over philosophy.)[9] Matters are very different from this in the Islamic and Jewish traditions. Because the focus of jurisprudence is in the first instance on action, opinions are to some extent more up for grabs in Islam and Judaism than in a more theological tradition such as Christianity. As Strauss puts it, philosophy possessed privacy and independence in Islamic and Jewish medieval philosophy; Scholasticism, in contrast, kept philosophy in subordination. The result has been an appearance of greater continuity of philosophy in the Christian West than in the so-called Islamic East (in which we include here Andalusia). Yet it can be argued that only in the latter was philosophy carried on in its pure form (*PAW*, 20).

Let us recapitulate briefly the disagreement between Wolfson and Strauss (with some additions): Wolfson holds that there is a synthesis (perhaps he would even admit one in which revelation looms victorious) across all three monotheistic faiths; Strauss claims that though such a synthesis exists in Scholasticism, it does not in Islamic and Jewish medieval philosophy (nor does revelation loom victorious in this Farabian tradition).[10] What I would like to show, then, is that based on this divergence a series of other disagreements in interpretation of Islamic and Jewish medieval philosophy occurs between Strauss and those whom he opposes. These disagreements fall roughly into two groups: thematic and methodological.[11] Of course, it would seem more natural to begin with methodological issues. In the case of Strauss and his opponents the methodological disagreement is all too evident—Strauss argues for esotericism; his contemporaries deny its existence. Rather than start with what, at this point, could only be a dead end, let us begin with some of the thematic disagreements and work our way around to the methodological ones. I hope to show ultimately, however, that the methodological disagreements are traceable to the original thematic disagreement that we have already seen between Strauss and his contemporaries.

Allow me to briefly anticipate that conclusion: if, as Strauss argues, revelation is not victorious among Islamic and Jewish medieval philosophers, then philosophers within those communities run the risk of persecution if they do not conceal their unwillingness to accept the victory of revelation. In other words, they must adopt esotericism. But if, as Strauss's opponents argue or assume, revelation is just as victorious among Islamic and Jewish medieval philosophers as among Scholastics, then there is no need for esotericism. I should underline, however, that I do not mean to suggest that Strauss's claim about Islamic and Jewish medieval philosophers eschewing synthesis is an assumption from which we might deduce esotericism. These thematic and methodological issues are inextricably bound up with one another. I do not believe that there is a neutral methodological starting point from which we could begin that would not prejudge the matter. Both thematic and methodological issues are more or less constantly in play. The dispute between Strauss and his opponents is not, however, irresolvable. The key to resolving the dispute is to determine who does a better job of explaining the medieval thought, which Strauss, his contemporaries, and we seek to understand. Although thematic and methodological issues are intertwined, let us begin by focusing on the thematic issues and work our way around to the more contentious methodological ones.

Synthesizing Reason and Revelation or Not?

Having already explained the basic sense of the fundamental thematic disagreement, we refer the reader to those passages in the synthesizing interpretations where its proponents, for example, E. I. J. Rosenthal and Richard Walzer, argue for such a synthesis of philosophy and revelation, or, for example, the corollary claim that Alfarabi is obviously a devout Muslim.[12] Before turning to other themes, however, it is worth reconsidering at least one of the original sources, Maimonides's *Guide of the Perplexed*, to determine why most interpreters take it for granted that Islamic and Jewish medieval philosophers sought a synthesis of reason and revelation much as Scholastics such as Thomas Aquinas sought. An obvious reason for assuming such a synthesis is that works such as the *Guide* defy easy classification as a work of philosophy or theology. In part this is because the theology found in Judaism and Islam is different in character from much of what is found in Christianity. The greatest examples of Christian theology, in Western Christendom especially, were far less apologetic than the Islamic and Jewish equivalent, kalām (dialectical theology). In turn this divergence between the approaches to theology is due at least in part to the different status of theology in Judaism and Islam vis-à-vis jurisprudence, which we have already mentioned.

When contemporary students read Maimonides's overview of Islamic kalām in *Guide*, 1.73–76, they are amazed to discover the extremes to which these theologians were willing to go to defend Islam, including having recourse to bits and pieces of ancient arguments borrowed from materialist opponents of Aristotle.[13] They are even more surprised to discover that the perceived opponent of Islam (and Judaism and Eastern Christianity) was philosophy itself (1.71, 177). In contrast, western Scholasticism confidently coopts reason into revelation—thus silencing any argumentation from philosophy—by declaring sacred doctrine or revealed theology superior to pagan metaphysics.[14] The relation between philosophy and Judaism is far more complicated in the thought of Maimonides. At first glance it would appear that his elusive *Guide* must be an odd blend of philosophy and theology, somehow privileging revelation, as does Scholasticism. That Maimonides defends Judaism is undeniable. Indeed, he underlines the necessity of such a defense (1.71, 179). But at the very moment that he announces the necessity of such a defense, he also underlines the necessity of engaging in such a defense without violating what he calls the "nature of existence" (*ṭabīʿa al-wujūd*) (cf. 178–79 with 182). When Maimonides goes on in chapters 73 through 76 of the first part to criticize the arguments employed by the *mutakallimūn* (dialectical theologians), he criticizes at great length their attempt to replace Aristotle's understanding of the necessary, possible, and impossible with their own fanciful version of the necessary, *admissible*, and impossible.[15] When one combines Maimonides's appeal to the nature of existence, its peculiar dependence on the philosophic notion of the possible, and his frequent admission that all that Aristotle argues about what is beneath the sphere of the moon is correct (2.22, 319), one is left at least with doubts that Maimonides has conceded, as Aquinas does, the subordination of reason to revelation.[16]

Synthesizing Sources or Not?

A corollary thematic issue to the putative synthesizing of reason and revelation is the putative synthesizing of a highly eclectic array of sources. Alfarabi and Maimonides are frequently identified variously as Neoplatonists, Platonists, and Aristotelians because they seem to draw so amply from all of these.[17] It is worth wondering, however, whether some of their sources serve to tone down or cover over the obvious tensions between one of these sources and revelation, for example, Aristotle and the Qurʾān. Neoplatonism is the preferred source in any such effort. E. I. J. Rosenthal is quite insistent that the so-called *Theology of Aristotle*, which he views as a commentary on Plotinus, makes possible for Alfarabi a genuine synthesis of Plato and Aristotle—thus, Neoplatonism is used to harmonize Plato with Aristotle.[18] After all, Alfarabi composed a work called the *Harmonization of the Two Opinions of the Two Sages: Plato the Divine and Aristotle*, which seems to achieve just such a synthesis by means of the *Theology of Aristotle*—not only a synthesis of Plato with Aristotle but also a synthesis of the two of them with revelation.[19] In contrast, much as Strauss doubts the more overarching synthesis of reason and revelation, he also doubts the sincerity with which Alfarabi harmonizes Plato and Aristotle in the *Harmonization*, for several reasons.[20] First, in another writing by Alfarabi, his *Philosophy of Aristotle* (the third part of his trilogy, the *Philosophy of Plato and Aristotle*), he makes no mention of the so-called *Theology of Aristotle*—thus, indicating to the attentive reader that he knows that the *Theology* is not really (of or) by Aristotle but by a Neoplatonist. Second, in the trilogy, Alfarabi notes, however subtly, the nonequivalence of Plato and Aristotle (though they share a common "purpose"—that is, the pursuit of wisdom—their "results" were different (cf. *PAW*, 12, that is, their opinions are less in harmony than the *Harmonization* implies). Third, as has already been mentioned, at the end of the first part of the trilogy, the *Attainment of Happiness*, Alfarabi states that in the trilogy he is setting forth the way of "restoring" philosophy when it has been lost—thus indicating that he does not see himself as continuing Neoplatonism but as reviving Socratic philosophy. Finally, anyone who has read the trilogy has detected that although the *Attainment of Happiness* has some Neoplatonic elements, the *Philosophy of Plato* and the *Philosophy of Aristotle* are relatively free of much of the Neoplatonic accretion we find in other Farabian writings (such as the *Political Regime* and the *Virtuous City*)—thus indicating that Alfarabi can tell Plato and Aristotle apart from the harmonizing rhetoric provided by Neoplatonism. Some or all of these reasons led Strauss to believe that Alfarabi uses the *Theology* to create an appearance of harmony between all parties, while pursuing a revival of Socratic political philosophy.[21]

Differences in Degree of Esotericism

Strauss has already begun to lead us toward a methodological corollary to esotericism, namely, that a single author may write some works that are more popular or exoteric and others that are less so. Even those with a methodological revulsion toward esotericism cannot but admit that the disjunction between Alfarabi's trilogy and the *Harmonization* is great—indeed, it is so great that there is a movement afoot in recent scholarship to deny the authenticity of the *Harmonization*![22] One of the alternatives to acknowledging such disjunctions within the Alfarabian oeuvre is to claim, as E. I. J. Rosenthal does, that Alfarabi's writings are "diffuse, repetitive and lacking in clarity and precision."[23] Even though Rosenthal evinces awareness of Maimonides's famous letter to Samuel Ibn Tibbon, which suggests to Samuel what authors he ought to take most seriously, Rosenthal seems not to have taken Maimonides's assessment of Alfarabi in that letter to heart: "Everything that he [Alfarabi] composed . . . is . . . finer than fine flour."[24] Of course, fine flour slips easily through the hands, and all of it seems to be the same. It is true that Alfarabi treats similar themes again and again. Yet no two treatments are exactly the same. To learn from Alfarabi we must learn to read with painstaking attention to the smallest differences between texts. Small differences when put together can indicate radically different intentions. Alfarabi's writings are not lacking in clarity and precision; the appearance of repetition is precisely that, merely an appearance.[25]

The Search for Alfarabi's Putative Lost Predecessors

The thematic disagreement about what Alfarabi is synthesizing carries over into other methodological issues. What kinds of sources really count for Alfarabi? According to the interpretation that we have just drawn from Strauss, Plato and Aristotle are the sources that count the most—perhaps Plato most of all. Many Farabi scholars, however, have devoted enormous amounts of time and energy in search of the missing Middle Platonist or Neoplatonist precursor that would help explain the features of Alfarabi that depart radically from all the "Platonist" (in other words, Neoplatonic) currents alive in his place and time—especially his focus on politics. Even some of those who attend to Alfarabi's claim about "restoring" philosophy at the end of the *Attainment of Happiness*—which implies that philosophy in its prevailing Neoplatonic form was somehow untrue to Socratic philosophy—continue to insist that he must have had a Neoplatonic or Middle Platonic predecessor.[26]

Yet another related methodological issue is that the anti-Straussian interpreters of Islamic and Jewish medieval philosophy tend to have a rather low estimate of the possible originality of the authors they study—especially of the so-called Islamic authors. Again and again, Richard Walzer, E. I. J. Rosenthal, and Franz Rosenthal insist that Farabian arguments without precedent, at least in Alfarabi's time, are anything but that—even though none of them was ever able to uncover his putative predecessor.[27] Here, we touch in passing on an important methodological issue: can the search for earlier sources, which played such a prominent role in late nineteenth- and early twentieth-century scholarship, lead us to understate the originality of these medieval thinkers? At least in the case of scholarship on Alfarabi, this seems to have been the case—at least among Strauss's opponents.

The Relation between Theology and Politics in Alfarabi and Maimonides

The second major thematic disagreement (of comparable importance to whether Alfarabi synthesizes reason and revelation) between Strauss and his contemporaries concerns how to interpret the political character of the majority of Alfarabi's writings. Strauss claims that Alfarabi places "the whole of philosophy proper within a political framework" (*PAW*, 9). In contrast, E. I. J. Rosenthal claims that Alfarabi's "political thought . . . is only a part of a whole philosophy . . . [and that his *Virtuous City*] is indicative of this dependence of politics on philosophy as a whole."[28] Strauss stresses the primacy of the political, Rosenthal the primacy of the metaphysical. The anti-Straussian interpreters add to the stress on the grounding role of the metaphysical the claim that Alfarabi views the individual human being, the city or nation, and the cosmos as nestling each within the other—in the spirit of the "animal" that is the cosmos in Plato's *Timaeus*.[29] This image, so potent throughout the history of Stoicism and Neoplatonism, recurs often in Alfarabi as well as in Maimonides.[30] In sum, these interpreters interpret Alfarabi (and Maimonides) as embracing central claims of Neoplatonism—what we refer to in brief as "theory dictates practice" and the "similarity of microcosm to macrocosm." The initial impression that both of these leave us with is of overwhelming confidence in divine providence.

In contrast, what would framing the whole of philosophy within politics, as Strauss interprets Alfarabi, suggest? In the introduction to *Persecution*, Strauss engages in a long and complicated analysis of the relation between two elements of Alfarabi's thought, namely, "a certain science and . . . a certain way of life" (*PAW*, 12). He concludes that the combination of philosophy and the royal art (the arts that provide the relevant science and way of life, respectively) in the *Philosophy of Plato* at first seems orthodox because it requires a supplement to philosophy; that is, it seems that philosophy requires some external (perhaps divine) aid. Strauss argues, "Yet the supplement to philosophy which, according to [Alfarabi], is required for the attainment of happiness is not religion or Revelation but politics, if Platonic politics. He substitutes politics for religion" (15). This is the ultimate significance of Strauss's description of Alfarabi's philosophy as placing "the whole of philosophy proper within a political framework." It amounts to an admission that the decisive form of providence, particular providence for man's well-being, is lacking. Framing philosophy within politics suggests that one should not rely on external (divine) aid to support human life.[31] In contrast, the opponents of Strauss see, in the writings of Alfarabi, pious Neoplatonic confidence that metaphysics dictates practice and that the macrocosmic order can underwrite a rigid and hierarchical political order.

One subtle theme in both Alfarabi and Maimonides gives the lie to the neat nestling of microcosm within macrocosm favored by the opponents of Strauss, namely, the evident disorder in human life.[32] As we saw in chapter 3, the most obvious symbol of this disorder in Platonic philosophy is the death of Socrates. He is alluded to, though not by name, in Alfarabi's *Political Regime* in the form of the "weeds."[33] Although Alfarabi appears at first to present a perfectly harmonious Neoplatonic hierarchy in works like the *Political Regime*, in that work in particular he offers two examples of departures from the perfectly ordered hierarchy: vipers and weeds. In the first, cosmological half, he describes many a rise and fall through a quasi-Neoplatonic hierarchy seeming to assure us of a providentially ordered hierarchy, but toward the end with the example of the vipers he highlights evidence, subtle though it may be, of the lack of such an order. In the second, political half, the weeds infest not just any city but, shockingly, virtuous cities! These weeds, as Alfarabi describes them, include both potential philosophers and far less desirable human beings such as sophists. Even in virtuous cities, where one would expect perfect order, the higher tends to fall prey to the lower—rather than to rule easily over it, as one might hope. Rather than philosophers being celebrated as saviors, they are put to death by those worse than they. Despite appearances to the contrary, and in keeping with Socratic philosophy, all is not orderly and neat in Alfarabi's world.

Similarly, in Maimonides's *Guide* in 1.72, after describing the cosmos as "this whole of being [that] is one individual and nothing else," he notes in a vein similar to Alfarabi's vipers:

> Now similarly in being as a whole, there are species whose generation is intended, stable, and subsisting according to an orderly arrangement, and between which there are only small differences to the extent of an accident that may have befallen that particular species with regard to its quality and quantity; and there are species that are not intended, but are consequent upon the nature of universal generation and corruption—for instance, the various species of worms that are engendered from dung. (188–89)

Of course, we are not concerned here with the scientific accuracy or inaccuracy of Maimonides's handling of what he thought was a case of spontaneous generation. Rather, we are interested in the way that Maimonides concedes the existence of things in the world that are "not intended"—as in Alfarabi, this is a crucial moment when he drops the apparently perfect harmony of the whole he is describing.[34] If this had implications merely for Maimonides's physical views, we would not have brought it up. Within a page of noting this lack of intention, he turns to humanity and shows that the order (and disorder) found in the cosmos is mirrored in peculiar ways by the human realm. He says, "Know that it was not because of all that we have mentioned in comparing the world as a whole to a human individual that it has been said about man that he is a small world. For this whole comparison can be consistently applied to every individual animal that has perfect limbs; but you never hear that one of the ancients has said that an ass or a horse is a small world. This has been said only about man. This is because of that which is a proprium of man only, namely, the rational faculty."[35] The rest of this paragraph is one of Maimonides's most extended discussions of practical intellect or prudence—though he studiously avoids using either of the Arabic equivalents of these terms, using instead the vague phrase "ruling faculty." One might be tempted to interpret the provision of such a ruling faculty as part of a providential plan to achieve the very hierarchy championed by proponents of the Great Chain of Being. Matters, however, are not so simple—as is evident from the ongoing disputes about whether Maimonides even has a conception of prudence.[36]

In *Guide*, 1.2, Maimonides argues as if matters of good and evil were somehow up to the imagination. As I have argued elsewhere, 1.2 is only the beginning of his account of how man apprehends good and evil, as one might expect since the account of the Garden of Eden is just the beginning of any account of such apprehension.[37] In 1.7, while discussing Seth's having been created in the image and likeness of Adam, Maimonides outlines what happens when human beings fail to develop that which is most peculiarly human (namely, reason): they become worse than other animals. Like Aristotle, Maimonides indicates that reason without proper orientation is merely a dangerous tool of the desires—indeed, one might even go so far as to deny that such merely instrumental reason qualifies as reason for Aristotle or Maimonides.[38] It might instead be properly understood as imagination. Be that as it may, the pressing issue for us is to see that Maimonides confronts the same challenge to order highlighted by Alfarabi in his images of vipers and weeds. As we have seen, the distinctive feature of Alfarabi's account is that the disorder in the whole appears even at the highest level in connection with the weeds, including the philosophers. Similarly, Maimonides shows that disorder (viz., evil) in human life is not traceable to man's materiality alone. Reason, though it is central to the right ordering of human life, is connected to these very disorders. In brief, Maimonides resists the Neoplatonic tendency to blame the body—contrary to those who would claim that Maimonides confidently insists on an orderly Great Chain of Being and a neat nestling of microcosm into macrocosm.

At this point, some readers are likely to object that Maimonides does blame materiality or the body profoundly in the *Guide*. Although Maimonides does wax ascetic in the *Guide* at times (for example, 2.36 and 3.8–9), his most considered views of the body and sensation oppose the Neoplatonic disdain of the body (1.46–47, 3.10–12). This is clearest in 3.10, in his assertion that evil is a privation, which evidently contradicts assertions such as in 3.8 that the "impulse of matter" is itself evil.³⁹

The Divide between Philosopher and Believer in Medieval Jewish Philosophy

Having begun the turn toward Maimonides in the interpretations of Strauss and his opponents, I return to the central thematic problem: does Strauss argue about *Jewish* medieval philosophy what he at least implies about *Islamic* medieval philosophy, namely, that the divide between philosophy and revelation is a great one—in other words, is there not in this tradition the same tendency to synthesize reason and revelation as in Christian Scholasticism? In fact, Strauss states this more explicitly about Jewish medieval philosophy than he ever does about Islamic medieval philosophy. In *Persecution*, he writes, "Jews of the philosophic competence of Halevi and Maimonides took it for granted that being a Jew and being a philosopher are mutually exclusive" (*PAW*, 19; cf. 11–13, 43). The moment that Strauss asserts this, the reader becomes curious about where Halevi and Maimonides each fall in this dichotomy. Previously, Strauss left the reader with the initial impression, or perhaps he began with the reader's initial impression, that Halevi and Maimonides form common cause against Islamic medieval philosophers such as Alfarabi (11). We cannot help but wonder whether that initial impression was correct.

To begin with, however, we must assemble the evidence Strauss evinces that such a divide exists in Jewish medieval philosophy between believer and philosopher. If so, then many other things would seem to follow in the wake of this key thematic dispute, including methodological implications for esotericism and so on. As Strauss observes, within the opening pages of the *Kuzari*, Halevi has the philosopher reveal his indifference to religion, though he acknowledges the likelihood that a philosopher would at least appear to adhere to some religion—if only the rational nomoi of the *falāsifa* (*PAW*, 114–15). The Khazar king has no use for conversing with the philosopher thereafter because he is interested in receiving guidance about the fitting actions. Philosophy's ongoing inquiry into the dis/order of the whole isn't conducive to a life of action such as the king's.⁴⁰ Apparently to receive clear guidance about action, such as the Khazar king desires, one must have already settled the highest theoretical matters so that the fitting actions might be inferred.⁴¹ At least if we may trust Judah Halevi, philosopher and believer are divided over what is most pressing, the fitting actions or understanding by one's own means. Consequently, Strauss makes one of his most shocking and perceptive claims about the divide between the two in his "Law of Reason in the *Kuzari*": "The philosopher ... asserts the superiority of contemplation as such to action as such: from the philosopher's point of view, goodness of character and goodness of action is essentially not more than a means toward, or a by-product of, the life of contemplation"; and later, "moral man as such is the potential believer" (114, 140). This is not to say that the philosopher is an immoralist but merely to say that he is not moral according to the Aristotelian standard; that is, he does not pursue moral action as itself an end of life.

That Maimonides shares this view about the divide between philosophy and religion is evident from many things. I limit myself to two obvious points. In the closing pages of the *Guide* (3.54), Maimonides ascribes to the "ancient and modern philosophers" the same (perhaps even a slightly more) severe view of morality (than the one) Strauss describes: "[The perfection of moral virtues] is, as it were, only the disposition to be useful to people; consequently it is an instrument for someone else."[42] I do not argue here what I assume is obvious, namely, that this view of the perfection of moral virtues is *not*—forgive the anthropomorphization—the Law's "self"-understanding of moral virtue. The other obvious point indicating Maimonides's view on the divide between philosopher and believer is the well-known disagreement over eternity versus creation. Across the board, the philosophers believed in the eternity of the world (see *PAW*, 124n92, citing *Guide*, 3.29, 516). When it comes time to justifying the Jew's belief in creation, Maimonides insinuates that between eternity and creation matters are at a stalemate regarding demonstration. Consequently, the Jew must believe more or less literally what the prophetic books teach, namely, creation (*Guide*, 2.25).

Yet the reader remains confused about the accuracy of the initial impression of Maimonides and Halevi. If an Islamic medieval philosopher (one of the *falāsifa*) such as Alfarabi is a philosopher, then Maimonides must as a Jew be opposed to him. Two questions indicate ways of settling this question. Does Maimonides side with Halevi's Khazar king, and thus with Judaism, against the life of contemplation? Although Strauss has already awakened our attention to the surface of the *Guide*, that it is in the first instance a defense of Judaism, not a vague congeries of theology and philosophy (see *PAW*, 38–46), we must wonder whether the *Guide*'s inquiry into the "true science of the Law" is essentially Jewish or perhaps essentially philosophic.

Over the course of *Persecution*, in his chapters on Maimonides and Halevi but especially in his very difficult chapter on Halevi, Strauss offers answers to these questions. He prepares the reader's response to the first question as early as the introduction, however, by underlining the divide between believer and philosopher as the divide between adherents of "rational commandments" or "natural law," on the one hand, and those who speak of "rational laws" or merely "generally accepted opinions," on the other (*PAW*, 10–11). In the opening pages of the difficult "Law of Reason in the *Kuzari*," Strauss returns to this same divide, though without the benefit of any appeal to the divide between believer and philosopher. Here, amid two of the most note-filled pages in Strauss's entire corpus, he adumbrates, however obscurely, the same divide that he mentioned in the introduction: Maimonides is grouped together with Marsilius of Padua in opposition to Thomas Aquinas and Saadya Gaon, both proponents of "natural law" (96–97). By the end of the "Law of Reason," Strauss has taken full advantage of the fact that "law of reason" can mean at least four different things to conceal the fact from the inattentive reader that, according to him, Halevi sides with the Mu'tazilite kalām regarding the existence of rational or natural laws. In short, over the course of the "Law of Reason" Strauss establishes lines of battle between the *falāsifa*, Maimonides, and Marsilius, on the one hand, and Thomas Aquinas, Saadya, the Mu'tazilite kalām, and Halevi, on the other. Thus, Strauss adds confusing nuance to the simple divide between Christians who synthesize reason and revelation and Jews and Muslims who reject such a synthesis, with which this chapter began.[43] It would seem that proponents of natural law are at the bottom believers, while those who speak of "generally accepted opinions" side—on the decisive point—with the philosophers.

Everything that Maimonides wrote (from the *Commentary on the Mishnah* to the Code to the *Guide*) seems to bear out the notion that he privileges contemplation over action—from the shockingly contemplative framing of the Code to the radical denigration of morality throughout the *Guide*.[44] One of the only moments of apparent backtracking occurs at the end of the *Guide*, in the renowned final four chapters (3.51–54).[45] There, Maimonides extols the value of imitating God's ways or actions. Throughout the *Guide*, he is at great pains to insist that God as an incorporeal being could never be "moved" to action by any "passion" (esp. 1.36 and 54). Thus, he leads one to wonder whether such passionless rule is exemplified by the God of Exodus and Deuteronomy or by divine rule of nature and especially to wonder how human beings can truly emulate such transcendence of passion (cf. 1.54, 3.18, 3.32). It is tempting to interpret this imitation as being exemplified by morality. After all, Maimonides happily invokes the Hebrew words with the heaviest moral weight (*ḥesed* [loving-kindness], *mishpat* [judgment or justice], and *ṣedakah* [righteousness]; 3.53–54, citing their invocation in Jeremiah 9:23). I wonder, however, whether Maimonides is alluding to something moral or rather political—especially considering that in attempting to characterize these morally weighted terms he appeals not to the God of Exodus or Deuteronomy but to the divine rule of nature (3.53, 632). Just as Alfarabi's Plato or Socrates supplements a certain science (philosophy) with a certain way of life (kingship or the royal art), perhaps Maimonides supplements the true science of the Law with a comparable royal art.[46] *Guide*, 3.51–54, then, is less concerned with moral exhortation than it is with extolling the royal art. This would fit well with what we have already seen of Maimonides's views on the prevalence of evil in human life due to human deficiencies related to reason. These are human, not divine, tasks. In addition, we seem to have stumbled upon a possible answer to the question we had about the true science of the Law: that science is philosophy or at least political philosophy broadly understood. Although the *Guide* is in the first instance enlightened kalām, in the second instance it is political science or political philosophy.[47]

Learning to Speak Greek

Let us begin to bring this chapter to a close by turning once more to the methodological disagreements between Strauss and the contemporaries with whom he disagreed. I work my way around to the central issue, esotericism, by way of related methodological issues, namely, irony and what I would like to call "speaking Greek." It is widely recognized that Socrates employs so-called Socratic irony—he sometimes holds things back, especially his own knowledge, to promote the learning of his interlocutors. The Jewish scholars of Islamic thought opposed to Strauss, however, almost never entertain the possibility that Alfarabi is less than perfectly frank—in other words, that Alfarabi might employ irony. I am aware of only one instance of a deviation from this rule: Richard Walzer's discussions of Alfarabi's views on bodily resurrection. In two discussions, he acknowledges that Alfarabi must not have believed in resurrection, despite apparent affirmations of it.[48] He argues that Alfarabi distinguishes between the imagery used in religion and the demonstrative arguments employed in philosophy, as Alfarabi does perhaps most clearly in the *Attainment of Happiness*—indeed, there Alfarabi goes so far as to claim in Plato's name that religion is an image of the philosophic truth (sec. 55). In spite of these reservations about resurrection and acknowledgments of the difference between religious and philosophic arguments, Walzer takes utterly seriously both that Alfarabi must adhere to "Plato's theory" of the immortality of the soul and that he must have been a devout Muslim the "whole of his life."[49] I realize that bodily resurrection strains the credulity of philosophers even more than immortality of the soul. Nevertheless, as Strauss notes, Alfarabi in his *Philosophy of Plato* never mentions immortality—implying that Socrates or Plato did not view immortality as rising to the level of a philosophic "theory" (*PAW*,

13). Of course, in other writings Alfarabi can be seen making very pious pronouncements about immortality—and in yet others, especially the lost commentary on the *Nicomachean Ethics*, he makes apparently even more boldly impious claims. All this is to suggest that Walzer came close, at least regarding one thing, to acknowledging that Alfarabi is not always perfectly frank in all that he writes—in other words, he came close to acknowledging the existence of irony and even esotericism in Alfarabi's writings.

What do I mean by "speaking Greek"? I refer to the care with which Alfarabi employs terms in Arabic as comparable to terms in Greek. He evinces very fine attunement to differences between, for example, household, city, nation, group of nations, and the inhabited world. Nevertheless, opponents of Strauss refer to Alfarabi's virtuous city (*al-madīna al-fāḍila*) as his "ideal state" or his "perfect state"—and that Alfarabi was wholly committed to the realization of such a state and on the scale of the inhabited world.[50] Furthermore, whether or not one believes that the existence of the "ideal state" is a precondition of philosophic perfection is used by E. I. J. Rosenthal as a litmus test for sorting medieval Islamic philosophers.[51] This anachronistic usage among German-speaking Jews should not come as much of a surprise. Talk of the "ideal" and the "state" was almost second nature to these scholars, which is not to say that it was inevitable for them, as Strauss shows.[52] I don't belabor the obvious point that the "state" referred to in Alfarabi's writings is often not the Islamic nation but just as often Plato's *tiny* city—which could never be confused with a "state." I don't belabor that Arabic words such as *madīna* were intended as equivalents of the Greek *polis* or that Alfarabi was highly attuned to the difference between such a small entity and what should be rendered as "nation" (*umma*). The main difficulty is that by combining "ideal" with "state," that is, by failing to "speak Greek," these scholars cement a particular interpretation—indeed, one utterly lacking in a sufficient appreciation of Farabian irony. I do not attempt, here, to persuade you that Alfarabi does not at all believe in what Walzer calls "the perfect state." I have already devoted a whole book to that. But I underline what I take to be obvious: the only way that Alfarabi could look critically at his own community's ambition to rule the world was to try to think through what would be required to achieve that and what would be the result of that achievement. He could not openly declare the absurdity of such an ambition. And if he truly and honestly believed in realizing such a state throughout the inhabited world, the dream of Islam, then why would Maimonides have considered his writings worth the time of day?

Finally, I must confront the issue of esotericism more directly than heretofore. We recall the obvious: if reason and revelation are synthesized (or revelation is victorious over reason), then there would be no need for esotericism.

It is, at least to a great extent, because of this underlying presupposition that Strauss's opponents consider esotericism so implausible.[53] If one adopts Farabian nonsynthesis of reason and revelation, then esotericism becomes incumbent on the philosopher. Why should the victory of revelation preclude the need for esotericism? As I have already said, Strauss argues in *Persecution* that the "moral man as such is the potential believer."[54] He meant in the context that he is the potential believer in revelation. For this very reason, proponents of revelation ultimately privilege action (morality) over contemplation. This privileging constitutes what might be called the medium of public life. The believer has nothing to hide. In contrast, the philosopher's willingness to question opinions or beliefs whose truth the believer takes on faith leads the philosopher to have something to hide. Although the philosopher is motivated in part by a desire to avoid persecution, this is hardly the only or the most interesting motive for esotericism. Like Socratic irony, the most interesting motive of esotericism may be its educative purpose. Shouting doubts from the rooftops may inspire action; it rarely if ever inspires reflection.

CHAPTER FIVE

Spinoza's Scholasticism and Alfarabi's Platonism

The problem inherent in the surface of things and only in the surface of things is the heart of things.
—Strauss, *Thoughts on Machiavelli*

In *Philosophy and Law*, Strauss claims that the "medieval Enlightenment" had certain advantages over the "modern Enlightenment." It is not easy, however, to articulate which problems he thought the medievals—his medievals, which he refers to as "Islamic and Jewish medieval philosophers"—might have superior "solutions" to. The title *Philosophy and Law* adumbrates what Strauss will eventually articulate as the title of one of his other books, namely, the problem of *The City and Man* (or man and city in the earlier title)—or the theologico-political problem. There are, however, at least two sides to this problem: the political solutions of the human problem, which are all necessarily less than fully adequate, and the philosopher's relation to the city or state. In recent scholarship on Strauss, a great deal of stress has been placed on the latter, that is, the large gap between philosopher and city that appears to be a mainstay of both premodern and, at least, early modern philosophy (cf. *PAW*, 7–8). Previously, a great deal of stress was placed on the former, that is, the discontinuity between the typically "ancient" and typically "modern" political solutions of the human problem—and thus the "problem of ancients versus moderns" in Strauss. The premodern political solution privileges some form of aristocracy or virtuous monarchy, even if tempered by realism about the need for a mixed regime, while the modern political solution is first typified in Spinoza as liberal democracy.

Based on what I know of his explorations of the medieval Enlightenment, I doubt that Strauss ever thought that the political solution of the medievals (or the ancients) was unambiguously superior to the political solution of the moderns. As he observed in his 1962 preface to *Spinoza's Critique of Religion*, "Finite, relative problems can be solved; infinite, absolute problems cannot be solved. In other words, human beings will never create a society which is free of contradictions" (*SCR*, 6). Strauss seems, however, to have detected in early modern political solutions the causes of deleterious effects for philosophy as a way of life in late modernity. As the drive toward liberal democracy increased, certain essential features of philosophy faded from view. What shows up first as an increasing forgetfulness about the very possibility of the philosophic way of life, however, comes eventually to be closely connected to a surprising ineptitude in understanding political problems. The two sides of the problem of philosophy and law or individual and city—the political solution and the status of philosophy—prove to be linked profoundly, though they are not identical. We will first explore Strauss's understanding of the process of philosophy's fading from view and the increasing inability to grasp the political phenomena; then we will explore his turn to medieval Islamic political philosophy as a means of recovering an understanding of the philosophic life as well as the attendant increase in the understanding of human things.

Spinoza and the Rise of Historicism

According to Strauss in *Persecution*, Spinoza, as a proponent of liberal democracy, advocates a new approach to esotericism. Although premodern esotericists held that the gap between few and many is permanent, modern esotericists sought to bridge the gap and to spread enlightenment (*PAW*, 33–35, esp. 35n17). Whether Spinoza intended ultimately to efface completely the distinction between philosopher and citizen is difficult to determine. It is not difficult to see, however, that he, like Locke, sought to cultivate a new intermediary class between few and many, which can be labeled "intellectuals." (This seems to have had the long-term effect, intended or unintended, of obliterating the distinction between few and many.) By intellectuals, we mean especially ministers of religion and professors of philosophy and theology, who were the intended addressees of works as different as Locke's *Reasonableness of Christianity* and Spinoza's *Ethics*. These addressees were exhorted more or less directly to preach the new dogma of religious toleration as a means of achieving many of the most important intended effects of the new political solution: not only the reduction of political friction between religious groups but also an unprecedented level of openness to the expression of philosophic speech and thought. (Consider, for example, the subtitle of Spinoza's *Theologico-Political Treatise*.)[1]

Among the most important of Spinoza's novelties for the fate of awareness of the philosophic life was his elaboration of a new method of scriptural interpretation. As Strauss shows in *Persecution*, one of the main effects of this new method was to establish a clear division between "unintelligible" and "intelligible" writings or, as Strauss more colorfully puts it, "hieroglyphic" and "intelligible" writings (*PAW*, 147–49). Of course, Spinoza classified the Bible as "unintelligible" insofar as it was the product of prophecy, which itself was simply the product of the human imagination. The task of the new method of scriptural interpretation was to extract from—or more honestly to inject into—scripture the ethical tenets of the new political solution: a new ethic of loving your neighbor by loving and jealously guarding your own material advantage. Leaving aside Spinoza's ethical teaching, what is important here is one of the effects of the new mode of scriptural interpretation. Through this process of segregation of the unintelligible from the intelligible, Spinoza seems to have inadvertently set the stage for the forgetfulness of esotericism itself. Since works like Euclid's *Elements* were constantly trumpeted by Spinoza and his colleagues as exemplifying intelligibility, one should not be surprised that philosophic works should one day come to be measured by this deductive standard, emulated to such strange effect by thinkers such as Hobbes and Spinoza. In effect, Spinoza established a standard against which many forms of esotericism could not but come to be viewed either as unintelligible or as failing in elementary ways to meet the deductive standard.

Although Spinoza learned what it meant to write esoterically by reading not only Descartes but also Maimonides, subsequent thinkers were hardly so lucky. Kant, whose case Strauss singles out in *Persecution* as "in a class by itself," though he likely hid his own sympathy for the French revolution by writing somewhat esoterically in its favor, may be the first thinker to insist that he could understand his predecessors better than they understood themselves.[2] It is not difficult to see how this would lead to the forgetfulness of esotericism as a phenomenon, especially when the thinker who espouses the view, like Kant, is so obviously a proponent of the formulation of massive synthetic, if not strictly deductive, systems of thought. The eclipse of esotericism, especially premodern esotericism, brings with it the rise of historicism, since the underlying presupposition of the claim that one can understand one's predecessors better than they understood themselves is the view that our time represents a clear and obvious progress over prior times with respect to the arts and sciences as well as morals and politics.[3]

Affinities between Historicism and Scholasticism

When we turn from this history of the decline of esotericism to consider the modern study of Islamic philosophy, we are not surprised to see how disruptive was Strauss's approach to what he awkwardly calls "Islamic and Jewish medieval philosophy." As he explains in the opening pages of *Persecution*, contemporary sociology of knowledge views the philosopher "as a member of a motley crowd which they called the intellectuals or Sages." In other words, the philosopher has been conflated with intellectuals, as anticipated earlier. Because these sociologists of knowledge presuppose the "essential harmony between thought and society, . . [they] see in the different philosophies, exponents of different societies or classes or ethnic spirits." In other words, they understand the philosopher on the model of the intellectual as merely an expression of the milieu or ideology of his city.

The consequences of this assimilation of thought to society go undetected when it comes to the study of medieval Christian philosophy or Scholasticism. After all, the characteristic feature of Scholasticism was that it achieved a harmony between thought and society or between philosophy and Christian theology—in which the needs of society as expressed in Christian theology achieve their full victory through the Christian formulation of the superiority of faith over reason, as well as the putatively perfect harmony of faith with reason. The historical-critical study of Scholasticism of the first half of the twentieth century, when Strauss wrote *Persecution*, hardly distorted its object of study because the underlying assumptions of many contemporary scholars and many of the Scholastics were, despite obvious differences, so similar in important ways. Scholasticism, like the modern historical-critical method, had little use for esotericism. Thomas Aquinas, for example, though he touches on esotericism in his commentary on Boethius's *De Trinitate*, seems to have considered its use in the spirit of the esotericism of the parables of Jesus—rather than the philosophic esotericism rediscovered by Strauss. That is, although a certain amount of esotericism might be necessary to guard the truths of revelation from the ears of those hostile to it for their own religious or antireligious reasons, those truths are not made inaccessible to potential believers, despite that esotericism. In brief, modern historical scholarship and Scholasticism, then, have similar views of the truth. It is or should be open to all (for Scholasticism, at least to all potential believers).

The same cannot be said for any harmony between modern historical methods and methods suited to the study of "Islamic and Jewish medieval philosophy." By the 1950s, when Strauss published *Persecution*, the study of Islamic and Jewish medieval philosophy had not experienced a reawakening of interest as had Scholasticism at the end of the nineteenth and over the course of the twentieth centuries. On the contrary, Islamic and Jewish medieval philosophy was of interest primarily as a part of the renewed interest in Scholasticism. Consequently, it was viewed as of primarily antiquarian interest, and it tended to be seen through the same interpretive lens as Scholasticism (*PAW*, 8). The mismatch between this interpretive lens and Islamic and Jewish medieval philosophy was profound. Contemporary historical scholarship, which expected authors to express their thoughts openly and on the surface, was not prepared to see premodern esotericism for what it was—thus the furor surrounding Strauss's inquiries.

(It is sometimes supposed that Strauss claims to have discovered esotericism. In *Persecution*, as in all his writings, Strauss chooses his words carefully, saying that he became "familiar" with the phenomenon of esotericism while studying Islamic and Jewish medieval philosophy [5]. The reason that he says he became "familiar" as opposed to, say, "discovered" is surely that Nietzsche had already made him aware of the existence of premodern esotericism.[4])

"Islamic and Jewish Medieval Philosophy" and the Rediscovery of the Theologico-Political Problem

As Strauss explains in the opening pages of his introduction to *Persecution*, his study of Islamic and Jewish medieval philosophy made him aware that philosophy and politics or thought and society are not always and everywhere in harmony, as was assumed by contemporary sociologists of knowledge. Why hadn't Strauss discovered this disharmony between philosopher and city through his own study of Plato, which he indicates elsewhere he had taken a passionate interest in since his youth, before he studied Nietzsche seriously?[5] Presumably, he had not discovered this disharmony and the attendant premodern esotericism because either he had been taught to read Plato in the spirit of the modern school of text criticism, or he had assumed that Plato wrote in the same manner as did people alive in his own time.

Strauss's talk, in the preface to *Persecution*, of becoming "familiar" is quite understated; in the introduction the Islamic political philosophers, the *falāsifa* in general and Alfarabi in particular, play a decisive role in his recovery of premodern esotericism. As Strauss says, "It is significant that Fārābī was definitely less known to Christian scholasticism than were Avicenna and Averroes" (*PAW*, 9). The writings of Avicenna and Averroës that scholars of Scholasticism took an interest in were metaphysical. It is not by chance that Alfarabi was almost completely passed over by the Christian tradition. He was passed over precisely because he focuses on the disjunction between philosophy and politics or the theologico-political problem in all his "political writings." Rather than seeming to exemplify the harmony of thought and society that Avicenna and Averroës's metaphysical works could appear to exemplify when taken in isolation from their writings as a whole, Alfarabi's focus on this disjunction made him the key to Strauss's recovery of ancient political philosophy.[6] The meaning of this disjunction rather than any specific political solution of premodern thinkers is what Strauss believed premodern political philosophy in general and Islamic and Jewish medieval philosophy in particular reveal in an unparalleled way. Of course, it is this very disjunction that is evident in the surface of things, alluded to in the epigraph we've drawn from Strauss's *Thoughts on Machiavelli*—that surface being amply evident, for example, in the life and death of Socrates. How could such obvious testimony to the disjunction between philosophy and the city, with such fertile implications for philosophic esotericism, as the death of Socrates have been so widely misunderstood, indeed, in effect overlooked? Rather than being seen as an indicator of this disjunction, the death of Socrates came to be interpreted in light of the Neoplatonic and Christian teachings that followed it. Because the appearance of the Christ was meant to heal this disjunction between philosophy and the city, it should not be surprising that it would come eventually to be viewed as a nonexistent disjunction.[7]

Strauss came to understand the life of Socrates in the spirit that Plato had intended it, primarily through his study of Alfarabi's *Philosophy of Plato*. Alfarabi's evident refusal of all Neoplatonic healings of the rift between philosopher and city is what sets his approach to Plato apart from the primarily Neoplatonic milieu in which he emerged. He claims at the end of the *Attainment of Happiness*, which of course immediately precedes the *Philosophy of Plato*, to have recovered philosophy in the face of forgetfulness of what philosophy really is—a forgetfulness that should remind us of the modern scholarly forgetfulness of philosophy as a way of life, in tension with the city. Although he does not use our relatively modern term "Neoplatonism" to characterize the forgetfulness of philosophy, Alfarabi insinuates as much as that he is alone in recovering the original meaning of philosophy. After all, he states at the end of the *Attainment* that true philosophy has been handed down only by Plato and Aristotle. We can be confident that he does not mean by "Plato and Aristotle" the Neoplatonic harmonization of the two because as Strauss says in *Persecution*,

> From here [the insight that "political" philosophy protects philosophy] we shall perhaps understand sometime why Fārābī presented the whole of philosophy within a political framework, or why his most comprehensive writings are "political books." It is not impossible that the titles "the two philosophies" by which his treatise *On the Purposes of Plato and Aristotle* [that is, the *Philosophy of Plato and Aristotle*] was known, intimated the difference between "the two philosophies" or "the two doctrines": the exterior and the interior. This possibility cannot be neglected in any serious evaluation of the Platonism or rather Neo-Platonism of the *falāsifa*, and in particular of the use which they sometimes made

of the Neo-Platonic *Theology of Aristotle* [for example, Alfarabi in the *Harmonization*]. It suffices here to remark that Fārābī's [*Philosophy of*] *Plato* shows no trace whatever of Neo-Platonic influence.

In other words, despite his use of Neoplatonic tropes throughout his writings, Alfarabi gives every indication of being fully aware of the differences between Plato and Aristotle, on the one hand, and Neoplatonism, on the other. He evinces this awareness by offering his trilogy, the *Philosophy of Plato and Aristotle*, which does not Neoplatonize regarding either Plato or Aristotle—in contradistinction to his *Harmonization of the Opinions of the Two Opinions of the Two Sages: Plato the Divine and Aristotle*, which has left many interpreters thinking that he doesn't know whether the so-called *Theology of Aristotle* is really Aristotelian or Neoplatonic!

Indeed, the opposition between the *Philosophy of Aristotle* and the *Harmonization* is so pronounced that scholars have concluded in recent years that the latter must be spurious.[8] They have done so in apparent obliviousness of Miriam Galston's fine "A Re-examination of al-Fārābī's Neoplatonism," which focuses on the differences between the occasions when Alfarabi uses Neoplatonic readings of Aristotle and the occasions when he adheres closely to the Stagirite.[9] Galston shows the system in Alfarabi's use of Neoplatonizing readings of Aristotle. How did Strauss rediscover a non-Neoplatonic Plato in the *Philosophy of Plato*? Strauss argued in his "Farabi's *Plato*" that Alfarabi's Plato is so far from the traditional (that is, Neoplatonized) portrait of Plato or Socrates that he discusses neither the so-called theory of ideas nor the immortality of the soul (FP, 360, 364, 374–75, 376, 389, 391). Instead, Alfarabi focuses on how the philosopher Socrates (and Plato) is at odds with his city and how Socrates chooses to die rather than continue to live if it means living like an animal without philosophy, that is, like a fish—in other words, Alfarabi concerns himself with the very feature of philosophy that is the lost surface of things, obscured by Neoplatonism. By harmonizing philosophy and city, Neoplatonism not only obscures the significance of philosophy as a way of life, assimilating it more to a mystical path in ultimate harmony with society, but also loses the capacity to reflect on political life. How odd that we should find in the first millennium of the Common Era a way of thinking so strangely resonant with the distortions of our own times.[10]

Will the Philosopher among the Jews Please Stand Up?

Strauss imitates Alfarabi's reading of Plato in his own interpretation of the writings of Maimonides, Halevi, and Spinoza in *Persecution*. By recovering this imitation, we learn more about not only Strauss's recovery of medieval Islamic political philosophy but also its implications for his more prominent study of medieval Jewish political philosophy. Strauss approaches Alfarabi's disjunction between philosopher and city through a complex comparison of philosopher and believer. In *Persecution*, the *falāsifa* are—above all, Alfarabi is—cast in the role of the philosopher, and the Jewish believer in the Law is cast in the role of the city. In other words, rather than appeal to Islamic spokesmen for Islamic Law, Strauss turns to Jewish thinkers, namely, Judah Halevi and Maimonides, who seem to be the opponents of the *falāsifa*—adding complication to complication. (Indeed, one of the key intended effects of the introduction to *Persecution* is to induce fruitful confusion about whether any Jewish thinkers qualify as "medieval Jewish philosophers," leaving some with the comforting suspicion that only Muslims can be *falāsifa*.)

From this moment forward in *Persecution*, one is left wondering where these Jewish thinkers fit in the opposition between the *falāsifa* and Scholasticism. Of course, by identifying "Islamic and Jewish medieval philosophy" as he does in the opening pages, he lends some credence to the view that these Jewish thinkers side with the *falāsifa*. But . . . among the most startling statements in *Persecution* is one that almost none of the scholars of Islamic and Jewish medieval philosophy of his generation and not many more in ours accept—namely, that "being a Jew and being a philosopher are mutually exclusive" (19). Because this is put so bluntly, the typical reader of *Persecution* assumes that Maimonides and Halevi are aware of the possibility of philosophy as a way of life, but choose in favor of revelation. At this point in *Persecution*, aside from the lumping together of Jews and Muslims into Islamic and Jewish medieval philosophy, one is not given any other clues that there might be a strong affinity between either Halevi or Maimonides and the *falāsifa*. Early in the course of "Law of Reason in the *Kuzari*," the third chapter in *Persecution*, the reader is led to consider Halevi as a thinker who chose in favor of revelation: "In the case of a man such as Halevi, however, the influence of philosophy on him consists in a conversion to philosophy: for some time, we prefer to think for a very short time, he was a philosopher. After that moment, a spiritual hell, he returned to the Jewish fold" (109). This is one of the most important bases for the view often associated with Strauss that the difference between philosopher and believer or philosopher and theologian is a matter of choice or decision.[11]

We may begin to sort out the significance of this putative choice by considering one of Strauss's other most startling statements, also in *Persecution*, voiced near the end of "The Law of Reason in the *Kuzari*": "One has not to be naturally pious, he has merely to have a passionate interest in genuine morality in order to long with all of his heart for revelation: moral man as such is the potential believer" (140). What motivated Halevi's decision against philosophy, then, appears to be his passionate interest in genuine morality, and this passionate interest also appears to be what distinguishes the believer from the philosopher and thus the city from philosophy. Does this then mean that the philosopher must be an outcast and opponent of the city and morality? If we consider what Strauss is arguing more in the light of Plato, Aristotle, and Alfarabi than in the light of a vulgarized Nietzsche of the sort one finds in Shadia Drury or William H. F. Altman, one can begin to see how the "alienation" or, to use a term of art of Alfarabi, the "solitude" of the philosopher in the city need not always eventuate in all-out rebellion against the city. Perhaps what differentiates the philosopher from the believer is less a decision for one way of life over the other than it is a more passionate interest in all that is than in genuine morality. The interest in all that is should, far from preventing one's understanding of morality, increase it. But it would also likely put the passionate interest in genuine morality in perspective—a perspective that deviates from that of the city.

So far we have seen indications that Halevi, though he might have entertained the way of life of the philosopher for a time, fell back into passionate interest in genuine morality.[12] Regarding Maimonides's status, Strauss is far more elusive in *Persecution*. He shifts focus to the surface of Maimonides's *Guide*, in which Maimonides shows up as a practitioner of kalām (dialectical theology) if "enlightened *kalām*" (*PAW*, 41). In contrast, Strauss characterizes Halevi or his Jewish scholar as an "atypical mutakallim," indebted in some ways to the Muʿtazilite kalām (99–100n14, 138n136). Having set forth the radical opposition between Jew and philosopher in the introduction to *Persecution*, Strauss shows just how complicated a matter it is to determine who might really be a Jew and who a philosopher. Above all, he shows not only the value but also the necessity of using extreme care in exploring the history of Islamic and Jewish medieval philosophy. One cannot but distort what has really been thought by employing the broad brush of "Jewish philosophy" or "Islamic philosophy" to capture the status of thinkers as different as Alfarabi and Halevi.

The Crux of the Dispute between Scholasticism and Alfarabi

Let us consider briefly what connection might exist between Alfarabi's awareness of the gap between philosopher and city, on the one hand, and his ability to grasp political phenomena, on the other. The profundity of Alfarabi's grasp of political phenomena is one of the great discoveries of Strauss and his students, especially Muhsin Mahdi. Too often, Alfarabi has been viewed as a metaphysically impoverished precursor to Avicenna and Averroës. Such a view is possible only if one takes one's lead on how to approach Islamic and Jewish medieval philosophy from Scholasticism. When interpreters of it follow Scholasticism, they nearly universally overestimate the determinative character of metaphysics, as if one could understand the human things by presupposing various truths about the whole. This nonphilosophic approach to the human things, which Alfarabi captures in his characterization of "certainty" in the opening of the *Attainment of Happiness*, reveals its own limitations. This approach leads to the excessive hopes for world rule explored in that work.

Those who would have us approach Alfarabi as a traditional Neoplatonist fail to see the profound critique of religion to be found more broadly in Islamic and Jewish medieval philosophy but in its most pristine and straightforward form in Alfarabi—at least in part because of the way in which Alfarabi cloaks his teaching in the garb of Neoplatonism, as Strauss argues in *Persecution*, citing the work of Louis Gardet and M.-M. Anawati,

> The philosophic intransigence of the *falāsifa* is not sufficiently appreciated in the accepted interpretations of their teachings. This is partly due to the reticence of the *falāsifa* themselves. The best clues to their intentions are found in the writings of men like Yehuda Halevi and Maimonides. The value of the testimony of these great men may be thought to be impaired by the fact that they opposed the *falāsifa*. Yet at least some writings of Fārābī confirm the interpretation which Halevi and Maimonides suggest. In the present state of our knowledge it is impossible to say to what extent Fārābī's successors accepted his view in regards to the crucial point. But there can be no doubt that those views acted as a leaven as long as philosophy exercised an influence on Islamic and Jewish thought. (11)

Leaving aside the insinuation that Halevi and Maimonides are on the same page in their opposition to Alfarabi, it is worth considering the most obvious feature of Alfarabi that Halevi and Maimonides bring forward. As Strauss goes on to show in "Law of Reason," Halevi accuses the *falāsifa* of indifference toward religion (114)—a view that is in no way compatible with the Neoplatonizing reading of Alfarabi. Similarly, Maimonides makes it amply evident that, what Strauss calls the "most fundamental point" (121n78), namely, the eternity or createdness of the world, is the center of the dispute between reason and revelation. Despite the halfway houses between eternity and creation that various Neoplatonists and Scholastics have erected, the Islamic and Jewish medieval philosophers, in works such as Alfarabi's *Philosophy of Plato and Aristotle*, reveal their dogged concern for the truth over facile harmonizations of thought and society. Although one might assume that the way to achieve what is best politically is to strive for just such a harmonization, it seems more likely that such harmonizations only blind one to the depth of disorder and disorganization to which human affairs are prone. Among other things, without a sufficient awareness of the depth of the gap between philosopher and city, thinkers grow complacent about how much human effort is required to secure even a modicum of political well-being.

Even if Spinoza did not intend to eliminate the gap between philosopher and state, his aggressive critique of religion seems to have facilitated our forgetfulness of this gap—not only by establishing the mediating role of the intellectual but also by launching an approach to books or texts that contributed mightily to the rise of problematically subversive approaches to reading philosophical writings. We turn back to Alfarabi, Maimonides, and Halevi not because we find in them ready-made political solutions for our time but because they enable us to look anew at our own world. Because the leading modern political solutions include a large mechanical or institutional component, they make us prone to forgetfulness and complacency about the great challenges posed by human nature. Strauss offers us Islamic and Jewish medieval philosophy that can awaken us from our stupor rather than lulling us into complacency.

CHAPTER SIX

The Differing Places of Metaphysics in Alfarabi and Thomas Aquinas

According to chapters 1 and 3, the most widely accepted interpretation of Alfarabi is that he grounds his politics on his metaphysics. And as we saw in chapter 3, E. I. J. Rosenthal argued that Alfarabi's "political thought . . . is only a part of a whole philosophy . . . [and his *Virtuous City*] is indicative of this dependence of politics on philosophy as a whole."[1] Indeed, it would appear that the *Virtuous City*, by placing metaphysics before politics, confirms Rosenthal's suggestion. Majid Fakhry has gone on much more recently to affirm that Alfarabi's politics is "an extension or development of metaphysics or its highest manifestation, theology."[2] By similarly devoting the opening portions of his *Political Regime* to metaphysics, Alfarabi seems to confirm the impression left by the *Virtuous City* that metaphysics provides the ground for politics.

Since I titled my first book *Metaphysics as Rhetoric*, I have sought to raise doubts about this prevailing interpretation of Alfarabi. In that book, I spoke in a postmodern vein, not because I was myself a postmodernist but because I hoped to catch the attention of postmodern readers. I never argued that Alfarabi does not have any metaphysical views or that metaphysics is ultimately irrelevant. Rather, I sought to raise doubts about whether Alfarabi intended the openings of the *Virtuous City* and the *Political Regime* as demonstrative metaphysical grounds for his politics. The most obvious evidence in support of the claim that Alfarabi grounds his politics on metaphysics is that metaphysics precedes politics in *Virtuous City* and *Political Regime*. Since Rosenthal argued as he did, however, another writing by Alfarabi has come to light, his *Book of Religion*.[3] In that work Alfarabi reverses the order of metaphysics and politics, placing politics before metaphysics.

Although the order of presentation of metaphysics and politics is not sufficient for determining Alfarabi's views, it remains a crucial clue in this inquiry into the relation between metaphysics and politics. In addition to considering the significance of this clue, we will need to determine, among other things, the following: Why did he present metaphysics before politics in *Virtuous City* and *Political Regime* but politics before metaphysics in the *Book of Religion*? What is the status and character of these different works? Eventually we will address these questions. For now, let us consider more generally the issue of the order of inquiry, which was so important in premodern philosophy and theology.

Differences in the Order of Inquiry in Philosophy and Theology

In his translation of Thomas Aquinas's *Summa contra gentiles*, (Fr.) Anton Pegis (FRSC) notes that, according to Thomas in that work he follows the order of inquiry of the "teaching of the faith," as opposed to the order of "human philosophy."[4] Comparison of the *Summa contra gentiles* with Aristotle's *Metaphysics* will, I hope, suffice to draw the distinction between these two orders of inquiry. Of course, the order of the *Summa contra gentiles* is God, creation, providence, salvation. Without going into any detail, we need only observe about the *Metaphysics* that Aristotle does not get around to addressing God directly until book 12. (Here, I leave aside all the debates about the composition of the *Metaphysics* because I, like most contemporary interpreters who follow in the footsteps of Joseph Owen and Giovanni Reale, prefer to see the work as a more or less coherent whole.) In brief, the difference between the "teaching of faith" and "human philosophy" is that the former begins with God and the latter (almost) ends with God. Of course, the comparison of the *Summa contra gentiles* with the *Metaphysics* is far from perfect. The former is far more wide ranging than the latter. Most important, the *Summa contra gentiles* addresses practical matters in a way that the *Metaphysics* does not. As reference to the "teaching of the faith" would seem to suggest, the *Summa contra gentiles*, as well as the later *Summa theologiae*, follows the order of scripture itself. The Bible begins with God, followed immediately by creation and culminating ultimately in guidance to humankind about practical affairs. Consequently, Thomas argues within the first question of the *Summa theologiae* not only that sacred doctrine or revealed theology is a science but that it is both theoretical and practical.[5]

So far two issues of ordering have emerged: the order internal to theological as opposed to philosophical inquiries into God and the order in the relation between theoretical (metaphysical) and practical (political) inquiries. It is possible (and we will argue very much the case in Alfarabi) that philosophy and religion (or revelation or faith) differ regarding not only the order of inquiry into God but also the relative order of inquiry into theoretical and practical matters.

For now, let us consider the origin of the divergences over order of inquiry into God. They are traceable, at least on the side of philosophy, to what

Aristotle captures in his contrast between what is first for us and what first by nature.⁶ This contrast has taken on many forms over the history of Western thought, perhaps most familiarly as the contrast between the *ordo cognoscendi* and the *ordo essendi*, or the order of (human) knowing or instruction and the order of being. Of course, since God is remote from human knowing, philosophy never begins with God. Rather, it begins its inquiry with the beings familiar to us through sensation—an inquiry somewhat mysteriously labeled the study of being qua being or general metaphysics or the like—and works its way around to God. In other words, philosophy begins with what is first for us or follows the order of instruction because we cannot follow the order of being directly, as we would all prefer to.

In contrast, "the teaching of the faith" or religion follows the order of being. Although there are many motives for following the order of being, we need only consider the most obvious one: human beings desire and are even impatient to know the order of all things (see *Guide*, 1.34). Such impatience also has a few sources, but the most important one here is that knowing of the highest kind (theoretical knowledge) is posterior to doing or acting (*praxis*). Human beings are thrown into a world of action, if not the highest kind of action, almost from birth. All such action—and here we temporarily abstract from the opinions championed by our given family, society, religion, and nation—leads us to feel and think certain things about the world. We are prone to leap to certain conclusions about the highest things because opinions about the meaning of our actions and the world's response to them gradually, increasingly color our actions. While working through the question, why religion or faith, unlike philosophy, turns directly to God, we have hit upon a connection to the other issue of ordering: why does religion begin with theory and then turn to practice? Once again, religion follows the order of being; philosophy follows the order of knowing.

Although it is relatively obvious that beginning with the beings around us and then moving to God amounts to following the order of knowing, it is slightly less obvious that, for philosophy, practice or practical science is somehow prior to theoretical science in the order of knowing; that is, practical science is or should be first for us. In passing in the previous argument about the motives for following the order of being, we hit upon the most obvious reason that practical science should precede theoretical science, namely, that practical affairs are more urgent and thus more evidently pressing for everyone. Two additional observations support the view that practical affairs and science precede theoretical science in the philosophic order of inquiry: the structure of each of the Platonic dialogues and the way teachers (or professors) of philosophy usually teach Aristotle's philosophy. Platonic dialogues are, crudely speaking, framed in one of two ways: Either the reader is led to infer the existence of a frame for the conversation (as in the performed dialogues, most obviously the pattern in the putatively early dialogues) or Plato presents the frame directly at the beginning by describing certain actions in certain places and times and involving specific actors (as in a dialogue like the *Republic*). The frame then is both temporal and political, because it refers the informed reader to certain historical events, especially those relating to the rise and fall of Athens in the lead up to, during, and following the Peloponnesian War and those relating to the life and death of Socrates. This frame either comes first (though it is filled out at moments throughout the dialogue), as in the narrated dialogues, or it is implied from the first, as in the performed dialogues. In brief, the political frame precedes any and every strictly philosophical or theoretical issue in the dialogues.

As a far less abstract justification for the claim that, in philosophy, practical science is first and theoretical philosophy second in the order of knowing, let us consider teaching Aristotle, who is of course the inaugurator of a clear distinction between theoretical and practical science. It is far easier—that is, it follows the order of knowing or what is first for us—to begin with a work like his *Nicomachean Ethics* rather than his *Metaphysics*. This is not to deny that some philosophy professors might begin with theoretical science and then turn to practical science (this was especially popular, for example, at my Catholic institution, the University of Dallas, following the heyday of Neo-Thomism in the mid-twentieth century), but in doing so, it seems to me that a philosophy professor would be following the order of being rather than the order of knowing, and thus the order suited to faith rather than philosophy. It is also not to say that there is not good sense in returning to a work like the *Nicomachean Ethics* after studying the *Metaphysics*. Indeed, practical science is in some important respects more elusive than theoretical science—and therefore may ultimately require more "returning to."

In brief, the "teaching of the faith" or religion follows the order of being when it comes to inquiring into God and to the relation between theoretical and practical inquiry; however, human philosophy follows the reverse order, the order of knowing in both cases. The main means by which religion approaches matters so directly is metaphor. As Thomas argues within the very first question of the *Summa theologiae*, the truths of sacred doctrine are made known even to the simple by means of metaphor. The extrascriptural support he offers for this argument in the *Summa theologiae* is drawn from the renowned negative theologian Pseudo-Dionysius the Areopagite. Interestingly, in the *Summa contra gentiles* evidence abounds that Thomas relied in these things, namely, the reasons for revelation, on Moses Maimonides, that student of Alfarabi who is far more widely known to the West than his teacher.[7] Religion approaches being directly in a way that philosophy does not because it can shade the eyes of the believer through the veil of metaphor and image and because the multitude or the simple do not have the time, patience, or wherewithal to engage in such inquiries. In effect, even though religion may begin in accordance with the order of being, it does so in such a way as to confirm the basic insight of Socrates in Plato's *Phaedo* that the eyes of human knowing must be shaded from the brilliance of the truth of being. Socrates and philosophers in general achieve a similar effect by the different means of beginning with what is first according to human knowing.

Alfarabi's Transformation of Kalām into Dialectic

At last we may turn more directly to Alfarabi. He argues—more bluntly than Maimonides—religion deals in images, while philosophy deals in truths.[8] Maimonides insists on the prophet's need for a highly refined imagination precisely because religion deals in images.[9] When I denied that Alfarabi provides the demonstrative metaphysical grounds for politics in the openings of his *Virtuous City* and *Political Regime*, my intention was not to dismiss the *Virtuous City* and *Political Regime* but to underline Alfarabi's recourse in them to rhetorical arguments and even metaphors rather than demonstrative arguments. These Farabian works are religious presentations or follow the order of the teaching of the faith, at least in their opening cosmological musings. In contrast, when Alfarabi presents his thought in the reverse order, politics then metaphysics, as he does in the *Book of Religion*, he is following the order of instruction more suited to philosophy than religion. So far our main focus has been on correlates in the thought of Thomas to phenomena in Alfarabi. Because crucial differences exist between Thomas and Alfarabi, we need to begin to attend to some of those differences. After all, to offer a convincing interpretation of Alfarabi we should do more than merely posit claims about his various works.

For Alfarabi the tasks of theology are far more limited than they are for Thomas. These limitations derive from the fact that theology (kalām) was to play a far smaller role in Islam. It played a smaller role because Islam is a *sharīʿa*, or divine law. Rather than theology playing the role of queen of the sciences, as it does for Thomas in the Christian setting, jurisprudence (*fiqh*) plays that role. Consequently, theology is far less developed in Islam (and for that matter in Judaism because they are religions of divine law) than in Christianity. Indeed, at first glance, it might appear that theology or kalām is nothing but apologetic theology.

In the one work by Alfarabi that received the most attention in the West, his *Enumeration of the Sciences*, he describes the confluence of the Islamic sciences including dialectical theology and jurisprudence, on the one hand, and the newly arrived sciences of the Greeks such as metaphysics and political science, on the other. The result of this confluence was a certain amount of disorder among the sciences as they appear when Alfarabi arrives on the scene. In the *Enumeration*, kalām has precious little to do with metaphysics. Instead, it is poised to defend religion, especially against the theoretical challenges posed by philosophy. Maimonides confirms Alfarabi's portrayal of the initial role of kalām as defense of the faith against philosophy. He argues that this relation between theology and philosophy originated among the Greek and Syrian Christians and was subsequently developed by the Muslims and finally the Jews (*Guide*, 1.71). Although the apologetic character of theology was especially pronounced in Islam and Judaism, it was, of course, not exclusive to them.

In his *Book of Religion*—the work already mentioned because in it he presents politics first and metaphysics second—Alfarabi presents a different account of theology from the account given in the *Enumeration*. In effect, the *Enumeration* presents the sciences as they appear before Alfarabi has given them a new shape; the *Book of Religion* presents the sciences (not all, but the ones most relevant to us) as Alfarabi intends them to be after he has given them a new shape. In the *Book of Religion*, far from the kalām that attacks philosophy of the *Enumeration*, he puts "dialectic" (*jadal*) in the place of kalām (sec. 6). To be more precise, he puts dialectic and rhetoric at the service of an already transformed religion. (Dialectic leads the way in *BR*, sec. 6, but is quickly followed by rhetoric. For ease of reference and because Alfarabi puts dialectic out front, as it were, we refer to "dialectic" rather than "dialectic and rhetoric." Ultimately, Alfarabi does not seem to want to limit this endeavor even to dialectic and rhetoric; he seems also to want to include poetic arguments or the use of images, based on what has already been said about the connection between images, metaphors, and religion.) To recapitulate, in the *Book of Religion*, which describes the new Farabian versions of sciences and religion, dialectic is far from the kalām that attacks philosophy of the *Enumeration*. Indeed, dialectic in the *Book of Religion* supports the virtuous religion established on the basis of philosophy! The substitution of dialectic for kalām appears at first glance to be a mere name change—an impression only intensified by the typical translation of kalām as "dialectical theology." (The most common denotation of kalām is simply "discourse.")[10] On the contrary, the relation between philosophy and theology (or religion or faith) has undergone a radical transformation in the *Book of Religion*, behind our backs, as it were.

Leaving aside the change in name from kalām to dialectic, how does Alfarabi bring about a new relation between theology and philosophy—in effect turning theology into a subordinate supporter of philosophy? Like his follower Averroës, Alfarabi establishes a hierarchy among the forms of argument based on Aristotle's Organon, in which the highest position and the position identified with philosophy proper is demonstrative argument. Beneath demonstration, he ranges dialectic, and beneath dialectic he places rhetoric and poetic forms of argument.[11] In effect, then, Alfarabi develops a replacement for kalām that is a dialectical equivalent to it. By identifying it as dialectic, he clearly subordinates it to philosophy. (Though usually translated as "dialectical theology," traditional kalām was not careful in its use of dialectical argumentation in Aristotle's and subsequently Alfarabi's technical sense of the term—on the contrary, it used every weapon at hand.)

We must backtrack a bit in the *Book of Religion* to appreciate fully the extent to which Alfarabi is subordinating "dialectic" to philosophy—and thus abandoning the traditional antagonism between theology and philosophy identified by both Alfarabi and Maimonides. Alfarabi intensifies this subordination by arguing that virtuous religion is "similar" (*shabīha*) to philosophy. Virtuous religion contains theoretical and practical parts similar to the theoretical and practical parts in philosophy. They are not only similar, however. On the contrary, that which is universal in philosophy is presented as determinate or particularized in religion. Here, we have come back to a point of convergence with the arguments of not only Maimonides but also even Thomas. Religion contains particularized images—unlike philosophy, which deals only in universals. Among other things, Alfarabi and Maimonides part ways with Thomas, however, over the extent to which this matter of particularization refers then not only to opinions or beliefs but also to divine law as law and to the role of the prophet in the giving of the Law.

In many respects, law itself is universal. As Aristotle's *Nicomachean Ethics* indicates, law is universal when it comes to justice, that is, it says the same thing to all its adherents in a given community. Consequently, equity (*epieikia*) must be employed by the prudent judge in applying the law. Nevertheless, law is also characterized by particularity. After all, laws are given to a particular community—even if that community might have universal ambitions. Although particularity is sometimes linked dismissively with mere conventionality, laws always seem to require rootedness in particularity.[12]

Indeed, particularity or determination is the first word of Alfarabi's *Book of Religion*. "Religion is opinions and actions, determined and restricted with stipulations and prescribed for a community by their first ruler" (sec. 1). And how this determination occurs proves to be one of the most elusive and profound questions in the thought of Alfarabi, as well as Maimonides. As I have taken this up elsewhere at great length, I must limit myself here to the observation that Alfarabi attributes this particularization or determination characteristic of divine law to a variety of possible sources, including revelation, prudence, or imagination.[13] For our purposes, it suffices to say that the subordination of religion to philosophy flows to a great extent from the fact that Alfarabi argues for the derivation of religion from philosophy as particular is derived from universal. It should be obvious by now that that derivation does not take a scientific form. On the contrary, the recourse to revelation or prudence or imagination shows what is borne out throughout the history of Western thought but especially profoundly in premodern thought—namely, that scientific or theoretical reason or demonstrative argument is characterized by profound limits when it comes to what Socrates referred to as the human things.[14] Most obvious, the elusive nature of Aristotle's conception of prudence, especially the forms and modes of reasoning employed by prudence in navigating the human things, bears out this basic insight.[15]

Lest we become completely sidetracked on the nature and character of divine law, prophecy, and their origins, we need to return to the question: how does the newfangled dialectic differ from the previously existing pair, kalām and metaphysics? The new dialectic is no longer an antagonist to philosophy but its subordinate or ministerial supporter. Indeed, the new dialectic seems to function more or less at the level of virtuous religion as its adjunct. Rather than defending the religion against philosophy, it "defend[s], support[s], and establish[es] those [religious] opinions" for "most people" (sec. 6), against those who would deceive the adherents of the said religion. By comparison, the religion in the background in the *Enumeration* is never identified there as virtuous religion. Furthermore, everything Alfarabi argues elsewhere about religion being an imitation of philosophy (in *AH* and *Book of Letters*) and especially that philosophy precedes religion in time suggests that, until religion is brought into the relation to philosophy established in the *Book of Religion*, religion is not considered by Alfarabi to be truly "virtuous" religion. In effect, as long as religion is not yet virtuous religion, one should expect the differentiation and tension between metaphysics and kalām that one finds in the *Enumeration*. This opposition falls away once theology comes to be properly subordinated to philosophy. To check our interpretation of the dialectic in the *Book of Religion* and its relation to philosophy, we will pause to compare it with what we find in Maimonides, Alfarabi's follower.

In *Persecution*, Strauss has observed that the account of the division of the sciences in the *Enumeration* is "of decisive importance for the understanding of the *Guide*" (*PAW*, 40n9). Although Maimonides's *Guide of the Perplexed* is often misinterpreted as self-evidently a work of philosophy—if so-called Jewish philosophy—Strauss argues that it must be understood in the first instance as a work of kalām. Now far from being a work of "vulgar *kalām*"—which battles against philosophy and is what Alfarabi describes in the *Enumeration*—the *Guide* is in the first instance a work of what Strauss calls "enlightened *kalām*." As I argue in chapter 2, the "dialectic" described in Alfarabi's *Book of Religion* seems to be the philosophic paradigm of the enlightened kalām in Maimonides's *Guide*.

In stark contrast to the distinction between kalām and metaphysics we find in the *Enumeration*, Strauss observes, Maimonides "does not know of theology as a discipline distinct from metaphysics" (46). Indeed, this convergence of metaphysics and theology is the first and last word of the *Guide*. It is announced in Maimonides's famous and famously elusive claim that the Account of the Beginning and the Account of the Chariot (the mysteries of the Torah) are the same as natural science or physics and divine science or metaphysics (*Guide*, pt. 1, introd., 6). In effect, the secrets of the Bible are the highest theoretical truths of philosophy. More specifically, the Account of the Chariot (or the inner meaning of biblical theology) is metaphysics.

Alfarabi implies much the same view of divine science or metaphysics or theology in his account of dialectic in the *Book of Religion*. The only difference between the metaphysics of philosophy and the dialectic that defends religion is that "dialectic" employs dialectical and rhetorical arguments. In other words, in the *Book of Religion*, Alfarabi presupposes the equivalence of theology and metaphysics, except insofar as theology communicates through images and determination what metaphysics or philosophy grasps in universal form. Rather than truly different sciences, which metaphysics and theology are sometimes treated as being, in the *Book of Religion* Alfarabi treats them as using different kinds of arguments but arguing about the same truth.

The contrast between this view of the relation between philosophy and theology, on the one hand, and that of Thomas, on the other, could hardly be greater—at least according to his teaching in the opening of the *Summa theologiae*. In the closing sentence of the first article of the first question, Thomas argues that "the theology included in sacred doctrine differs in genus from that theology which is a part of philosophy." Of course, the latter theology is what Thomas relatively infrequently refers to as "natural theology," and the former is the revealed theology that is sacred doctrine. Thomas clearly intends for natural theology to be subordinate to revealed theology, as philosophy is the handmaiden to (revealed) theology. Roughly speaking, for Alfarabi, the reverse is true: religion (or theology) is the handmaiden to philosophy—except insofar as the theology of philosophy is identical to the theology of religion. Put most bluntly: Alfarabi does not envision a superior revealed theology.

Alfarabi's Understanding of the Relation between Metaphysics and Politics

Based on the *Book of Religion*, it is tempting to assume that Alfarabi argues that philosophy takes the place of revealed theology. Much as Thomas's sacred doctrine begins by setting forth the theoretical truths of the faith and then identifies the practical consequences of those truths, so one might assume Alfarabi would have philosophy play this role of comprehensive theoretico-practical science.[16] In spite of the confident manner in which philosophy guides religion in the *Book of Religion*, Alfarabi's ultimate views on philosophy undercut the initial impression that his philosophy holds the position of authority in his account that sacred doctrine holds in Thomas's. True, philosophy for Alfarabi has a theoretical and a practical part much as Thomas's sacred doctrine does; however, Alfarabi is far less sanguine about the completeness of the theoretical part of philosophy than Thomas is about the theoretical part of sacred doctrine. It will come as little surprise that Alfarabi questions the completeness of the highest reaches of philosophy, especially metaphysics. After all, among the reasons that Thomas declares sacred doctrine of a different genus from the metaphysics that is a part of philosophy is not only that sacred doctrine derives its superiority from the fact that it can draw on supranatural resources but also that human reason is somehow deficient in its efforts to acquire knowledge of the highest reaches of metaphysics. Of course, the recognition of some limits of human reason is not reserved to modern thinkers such as Kant.

Much like Kant, Alfarabi seems to recognize that human reason cannot acquire full possession of the highest reaches of metaphysics. Unlike Kant, however, Alfarabi writes only cryptically about where those limits might lie.[17] In the *Philosophy of Aristotle* Alfarabi enters into the upper reaches of theoretical science just at the cusp of metaphysics, including a discussion of the heavenly bodies and an account of the Active Intellect (so important for his accounts of prophecy).[18] Yet he announces before concluding the *Philosophy of Aristotle*, "We do not possess metaphysical science."

Now based on other writings by Alfarabi, we may infer that he did think that we possess some of metaphysics and likely far more than Kant would admit.[19] For our present inquiry, however, it is more important for us to determine what Alfarabi thought the consequences of these limits were for the relation between metaphysics and politics than it is to determine where are those limits with any precision.

There are at least three consequences of those limits: (1) As long as metaphysics is incomplete, philosophy as a whole is more dependent on inquiry into human things than it might otherwise be. (2) As long as metaphysics is incomplete, religion cannot receive from philosophy the universals that it particularizes with the confidence that might otherwise be expected. In other words, the less complete metaphysics is the less confident one can be that in giving religion to a community that that particular religion is a guide toward the truth. And (3) since revealed religions in particular aspire to bring one truth to all humankind, they in particular need to have their aspirations to universal acceptance tempered. Since I have already devoted my second book, *An Islamic Philosophy of Virtuous Religions*, to these interrelated second and third points, let us focus here on the first consequence: the interdependence of inquiry into human things and inquiry into the whole, otherwise known as the interdependence of politics or political science and metaphysics.

To some extent, all of Alfarabi's so-called political writings, *Book of Religion*, *Virtuous City*, and *Political Regime* and even his *Selected Aphorisms*, show that he recognizes the interdependence of metaphysical and political inquiry. What we are interested in, however, is how we are to understand that interdependence. In particular, we need to clarify the difference between the kind of dependency of the practical sciences on the theoretical sciences that we see in works such as Thomas's *Summa theologiae* and Alfarabi's writings. For purposes of clarity, one might say that *Summa theologiae* establishes a top-down relation, where theoretical science is the top and practical science is down. Because, according to Alfarabi, metaphysical science is incomplete, we must expect a less top-down relation from him. Although his more theological works such as *Virtuous City* and *Political Regime* appear at times to provide a top-down relation between metaphysics and politics, the *Book of Religion* suggests either the opposite or an ongoing, what one might call, a "dialogical" relation between metaphysics and politics. At a minimum, this chapter has shown—especially in light of the *Book of Religion*, unknown to authors such as E. I. J. Rosenthal—that Alfarabi's more philosophic view is that due to limitations in our knowledge of the highest things, politics does not flow down from metaphysics. In effect, what the *Book of Religion* reveals is a more Platonic view of the relation between metaphysics and politics, between theoretical and practical science—again, a more dialectical or dialogical relation between them.

At least two other features of Alfarabi's thought confirm this characterization as supporting a dialogue between metaphysics and political science. First, in the *Enumeration* and the *Book of Religion* he presents two accounts of political science. In the first (PS 1) he gives an account of politics reminiscent of Aristotle's *Ethics* and *Politics*—that is, he presents an account of human action from within the horizon of the ethically virtuous political actor, as opposed to that of the philosopher (whose horizon is alluded to, for example, only in *Nicomachean Ethics*, bks. 6 and 10, and *Politics*, bks. 4 and 10). In the second account (PS 2), he includes within this political science an account of the role of theoretical science as well as practical science and the peculiar importance of opinions, not only political but also theoretical, in politics.[20] In effect, PS 2 discusses politics with reference to the virtuous kingly craft of the philosopher-king of Platonic fame. The fact that Alfarabi's political philosophy is concerned with revealed divine law helps to explain why he would follow the lead of Plato rather than Aristotle. Revealed divine law places new emphasis on opinion, especially theoretical opinions, as compared with what one would find among pagan Greeks. Second, in the *Attainment of Happiness* Alfarabi goes so far as to characterize human or political science as part of man's theoretical perfection—thus, again, undercutting Aristotle's distinction between theoretical and practical science. We could bring forth other evidence that Alfarabi's view of theoretical and practical science in general, and metaphysics and political science in particular, are more dialogical than, for example, the tradition of political philosophy and metaphysics exemplified by Thomas.

At this point, however, we should turn briefly to Strauss to confirm that what we're calling a dialectical relation between theoretical and practical philosophy in Alfarabi may have influenced the way Strauss read not only Plato but also Aristotle—or, at least, that Strauss's view of Aristotle is similarly un-Thomistic as regard the relation between the theoretical and the practical. In "An Epilogue," Strauss opposes the commonly held view that for Aristotle metaphysics grounds politics. Precisely because Aristotle's account of politics establishes a prescientific horizon within which the political man considers the human things, Aristotle is able to establish a certain amount of autonomy of the political, especially the very core of politics, prudence, from the metaphysical. The task of metaphysics then is not to establish the grounds of prudence but to provide arguments against those "false doctrines about the whole" by which "prudence is always endangered."[21]

We began with a relatively wide-ranging discussion of the order of inquiry in philosophical and theological writings, noting that the former follows the order of knowledge while the latter follows the order of being or nature. Furthermore, we argued that when it comes to the order of inquiry in theoretical and practical matters a similar opposition prevails: the more philosophic begin with the practical and the more theological with the theoretical. We then used this contrast between the philosophical and theological approaches to help sort Alfarabi's writings into his more theological (*Political Regime* and *Virtuous City*) and his more philosophical (*BR* and eventually the trilogy). We began by challenging the view prevalent among scholars of Islamic philosophy from E. I. J. Rosenthal to Majid Fakhry. The *Book of Religion* bears out what I've been trying to argue, following my teacher Muhsin Mahdi, namely, that one fails to understand Alfarabi if one holds that his political science derives in top-down fashion from his metaphysics. As we've seen in these concluding pages, the trilogy also shows that we should not read Alfarabi in this way. As we have already seen in chapter 2, even in works such as the *Political Regime* Alfarabi gives the reader indications that the Neoplatonic metaphysics one finds at times in his writings, which is highlighted so constantly by interpreters such as Rosenthal and Fakhry, has more to do with the opinions of the inhabitants of the virtuous city than it has to do with the philosophic truth. In conclusion, Alfarabi is not the metaphysical foundationalist he is usually taken to be.

PART THREE

Strauss on Alfarabi and Maimonides in the 1930s through the 1950s

CHAPTER SEVEN

From Political Philosophy to Enlightened Kalām

The 1930s and 1940s

The end of the 1930s marked a turning point in Strauss's thought that Daniel Tanguay has aptly called his "Farabian Turn."[1] Although Strauss's most extended work on Alfarabi, Maimonides, and others in the 1930s is *Philosophy and Law* (1935), the turn Tanguay identifies is more evident in the smaller pieces that came out in the wake of *Philosophy and Law*—including "Some Remarks on the Political Science of Maimonides and Farabi" (1936) but especially "The Place of the Doctrine of Providence according to Maimonides" (1937).[2] In these two pieces, Strauss evinces a growing awareness of the depth of Maimonides's debt to Alfarabi. Tanguay identifies two main features of the Farabian Turn: the focus on the political in Maimonides and a growing awareness of the centrality of esotericism. Prior to the turn, in *Philosophy and Law*, Strauss elevated two features in his interpretation of Maimonides that fade into the background as early as the two pieces written in 1936 and 1937: the importance of Avicenna's account of prophecy and Maimonides's apparent reliance on supernatural resources for knowledge beyond the limit of natural human knowledge. Beginning in 1936 Strauss avoids any suggestion that the supernatural plays such a role.[3]

Our initial focus in this chapter is on how "Place of Providence" provides a missing piece in Strauss's effort to show that political science is central in Maimonides's *Guide*. Before the Farabian Turn, Strauss was bold in declaring this centrality. And with the beginning of the turn in 1936 and 1937, he remains bold in declaring its centrality and Maimonides's debt to Alfarabi regarding its centrality. Subsequently, however, and as early as his (1941) "Literary Character of the *Guide for the Perplexed*," Strauss speaks far more cautiously about the role of political science in Maimonides's thought.[4] Indeed in "Literary Character," his main reference to political science in the *Guide* is to how "there is practically complete agreement among the students of Maimonides" that the

Guide does not concern it (*PAW*, 44). Indeed, there are moments in the *Guide* (end of 2.39) as well as in Maimonides's *Logic* (end of chap. 14) that appear to exclude any concern with political science or philosophy.[5] Strauss moves from boldly underlining the importance of political science in and for the *Guide* in the 1930s to downplaying direct reference to political science in connection with Maimonides. As Tanguay notes, after the Farabian Turn Strauss decided more and more to emulate premodern esotericism.[6] That emulation includes writing in an increasingly esoteric manner about the character and objectives of the *Guide*. Because of Strauss's greater frankness in his writings in the 1930s, they provide an indispensable window into understanding Strauss's lifelong interest in Maimonides and especially his *Guide*. Although his insights into Maimonides deepened even into the last decade of his life, his earliest, at times ambiguous, insights were often proffered with the greatest frankness.

After our initial focus on the pieces on Alfarabi and Maimonides, we will turn to consider Strauss's writings from the 1930s on Isaac Abravanel. Strauss came to see that Maimonides had been too readily assimilated to medieval Christian philosophy.[7] Because Abravanel's approach to political philosophy was deeply indebted to medieval Christian thought, Strauss came to see that Abravanel's own thought as well as his interpretations of Maimonides followed Christian patterns. We will add Strauss's reading of Abravanel to our prior focus on his Farabian reading of Maimonides to paint a picture of Strauss's emerging understanding of Maimonides in the 1930s.

Arguably, the most striking insight overall in Strauss's writings on Maimonides, Farabi, and others of the 1930s is also the broadest structural insight: In *Philosophy and Law* Strauss shows that the prophetology (*Guide*, 2.32–48) is part of Maimonides's political science, and in the "Place of Providence" Strauss shows that his teaching on particular providence (3.8–24) is also part of his political science. In other words, Strauss argues that the central chapters of the *Guide* are part of political science.[8] A potential source of confusion is worth nipping in the bud: Maimonides states that after *Guide*, 3.7 (the culmination of what every reader of the *Guide* readily acknowledges is the most elusive discussion in this most elusive of books, the biblical Account of the Chariot [3.1–7]), "after this chapter, you will not hear from me even a single word about this subject." Strauss interprets this as Maimonides's establishment of the end of his discussion of divine science or metaphysics in the *Guide*. Maimonides implies thereby that *Guide*, 3.8–24, is not a metaphysical discussion. Now, if one overinterprets Strauss one could suppose that this implies that everything preceding *Guide*, 3.7, concerns metaphysics. This would obviously undercut the claim that the prophetology is part of political science. It is one thing to say henceforth I won't say anything more about *x*, and quite another thing to say that all I discussed previously was about *x*. And it is obviously false to suggest that everything prior to *Guide*, 3.7, concerns metaphysics or divine science. In short, it is at least conceivable that both the prophetology and the teaching on particular providence are part of Maimonides's political science.

Aside from the bold insinuation that the central arguments of the *Guide* are political, what is the significance of Strauss's claim that these two sections are part of political science? To answer this question, we begin by considering why one might have assumed that these two sections were a part of metaphysics or divine science. Throughout the *Guide* the exact content of divine science is in contention. After all, the introduction to the first part opens with the riddle that equates the biblical or rabbinic mysteries, the Account of the Beginning and the Account of the Chariot, with natural science or physics and divine science or metaphysics. There is little agreement among scholars about what this means. It could mean the secret teachings of the Torah are (a) these philosophic, theoretical sciences (cf. *Guide*, 1.71), (b) some revealed equivalent to these philosophic sciences, or (c) a blend or synthesis of philosophic and revealed teachings. Perhaps the most widely prevailing interpretation is some version of the third option. Strauss seems to have adopted some version of (c) in *Philosophy and Law*.

In keeping with some version of (c), one would think that the prophetology would be a part of the Account of the Chariot or divine science because of the central role that the Active Intellect, the lowest of the separate intellects, plays in the reception of prophecy by the prophet. To say that the prophetology is part of political science is to discount the centrality of the theoretical psychology of prophecy.[9] Strauss does not discount completely that psychology in *Philosophy and Law*, but he does begin a process of shifting more and more emphasis from psychology to political science. Similarly, one would think that Maimonides's teaching on particular providence would be part of his divine science. After all, who but God is responsible for particular providence? At this point, we may venture the conjecture that Strauss's break from his earlier stress on the role of the supernatural in prophetic action and human knowledge of the metaphysical and his turn to this unexpected approach to particular providence in "Place of Providence" are connected. As we will see, Strauss's analyses of prophecy and particular providence lead Strauss step by step back to Plato by way of Alfarabi, not only in *Philosophy and Law*, chapter 3, and "Place of Providence" but perhaps especially in "Some Remarks."

In *Philosophy and Law* Strauss begins the shift in orientation away from more theoretical inquiries toward political science in his analysis of Maimonides's

Guide well before he gets to chapter 3. In the introduction Strauss shows that what makes Maimonides's medieval enlightenment distinctive is that it, unlike the modern Enlightenment, takes as its "leading idea . . . the idea of Law" (*PL*, 39). Because the modern Enlightenment is oriented elsewhere, namely, the autonomous individual or the subjective consciousness, interpreters like Julius Guttmann, whom Strauss devotes so much attention to criticizing in chapter 1, treat "philosophy of religion" or "religious consciousness" as the central phenomena of all Jewish thinkers, including Maimonides.[10] Since at least Spinoza political philosophers have made every effort to transform religion into a part of man's private or social, as opposed to political, experience. Strauss discovers in Maimonides's concern with Law or the divine Law a different focus on something both public and total. The Law, unlike contemporary religion, covers every aspect of life. Consequently, the Law proves to be the natural counterpoint to philosophy as a total way of life (73). The more partial or less encompassing a religion's demands become, the less relevant they are as a counterpoint to philosophy.

In chapter 1 Strauss identifies in reverse order the two main steps of his argument: (chap. 3) the philosophic foundation of the law and (chap. 2) the legal foundation of philosophy (60). Already in chapter 2's focus on the legal foundation we can see the centrality of Law—and in a light that anticipates the focus of Strauss's subsequent studies of Platonic political philosophy. Any reader of Strauss's writings on not only Plato but also Aristophanes will be reminded by chapter 2 of the fate of Socrates in Aristophanes's *Clouds* and Plato's *Apology* and *Phaedo*. Through the lens of the city, the philosopher appears to be a renegade. The Law is the highest expression of the city's way of life.

The main focus of the legal foundation of philosophy (chap. 2) is sufficiently difficult to detect in Maimonides that Strauss devotes little attention to it (cf. *PL*, 89–92, approximately three pages in Adler's translation). Figuring prominently in the middle of it is a declaration that we will not find after *Philosophy and Law*: "human intellect has a limit which it cannot cross; for this reason man is obliged for the glory of the Lord, to halt at this limit and not to reject the teachings of revelation that he cannot comprehend and demonstrate. Philosophy is free—in its own sphere. Its sphere is nature, not super-nature" (90–91).[11] In every other respect, Strauss associates Maimonides's position with that of Averroës's.

Strauss presents Maimonides's legal foundation of philosophy as a mean between Averroës's defense of philosophy before the bar of the law in his *Decisive Treatise* and Gersonides's oddly protomodern claims to pursue philosophy in his *Wars of the Lord*.[12] Unlike Strauss's Maimonides in *Philosophy and Law* (66–67), Averroës defends philosophy before the law by tacitly assuming that all the relevant dogmas in the philosopher's confrontation with the law are "accessible to the unaided reason of man." Yet Averroës is notoriously circumspect about how much of the truth the philosopher should make available to the multitude. Rather than public teaching of the truth, he argues for the philosopher's bondage to the public teaching of scripture (88)—a bondage that, by the way, Strauss identifies as the main source of intellectual freedom in the premodern enlightenment. In contrast, though Gersonides appears oddly protomodern in his calls for "the *freedom of public communication* . . . of philosophic truths" (96); his understanding of the preexistence of the Torah undercuts any possibility of discovering truths at odds with it (100). Here, in *Philosophy and Law*, we already see hints of Strauss's teaching regarding esotericism. Although his argument regarding philosophy's bondage as the source of its freedom (88) clearly anticipates his more fully developed arguments about esotericism in *Persecution*, Strauss's understanding of esotericism in *Philosophy and Law* (102–3) has mixed in it another more widely recognized sense of esotericism, the esotericism of incommunicable mysteries (66–67, 95)—a sense that Strauss deemphasizes in his subsequent writings. Once again, Strauss's stress in *Philosophy and Law* on the supernatural element and the putative limitedness of human understanding of Maimonides's teaching undercuts his full embrace of esotericism.

We must renew our question as we turn to chapter 3 of *Philosophy and Law*: how and why does Strauss shift the emphasis in his account of the philosophic foundation of the Law (that is, the prophetology) from psychology to Law? Strauss answered this question in outline in his critique of Guttmann's approach to Maimonides in chapter 1:

> The philosophic foundation of the law, in spite of outward appearances, is not *a* teaching among others but is the place in the system of the Islamic Aristotelians and their Jewish pupils where the presupposition of their philosophizing comes under discussion. Now if they are following Plato in the philosophic foundation of the law, this means that these philosophers are Platonists not because they follow this or that Platonic theorem, however important—in this sense they are Aristotelians rather than Platonists—but because in the foundation of philosophizing itself, they are guided by Plato to answer a Platonic question within a framework laid out by Plato. Ultimately, they differ from Plato only in this, though decisively in this: for them the founder of the ideal state is not a possible philosopher-king to be awaited in the future, but an actual prophet who existed in the past. (75)

The prophet is understood in the light of Plato's philosopher-king. Even though Strauss insists in *Philosophy and Law* on the supernatural superiority of the prophet vis-à-vis the philosopher-king (66), his analysis of the prophetology leads him eventually to the striking admission that all or nearly all of Maimonides's account of the prophetology is natural rather than supernatural. And the remainder that is not natural is merely the possibility that God might withhold prophecy.[13] Maimonides so likens the revealed understanding of prophecy to the philosophic understanding developed by the Islamic *falāsifa* (esp. in *Guide*, 2.32) that Strauss is compelled to acknowledge that for Maimonides "prophecy as such is natural" (104). Wary of the possible implications of this, Strauss presses Maimonides's teaching, noting for example that in *Guide*, 2.38, he comes close to siding with Avicenna in insinuating that the difference between the prophet and the philosopher-king is that the prophet possesses "direct" knowledge of the "upper world," whereas the philosopher possesses only "indirect" knowledge, that is, through the study of nature (109, 116). This account of the difference between philosopher and prophet is a far cry from the earlier insistence on the supernatural insight provided by revelation. One of the most striking features of Strauss's account of Maimonides's prophetology is the way he finds again and again that apparent differences between Maimonides and the Islamic *falāsifa* prove ultimately to be just that, merely apparent.

In the last two sections of *Philosophy and Law*, Strauss focuses intensely on the exact sense in which prophecy is political rather than psychological. He frames this opposition by reference to the opposition between the mantic role and the political role of the prophet (120). Starting from the political center of the *Guide* (2.40), Strauss shows that Maimonides, by way of Avicenna and Alfarabi, characterizes politics in a manner that cannot but remind the reader of Aristotle's *Politics*.[14] Although Strauss no longer appeals to the modern Enlightenment here, it isn't difficult to see that the understanding of politics that he finds in Maimonides is one that emphasizes not only the well-being of the body but also of the soul, that is, of the intellect (124).[15] In other words, Maimonides's prophetology culminates in a political science that stresses the perfection of the individual intellect—which, of course, can be achieved only by the philosopher (cf. *PL*, 126, with *Guide*, 3.34). In the final section, Strauss famously argues that the Law so conceived enables those who live under it to "aristotelize" (*PL*, 133). Because they are no longer beset as were Plato and Aristotle by the task of discovering the "ideal state," believers in revealed laws may now turn their efforts to philosophy. It is as if the Jew under the Law lives in the end of days as described by Maimonides in his *Mishneh Torah*. One wonders, though, whether discovering philosophy in the Law or among its aims means that the Law has divined the insights of the philosophers. Even though the perfect Law has been given, its perfection may not be fully apparent without proper interpretation. Perhaps due to some residual influence of the supernatural, direct knowledge and neo-Pythagorean mantic elements that Strauss finds in Maimonides in *Philosophy and Law* (129), he is prevented from fully plumbing the depths of the Platonic political philosophy he has begun to uncover in *Philosophy and Law*. Indeed, a certain overemphasis on a traditional understanding of theoretical philosophy obscures the full depth of Strauss's insight even into the 1940s.[16]

We turn now to the "Place of Providence" to consider the political supplement to the prophetology, Maimonides's teaching on particular providence. In comparison with his account of prophecy, Maimonides's teaching on particular providence is extremely secretive. He is untroubled by stating openly that the true account of prophecy is equivalent to the philosophic view with the sole exception of divine withholding. In contrast, Maimonides's own views on particular providence are, according to Strauss, revealed elusively under the guise of his interpretation of Job (cf. PPr, 544n20, with *Guide*, 3.23, 3.17). Although all scholars acknowledge the surprising proximity of Maimonides's views on prophecy to that of the Islamic *falāsifa*, far fewer would assent to Strauss's claim that even with respect to particular providence Maimonides proves to be a "rationalist" (PPr, 544n20). It is likely that it was the very secretiveness of Maimonides's position on particular providence that makes "Place of Providence" and "Some Remarks" such fruitful ground in the development of Strauss's views on premodern esotericism.

Scholars have sometimes complained about Strauss's characterization of Maimonides in the "Literary Character" as a *mutakallim*, or dialectical theologian.[17] As has already been mentioned, "Literary Character" is itself far more elusive about the character and objectives of the *Guide* than his writings of the 1930s—apparently the closer Strauss got to the nerve of Maimonides's argument, the more uneasy he became about revealing it to his audience.[18] In "Literary Character" Strauss's point is neither that the *Guide* is devoid of philosophic content nor that Maimonides never adopts the viewpoint of the philosopher therein but that its *exoteric* surface is kalām (dialectical theology). Those who characterize the *Guide* as "Jewish philosophy" blend together the exoteric with the esoteric layers of this multilayered work—thus obscuring each of the layers and their relation to one another. In resisting the label "Jewish philosophy" (see *PAW*, 19), however, Strauss was deepening the insights of some his predecessors. In "Place of Providence," he underlines his agreement with Jacob Guttmann and Shlomo Pines in observing similarities in the structure of the *Guide* with the Muʿtazilite kalām (PPr, 542n16). Now Saadya Gaon's (892–942 CE) debt to this kalām is well documented.[19] Yet Maimonides is so critical of the dialectical theologians as a group (though somewhat more sparingly regarding the Mu'tazilites) that we cannot but be somewhat surprised to see that the structure of the *Guide* is highly similar to what he criticizes.

Unlike Guttmann and Pines, however, Strauss underlines a crucial Maimonidean departure. The Mu'tazilites are famous as proponents of the unity and justice of God. Consequently, they divide their theological treatises into a first part on God's unity and a second part on God's justice. The unity section covers God and the angels; the justice section covers prophecy, the Law, and (particular) providence. Strauss's key insight is that Maimonides's philosophic or political approach to the prophetology severs the connection between his account of particular providence and God's justice. In other words, Maimonides's account of particular providence falls within the ambit of political science rather than the Mu'tazilite kalām teaching on God's justice (PPr, 542). Although Maimonides imitates the Mu'tazilite kalām in his exoteric teaching, even that imitation is superficial. The surface structure of the *Guide* is similar to that of the theologians, but its meaning and intention is opposed to theirs. As Maimonides explains in *Guide*, 1.71, albeit somewhat indirectly, he will pursue a defense of Judaism that avoids the pitfalls of traditional kalām: its main pitfall was to defend a given faith using any means fair or foul.[20] Above all, the *mutakallimūn* were willing to violate the "nature of existence," which nature was discovered by the philosophers. Indeed, according to Maimonides, kalām originated less as defense of one revealed religion against others than as defense of revelation against philosophy (*Guide*, 1.71).

Although Strauss highlights the opposition between the exoteric surface of the *Guide* and its esoteric depths in "Place of Providence" (545), he does not yet insist as he does in "Literary Character" that Maimonides is a practitioner of "enlightened *kalām*." Rather, in "Place of Providence" Strauss speaks more boldly perhaps than anywhere else in his oeuvre about the subject matter of the *Guide*. He takes far more literally than most interpreters the significance of what Maimonides identifies in the introduction to the first part as its subject matter, namely, the "true science of the Law." According to Strauss, the theme of the *Guide* is the Law, and the Law is analyzed from within the philosophic discipline of political science (548).[21] Most interpreters view the true science of the Law as the study of the theological foundations of the Law or of the fundamental articles of faith (cf. *Pereq Ḥeleq*). In contrast, Strauss views the true science of the Law as the political philosophic study of the aims of the Law. As we saw in *Philosophy and Law*, the highest aim of the Law studied by political science or philosophy is the philosophic aspiration to intellectual perfection. It would appear then that the theological foundations stressed so heavily by other interpreters reappear in Strauss as the enlightened theological surface of the *Guide*.

We need to turn back momentarily to Strauss's main focus in "Place of Providence": particular providence. According to Strauss, from *Guide*, 1.1 to 3.7, at the end of which Maimonides announces his intention to cease theoretical discussions of the Account of the Chariot, Maimonides at times discusses providence but only or for the most part general providence (PPr, 539n9). The discussion of particular providence then is limited to nontheoretical or practical philosophy (540). A crucial consequence of this is that discussions such as of the "doctrine of divine reward and punishment" are part of Maimonides's "exoteric doctrine" (545–46)—or his "edifying doctrine[s]," as opposed to his "fundamental doctrine" treated in the prophetology. One must be careful then not to leap to the conclusion that Strauss's stress on the political character of Maimonides's teaching implies that there is nothing but edifying surface without any depth. The political (as well as superpolitical) end of the Law is, according to Strauss, "a true and demonstrable fundamental doctrine" (548–49).

It may seem odd that we turn back briefly now to Strauss's earlier "Some Remarks." After all, Strauss underlines an important development from "Some Remarks" (1936) to "Place of Providence" (1937).[22] Yet we do so because "Some Remarks" reveals more clearly than "Place of Providence" the interrelation of particular and general providence in the thought of Maimonides. Ultimately, Strauss argues for a shocking convergence of Maimonides's teaching on particular providence with *Laws* 10: a convergence emerges even though Plato moves from a more philosophic teaching toward a teaching oddly anticipatory of the revealed teaching, and Maimonides moves in the opposite direction. In both cases, the teaching on particular providence proves ultimately to be the exoteric face of a philosophic teaching on general providence. Their different contexts, however, demand opposite rhetorical strategies. We cannot consider the details of Strauss's investigation of Maimonides's possible sources for the development of his position on particular providence here. Let it suffice to say that he shows that Maimonides either knew of or divined by himself the teaching of Plato's *Laws* 10 with the help of intermediaries such as Alexander of Aphrodisias (SRMF, 22–24).

Strauss sets the stage for this linking of Maimonides to Plato by offering what may be the first glimpse of the thesis of *Persecution*. Although Strauss refers in *Philosophy and Law* to esotericism and even differences between modern and medieval types of esotericism (102–3), "Some Remarks" hints at the likelihood that the philosopher, like the prophet, is subject to persecution. Protecting oneself from persecution seems on the tip of Strauss's tongue here. Over the course of several pages (SRMF, 18–21), Strauss shows the striking similarities between the prophetic call to Israel to change its ways and return to God and the perfection of Zion, that is, the idea of the perfect city, on the one hand, and

Socrates's divining of a perfect city in the *Republic* as well as his philosophic call to his fellow citizens to strive for virtue, on the other. How ironic that the one who demands justice should be persecuted. Most notable of all, however, may be that the return to Zion in the end of days is reimagined by Maimonides. Contrary to Jewish tradition regarding the Messianic age, the lion does not lie down with the lamb—in other words, nature is not controverted. On the contrary, the key natural divide among men is not undermined; it is in a sense reinforced or deepened: "Only [when the Messiah has come will] ... the privileges of the philosophers be fully recognized" (20).

With Strauss's subtle adumbration of the differences between the prophetic, biblical view and the philosophic view still before our eyes, we turn to his analysis of the political teaching of Isaac Abravanel (1437–1508 CE), which includes Abravanel's transformation of Maimonides's political science. Because Abravanel is deeply indebted to Christian political thinkers, including most notably Thomas Aquinas, Strauss's "On Abravanel's Philosophical Tendency and Political Teaching" (1957) enables us to deepen our understanding of the key differences between Maimonides and the main line of Christian political thought.[23] Should the reader wish to have a more nuanced understanding of Strauss's interpretation of different trends in medieval Christian political thought he will have to wait for his "Law of Reason in the *Kuzari*" (1943) (see esp. *PAW*, 96–97). Be that as it may, two clear and striking oppositions characterize the lines between Abravanel and Maimonides in Strauss's 1937 piece: on the one hand, Maimonides is a "thoroughgoing rationalis[t]"; on the other, Abravanel sides with the "'mythical' or 'mystical' tendencies of the Midrash."[24] And, on the one hand, Maimonides adopts not only a promonarchical interpretation of the Bible but also a political interpretation of it; on the other, Abravanel adopts not only an antimonarchical interpretation but also an antipolitical one. The former opposition is evidently simpler and more straightforward. The character of Abravanel's mysticism is connected with what Strauss describes as "the fact that for him political philosophy loses its central importance" (104).[25] It has a "much more restricted field than it had for Maimonides" (105)—a field reminiscent of Aristotelian political thought, which, of course, takes the lead in medieval Christian thought in general (cf. 105 with 96–99).[26] As we saw in *Philosophy and Law*, the characteristically modern view of philosophy of religion as concerned with subjective religious consciousness is more closely linked to this restricted view of political philosophy than the total teaching of the Islamic *falāsifa* and Maimonides. Rationalism, then, is closely linked to (Platonic) political philosophy broadly understood.

The former opposition between Abravanel and Maimonides regarding the status of monarchy and politics is a bit more complicated than the opposition regarding rationalism and mysticism—though they are intimately connected, as is already evident from our inability to avoid referring to *political* philosophy to characterize that rationalism. The former opposition is more complicated because Maimonides's positive view of monarchy is characteristic of the vast majority of the rabbinic tradition (112, 119). Yet the biblical attitude toward politics and the founding of the city is far closer to Abravanel's view than Maimonides's (129).[27] Ultimately, Maimonides's positive attitude toward monarchy and politics is more deeply rooted in his philosophic orientation than the rabbinic attitude toward monarchy. He, like Alfarabi and other Islamic *falāsifa*, favors monarchy because it squares with his conception of Moses and prophets more generally as philosopher-kings. In contrast, not only does human kingship fill Abravanel with "disgust" (117)—indeed, so deeply that he can be found speaking somewhat favorably of a "'mixed' constitution"—but also Abravanel prefers the rule of judge and prophet or priest to that of philosopher-king (118, 126). In other words, Abravanel's animosity toward monarchy and politics is rooted in the view that "man's 'natural' state" is most analogous to Israel's life "in the desert, where Israel had to rely entirely for everything on miraculous providence" (110–11). Here, we arrive at the opposite pole to the convergence of Maimonides and Plato regarding particular providence we saw in "Some Remarks." Maimonides's rationalism places roughly as much stress on human self-reliance as Abravanel's mysticism places on faith in divine support.

In the 1940s Strauss began to write about Maimonides in such a way that his debt to Alfarabi in political philosophy became more difficult, not easier, to detect. I do not mean that Strauss did not consistently acknowledge this debt, but he did little in writing to explain that debt, especially from the side of Maimonides. In "Literary Character" Strauss moved away from the emphasis in his 1930s writings on the political character of Maimonides's teaching to an emphasis on the enlightened kalām surface of the *Guide*. At the same time, of course, Strauss began to make the difference between exoteric surface and esoteric depth a central theme of his writing. For those sympathetic to Strauss's insights, then, it is not difficult to see that he eventually argued that the *Guide* consists in an enlightened kalām surface and a political philosophic depth. To the unsympathetic, he appears to be making Maimonides into a mere dialectical theologian. That is because the unsympathetic tend to overstate the importance of the theological aspect of Maimonides's writings—thinking of him primarily as a "Jewish philosopher." Strauss insisted rightly that interpreters would never understand Maimonides properly until they understood the surface of the *Guide* for what it was, namely, enlightened kalām. It must be underlined that Maimonides learned from Alfarabi how to make and use a kalām surface.[28]

Fortunately, "A Lost Writing of Farabi's" (1936) has recently been translated into English.[29] This often dry explanation—of how Strauss discovered that what were thought to be parts of Alfarabi's *Enumeration of the Sciences* were in fact parts of the first part (the *Attainment of Happiness*) of a lost Farabian trilogy, the *Philosophy of Plato and Aristotle*—contains one of Strauss's frankest statements of the depth and significance of Maimonides's debt to Alfarabi. Strauss concludes this piece by arguing that now that we know the outlines of this lost trilogy, we are finally in possession of the "central writings" of Alfarabi—because we can add this writing to the *Enumeration* (or Encyclopedia), the *Virtuous City*, and his *Political Regime*.[30] In explaining the importance of this discovery, Strauss cites the letter Maimonides wrote to Samuel Ibn Tibbon explaining the unparalleled importance of Alfarabi's writings and especially his *Political Regime*. Strauss concludes this piece by stating that at last we are in a position to assess properly "the Islamic and Jewish philosophy of the Middle Ages: At the beginning of this epoch of the history of philosophy there stands not just any 'predecessor,' but a towering spirit [Alfarabi] who laid the ground for the later development and set down its limits by making his task the revival of the Platonic-Aristotelian philosophy as philosophy as such." The Farabian Turn set Strauss on the course to a Plato who was far less metaphysical than had been previously believed. In effect, it was through his study of Alfarabi and Maimonides that Strauss came to understand that Plato's "political philosophy broadly understood . . . [is] 'the first philosophy.'"[31]

This chapter has explored the more explicit declarations of Strauss's writings in the 1930s about the centrality of political science or philosophy in Maimonides's writings to facilitate a recovery of the distinctiveness of the "Islamic and Jewish philosophy of the Middle Ages," especially that of Alfarabi and Maimonides. The Farabian Turn in Strauss's thought, though often elusive in the written word, is there for anyone who can see and attend to Strauss's actions. Even while he grows quieter about the centrality of political science in Maimonides's writings, Strauss's exploration of Maimonides's enlightened kalām demonstrates a key, oft-forgotten aspect of political philosophy.

CHAPTER EIGHT

Maimonides's Secretiveness about Political Philosophy

The 1950s

Strauss's "Maimonides' Statement on Political Science" is among his shortest and strangest writings.[1] Its shortness reflects the brevity of the work on which it is based, Maimonides's *Treatise on the Art of Logic*, especially chapter 14, its final, brief chapter. The strangeness of Strauss's piece derives from three factors: First, the original Arabic of the *Logic* had not yet been found when Strauss wrote his article. It was based instead on Hebrew translations and Arabic fragments—leading inevitably to conjectural readings.[2] Second, Maimonides appears to argue that political science is not needed in his time! Third, Strauss's all-too-brief historical study seems initially to be out of place in a collection that includes such a substantive and provocative programmatic essay as "What Is Political Philosophy?," supplemented by somewhat less comprehensive though equally programmatic essays such as "Political Philosophy and History," "Classical Political Philosophy," and "Restatement on Xenophon's *Hiero*." In other words, the context in which Strauss chose to place the "Statement on Political Science" only intensifies the strangeness of the article itself.

Let us consider the first source of strangeness, the problematic texts at Strauss's disposal: at least two articles have been written commenting on the limitations of Strauss's article, both of which appeared after the publication of Arabic versions of the *Logic* not available to Strauss.[3] When relevant, I touch on those articles, but I do not focus, as they have, on Strauss's occasional faulty conjectures. After all, Strauss devotes an entire paragraph, the second paragraph of the piece, to underlining how conjectural his inquiry is (156).[4] Nevertheless, it is striking that Strauss would include in this collection a historical study filled with conjectures and some of his most "unscientific" speculations about numerology in the thought of Maimonides (see 165–68). A yawning chasm opens up between the kind of "data" considered in this historical study on Maimonides's political science and the kind considered in the contemporary, positivistic political science that Strauss discusses in "What Is Political Philosophy?" (17–26).

Why, the reader should wonder, does Strauss engage in such historical studies, which are foreign not only to contemporary social scientists but also to the very thinkers, such as Maimonides, that Strauss studies in these historical studies (also) on Alfarabi, Hobbes, and Locke (73–75)? According to Strauss, we live in an age in which "historicism" prevails. Historicism holds that the truth for our age must be different from that for other ages (71). Consequently, though it might embrace the study of former ages with an eye to clarifying our own present views, it rejects out of hand the possibility that insights acquired in another age could have permanent relevance. In addition, as denizens of the modern world, we are the recipients of a modern history of political philosophy that, even before the advent of historicism, relied on and criticized ideas about political things that it had received from premodern political philosophy (75, 79, 81). Consequently, contemporary political ideas and concepts often contain within them layers of sedimentation that impede our access to the original ideas, not to mention the original political phenomena (28, 74–75, 84). Strauss advocates historical studies of thinkers who themselves did not engage in such historical studies because in our contemporary situation we are able to gain access to the original phenomena only by peeling away the layers of sedimentation in our own ideas (75n4) and because he has become convinced through his own study of political philosophy that it has more to offer than historicism (26).

Why does Strauss choose to write on two medieval political philosophers and two modern political philosophers, and why these two pairs: Alfarabi and Maimonides and then Hobbes and Locke? The first question will be addressed shortly. For now, let us turn to the question why these particular pairs together. In each of these pairs, the reader is confronted by a less renowned but more outspoken political philosopher. As Strauss observes about Hobbes, like Machiavelli before him, "Hobbes's teaching was still much too bold to be acceptable. It, too, was in need of mitigation. The mitigation was the work of Locke" (49). In the case of the pair—Alfarabi and Maimonides—Strauss considers thinkers whose connection is less obvious than that of Hobbes and Locke.[5] Although Hobbes and Locke were divided over liberal *democracy*, it has been widely acknowledged for many decades, if not for centuries, that Hobbes and Locke were central to the American founding. Strauss explains the affinity between Alfarabi and Maimonides in "Restatement on Xenophon's *Hiero*" as engaging in "philosophic politics"—which despite the fact that Alfarabi engaged in such politics in the context of Islam and Maimonides in the context of

Judaism—proves to be a profound connection indeed (126–27). Is it possible that, in spite of their different religious contexts, Maimonides did for Alfarabi what Locke did for Hobbes, that is, mitigate his teaching?

This preliminary consideration of Maimonides brings to mind an obvious and yet shocking similarity between Maimonides's situation and our own. Much as historicism seems to deny the need for (and the very possibility of) political philosophy (26, 57), so many in Maimonides's time and place also denied the need for political philosophy—revelation, it seemed to them, made recourse to philosophy unnecessary.[6] Much of Strauss's article is devoted to showing that Maimonides, though he appears at first to be denying the relevance of political philosophy to a revealed community, is in fact showing subtly and indirectly just how much his revealed community needs the guidance of political philosophy. Although as inheritors of the secularization of politics by the Enlightenment, we would seem to have little or no need for the insights of Maimonides, it seems that the return of the gods under the auspices of historicism makes the untimely insights of Maimonides timely for us.

More broadly, why did Strauss choose to include these essays on two medieval and two modern authors? He seems to be drawing attention to the shift from medieval to modern with matching pairs of historical studies. In other words, "Maimonides' Statement on Political Science" is included in *What Is Political Philosophy?* to offer insights into that crucial turn in the history of political philosophy, the movement from premodern to modern, or, as Strauss more often refers to it, the difference between ancient and modern. Although Heinrich Meier is, I believe, correct that the central phenomenon with which Strauss is concerned is the theologico-political problem and especially the opposition between philosophy and revelation, as we will see later in this chapter, disagreement exists in Straussian circles about how important are the differences (or oppositions) between ancient or premodern and modern. The differences between medievals such as Alfarabi and Maimonides, on the one hand, and the moderns such as Hobbes and Locke, on the other, seem all too obvious. Yet Strauss shows again and again that the first modern, Machiavelli, has some odd connections with medievals, especially those whom the tradition has dubbed "Averroists." The reader is led to wonder, then, why Strauss connects such different thinkers as Machiavelli and Maimonides. Indeed, Strauss, though subtly and in so many words, even insinuates that Maimonides is an "Averroist."[7] What could possibly link one of the most outspoken critics of Christianity with one of the strongest defenders of Judaism?

In both "What Is Political Philosophy?" (41) and "Restatement on Xenophon's *Hiero*" (102), Strauss notes an important connection between medieval political philosophy, especially medieval Islamic and Jewish political philosophy, and Machiavelli: this bold founder of modernity, whose boldness Strauss frequently highlights, is not as original as Strauss's accounts might lead us to believe initially. According to Strauss, Machiavelli is the inheritor of a "critique of religion" that dates back beyond the medievals to the classics (41).[8] The medieval bearers of that tradition belong to the "Averroistic tradition," about which contemporary scholars, such as Eric Voegelin, are pardonably ignorant (102). The "Maimonides' Statement" is part of an effort to replace that ignorance with knowledge. One wonders why it should be important to make scholars more aware of the Averroistic tradition if the classics are bearers of the same teaching. There must be other points of discontinuity between ancients and medievals that make the existence of the Averroistic tradition important to Strauss's overall account of the history of political philosophy. The obvious point of discontinuity is the most relevant one: the Averroistic tradition is the adaptation of the classical teaching to the setting of the monotheistic faiths (cf. 127).

In *What Is Political Philosophy?* Strauss resists the suggestion by thinkers such as Kojève that monotheism, any more than tyranny, is a wholly unprecedented phenomenon that transcends or eludes the framework of classical political philosophy. He argues this in the face of Kojève's insistence that the classics were limited to the view of the master, the honor-loving view, which stood in need of its biblical complement, the view of the slave (96, 108). Strauss insists that Platonic philosophy as embodied in the character of Socrates cannot be confused with the honor-loving view. Socrates is already the synthesis or transcendence that Kojève claims to find in Hegel's synthesis of the ancient and modern Christian "(Hobbian)" teaching (cf. 105 with 109–10). What could serve as better support for Strauss's view as expressed in "Restatement" than the evidence we will find in the "Statement on Political Science" that Maimonides testifies to the continued relevance of classical political philosophy under monotheistic conditions. Strauss's strange forays into medieval Islamic and Jewish political philosophy support what may be Strauss's most lasting contribution to political philosophy, namely, his insight that classical political philosophy, its *framework*, remains relevant to all political phenomena in every historical period. Students of political philosophy should never confuse the political "solution" of the classics (132, cf. 126–27), however, with the range of political phenomena their framework can make intelligible.[9]

Strauss describes Averroism elsewhere as the "secular alliance between philosophers and princes friendly to philosophy." There, he also connects Machiavelli to his Averroist predecessors. According to Strauss, Alfarabi departed from Plato in transforming the open alliance between philosophy and kings in the *Republic* into the "secret kingship of the philosopher."[10] The reader is led to wonder why that open alliance became secret. Once again, the reason proves to be monotheism. The unprecedented authority of monotheistic or revealed texts made it incumbent on political philosophers to hide their philosophic activity—even more than had Socrates.[11] Maimonides's statement on political science in the *Logic* appears at first glance to deny the relevance of political science in the new revealed setting. The *Logic* does so because it needs to bow to the authority of revelation. Far from proving the irrelevance of classical political philosophy to the monotheistic setting, Maimonides's *Logic*, as long as one attends to its reasons for being secretive, reveals the continued relevance of the classics in the new setting.

Although Machiavelli's founding of modernity may emerge out of an Averroist critique of religion, I need hardly remind the reader of all his radical departures from his predecessors, which seem to render our political experience so different from the premodern (see 41–43). Machiavelli's mode of expression of his critique of religion is part and parcel of that radical departure: Machiavelli is the "great master of blasphemy" (41), whose blasphemy is fueled by "anti-theological ire" (44). Although Machiavelli may continue the secret alliance of philosophy and princes, he chose to broadcast his critique of religion—using techniques that the founder of his own religion had first employed (45–46). In contrast, Maimonides's critique of religion could hardly be more secretive. In effect, the most salient difference between Machiavelli and Maimonides is the immoderation of the former and the moderation of the latter. Although Machiavelli may have links to the classical critique of religion by way of Averroism, his approach gave rise to the secularization that led eventually to historicism. Perhaps moderation, a virtue that Strauss repeatedly associates with premodern philosophy, in such matters is the most important element in preserving political philosophy.

Strauss singles out three difficulties in the *Logic*: (1) Maimonides seems to repudiate "the philosophers on politics proper" as useless "'in these times,'" (2) he "divides politics proper in an unusual manner," and (3) he distinguishes the subject matter of ethics from that of politics proper, "assign[ing] the understanding of happiness . . . to politics proper" (156–57).[12] His discussion of these three difficulties is divided into six parts: (a) on whether and for whom the study of politics proper might be useless (157–59); (b) on the unusual divisions of politics proper (159–62); (c) on the rule of nomoi, living intelligence, and the "effects produced upon the character of laws by the change from paganism to revealed religion" (162–65); (d) the first look at the overarching division of the sciences in the *Logic*, including the relation between ethics, on the one hand, and politics proper and the issue of happiness, on the other

(165–67); and (e) the second look at the overarching division of the sciences, which "leads directly into the center of the fundamental problem" (167–69). Part (a) takes up the problem set forth as difficulty (1). Part (b) takes up the problem set forth as difficulty (2). Part (d) addresses difficulty (3), although its significance must apparently be seen in light of parts (c) and (e).

A. Is the Study of Politics Useless? (157–59)

It must be admitted that the Hebrew translations of the *Logic*, which Strauss consulted, led him more quickly than do the more accurate Arabic texts to the conclusion that, according to Maimonides, revelation repudiates the science of "politics proper." The question remains, however, whether that conclusion was not also implied by the more accurate Arabic. Strauss translates, based on what little he had, the following: "But we have no need in these times for all this, viz. for [the commands], the laws, the *nomoi*, the governance [of] [these] human beings in divine things [for the laws and the *nomoi*; the governance of human beings is now through divine things]" (156). In contrast, Mahdi translates based on dependable Arabic texts the following: "In these times, all this—I mean the regimes and the nomoi—has been dispensed with, and men are being governed by divine commands." The more restrained Arabic seems to leave open the possibility that aspects of the philosophic study of politics proper, other than the regimes and nomoi resulting from those studies, remain relevant. Although the latter translation based on the Arabic version is able to qualify "all this," further consideration of this qualified claim may lead, as Maimonides's *Logic* led Strauss, to the view that revelation repudiates the political science of the philosophers. In the preceding lines of chapter 14, among the regimes and nomoi given to the pagans, Maimonides singles out those given by philosophers. Those have been dispensed with. How do divine commands take their place? It would seem that God takes the place of philosophers in the giving of regimes and nomoi. If God can do this for man, it is unclear why human beings should feel any need to study politics proper.[13] Although Strauss's translation may have lacked the precision of translations based on the Arabic, difficulty (1) proves to be precisely as he first stated it: Maimonides insinuates that revelation purports to make political science unnecessary—which is the very thing necessitating Maimonides's secretiveness about political science.

In addition to objecting that Strauss has been too hasty about Maimonides's (apparent) rejection of political science, Joel L. Kraemer objects to Strauss's inference that "'the function of the Torah is emphatically political'" (157).[14] According to Kraemer, Strauss has inferred the political character of the Torah because of his misreading of Maimonides's repudiation of political science: if the Torah insinuates that revelation makes political science obsolete, then the Torah must be essentially political. Kraemer objects to Strauss's interpretation by claiming that there really is no comparison between pagan law and revealed law.[15] Initially, Kraemer seems to be on firm footing. At crucial moments in his *Guide*, Maimonides draws a clear distinction between nomoi, which are concerned merely with the well-being of the body, and truly divine Laws, which are concerned with both the perfection of the body and of the soul. Furthermore, he appears to identify pagan laws with perfection of the body—and to identify the Law of Moses with perfection of the soul (2.39–40, 3.27–28).[16] If this simple portrait were accurate, we would be left with the strange implication that the philosophic study of politics proper was relevant for the pagans and remains relevant to the revealed religions because it treats merely the perfection of the body.[17] If this were the case, then why would Maimonides indicate that the teaching of the philosophers about the regimes and nomoi is obsolete (esp. "in these times")? Furthermore, we would be left with the untenable suggestion that the philosophic study of politics proper concerns the well-being of the body only. Yet Maimonides states explicitly in the *Logic* that that study concerns happiness (cf. difficulty [3]). Not even the adherents of the "Averroistic tradition" held that happiness is merely a matter of the well-being of the body.

Finally, in response to Kraemer's interpretation, Strauss might appeal to one of his favorite passages in the Averroistic tradition, the passage he quotes from Avicenna's *On the Division of the Rational Sciences* as the epigraph to his final study of classical political philosophy, *The Argument and the Action of Plato's "Laws"*: "The treatment of prophecy and the Law (*sharī'a*) is contained in [Plato's and Aristotle's] books on the laws."[18] It may serve the enlightened kalām of the *Guide* to denigrate pagan laws, as Maimonides does in the penultimate paragraph of the *Logic* and the end of *Guide*, 2.39; however, even in the *Guide*, Maimonides hints to the attentive reader that a distinction should be drawn between traditional pagan laws and the laws of the philosophers.[19] Although one might dispute whether the laws or the education of the soul in Plato's *Laws* in fact perfects the soul, it is obviously false to claim that Plato's *Laws* is not concerned with the soul's perfection.

Leaving aside Kraemer's objections to Strauss, it is worth pausing to attend to Strauss's careful consideration of the audience of the *Logic*, which necessarily has bearing on the question for whom might political science be said to be irrelevant.[20] Over the course of pages 157 through 159, Strauss carefully considers the "we" to whom the *Logic*, and thus the repudiation of political science, seems to be addressed. He shows that previous commentators on the *Logic* had latched on to Maimonides's implied distinction between the ethics and politics proper. Among them, Moses Mendelssohn voices an all-too-modern interpretation of Maimonides. According to Mendelssohn, so long as the Jewish people lack a homeland, the political part of the Law is irrelevant.[21] In other words, Mendelssohn interprets Maimonides as dispensing with political philosophy due to the Jewish lack of a homeland (157). He seems to imply that the ethical teaching of the Law might be separated from the political to be used separately. In doing so, Mendelssohn adopts the modern (esp. late modern) view that happiness is the proper subject of ethics rather than of politics. In this subtle way, Strauss alludes to the radical difference between the premodern inclusion of ethics within politics and the modern separation of the two.

Strauss goes on to question the assumption of interpreters such as Mendelssohn that the "we" or the audience of the *Logic* is the Jewish people simply. After all, Maimonides refers to an audience that "in these times" has no need for these pagan philosophic works. Of course, "the Torah antedates philosophy, or Greek wisdom, by centuries. If it were the Torah which rendered superfluous the political books of the philosophers, those books would not have been needed by the Jewish people at any time" (157–58). Consequently, Strauss draws the important conclusion that the audience of the *Logic* is not likely as broad as "we Jews" but the far narrower grouping "we men of theory"—covering "the men who speculate about principles or roots."[22] Defenders of religion, in particular of monotheistic faiths, seem to be the target audience. Thus, Strauss expands his previous claim that "the function of the Torah is emphatically political" (157) to the broader claim "the function of revealed religion is emphatically political" (159). In addition, the identification of the target audience as persons above the vulgar, who are especially concerned to defend revealed religion, enables Strauss to refine the target of Maimonides's repudiation of political science. He separates "the most practical part of the political teaching of the philosophers" from "the theoretical understanding of revealed religion" (159).[23] How could the latter not be of interest to "the men who speculate about principles or roots"? We will see more of this aspect of the political teaching of the philosophers later.

B. The Divisions of Politics Proper (159–62)

Maimonides distinguishes, according to Strauss's accurate paraphrase, between the "governance of the city, and governance of the great [numerous] nation or of the nations" (155). Maimonides's possible sources for this striking division have already been discussed elsewhere.[24] Strauss notes that Alfarabi draws such distinctions primarily with reference to the size of the regimes ("city-nation-many [all] nations" [159]).[25] Maimonides seems to replace this "tri-partition" by size with a "bi-partition" involving religion (160, 165). It is not the overall bipartition (city versus great nation or the nations) that refers to religion so much as the second part of the bipartition, which is itself subdivided (great nation or [versus] the nations) that does so. Strauss, and before him Harry Austryn Wolfson, ruminated over this odd subdivision at great length.[26] According to Strauss,

> Wolfson has suggested that "the nation" stands for the ancient pagan nations, and "the great nation" stands for Israel, and therefore that Maimonides tacitly goes over from the distinction between political communities in regard to size to their distinction in regard to religion: the "city" stands for the "civil state," and the pagan nations and Israel stand for different forms of the "religious state." This suggestion necessarily implies that the governance, or guidance of Israel, i.e., the Torah, is a subject of political philosophy. (160)

Strauss agrees with the broad outlines of Wolfson's interpretation, especially the notion of a shift from size to religion (cf. 165) and with the inference that the Torah is a proper object of political philosophic study. Strauss goes on to argue that chapters such as *Guide*, 2.40, that "deal with the difference between the Torah and the *nomoi* of the pagans would belong to political science." Furthermore, he notes that the political scientific character of 2.40, as the central chapter of the prophetology of the *Guide*, confirms that the "prophetology as a whole is a branch of political science" (160).[27] All these observations run contrary to the initial impression that chapter 14 of the *Logic* leaves the reader with, namely, that classical political science is irrelevant to the revealed setting. The apparent rejection of political science in the penultimate paragraph—the last impression Maimonides leaves the reader with—is intentionally misleading. It is part of his secretiveness about political science, not to mention the secret alliance of philosopher and prince.

Regarding the subdivision into governance of "the great nation" and "the nations," Strauss disagrees with Wolfson's conjecture that the great nation is Israel. After all, Israel is hardly "great"—as Amos 7:7 confirms (161). Rather, "the great nation" refers to any one of the monotheistic religions and "the nations" to the pagan nations (162).[28] Although the *Logic* is written in Arabic, it seems plausible that "the nations" (*al-umam*) should refer to the pagans— after all, the Torah frequently refers to the pagans as "the nations" (*ha-goyim*). Above all, the difference between the singular form of "the great nation" (*al-umma al-kabīra*) and the plural form of "the nations," provides the needed bridge from the focus on size to the focus on religion. The monotheistic faiths are "universalistic religion[s]" (162)—all of which claim to possess *the* truth. The pagan nations do not make the same type of universal claims. Furthermore, in monotheism, politics serves religion; in paganism, religion serves politics (164). It is hardly surprising then that Maimonides makes no reference to the "rule of living intelligence," a political option so relevant to Plato and Aristotle (163). The Law's claim to possess the final truth makes reference to the rule of a merely human living intelligence into a potential affront to the divine. Consequently, the penultimate paragraph of chapter 14 voices just the kind of deference revelation demands. Before that, however, in his distinction between "the great nation" and "the nations," Maimonides divides practical philosophy in such a way as to emphasize the continued relevance of (classical) political philosophy to the study of revealed law.

C. A Faulty Conjecture and the Unprecedented Challenge of Doctrine in the Monotheistic Setting (162–65)

As Strauss explains, "as a rule" Maimonides concludes each chapter of the *Logic* with an inventory of terms that he has explained earlier. At the conclusion of chapter 14, according to Strauss, he discusses only two terms relevant to politics proper (and economics or household rule), namely, "'commands' and *nomoi*" (163). Strauss includes a footnote offering a conjecture regarding the Arabic equivalent to the various Hebrew terms by which translators had rendered the original Arabic, which he renders "commands." Note 14 reads as follows: "Ibn Tibbon: *haḥuqqim* [the commands or statutes]; Vives: *ḥahoq* [the command or statute]; Ahitub: *hahanhaga* [the regimen]. Could the original [Arabic] have read *ḥukm*?"[29] Strauss's conjecture about the Arabic equivalent of what he renders "command" is plausible, though apparently incorrect. The two terms listed that refer to politics proper, which appear as the last two words of the whole treatise in the complete Arabic versions to which Strauss did not have access, are "regime (*siyāsa*) and *nomoi*."[30] Based on this faulty conjecture, Strauss goes on to discuss the relation between "command" and "*nomos*" as that between genus and species. Nomoi are laws set forth without regard to time or place, implying that there are other commands that change in accordance with time and place—not only time and place but from individual to individual.[31]

Over the course of the next page and a half, Strauss follows out this conjectured contrast between *nomos* as general command and more particular commands in relation to two other themes: On the one hand, he discusses it in relation to another nonconjectural claim about the *Logic*. As mentioned previously, he is surprisingly silent about a key claim of Maimonides's predecessors

Plato and Alfarabi, namely, the rule of living intelligence (163–64). On the other hand, Strauss discusses the conjectured contrast in relation to the contrast between regimes ruled by nomoi (pagan regimes) in which religion serves politics and (regimes of) revealed law in which politics is made to serve religion (164). Even when Strauss overreaches in his interpretation of the *Logic*, he anchors his interpretation on solid ground in either the *Logic* or the *Guide*. Furthermore, the conclusion he draws from chapter 14 is a sound one. Maimonides intends here as in the much later *Guide* to focus the attention, at least of the thoughtful reader, on the "change from paganism to revealed religion" (165)—if only so that we might understand the new status and place of political science in the revealed setting.

In addition to the problematic monotheistic expectation that politics should serve religion, Maimonides highlights related new problems on the horizon, ones that would become especially acute in Christendom: "The public discussion of 'the account of the creation' [that is, the account of the beginning], i.e., of physics, did not harm the pagans in the way in which it might harm the adherents of revealed laws. The divinely revealed laws also create dangers which did not exist among the Greeks: they open up a new source of disagreement among men" (164).[32] Although the pagan world saw philosophers put to death for proposing opinions that called the laws of the city into question, it was not until monotheism that cities and nations were themselves torn from within by intestinal conflicts over opinions. Alfarabi and Maimonides both sought, among other things, to protect their religious communities from succumbing to such conflict. Their communities' focus on laws and actions—not to mention the lack of political power of the Jewish nation—made their task far easier than it would prove to be for their Christian counterparts. Christianity's emphasis on the spirit of the Law and thus on doctrine (as opposed to laws and actions) made the tendency toward such conflict more intense, as thinker after thinker in the medieval period could attest—until Machiavelli took his momentous turn to make the critique of religion so explicit that the political role of religious authorities was permanently undercut. Apparently, secularization could not prevent the return of the gods forever.

D. The Initial Impression Left by Maimonides's Division of the Sciences (165–67)

After Strauss summarizes the results of all his previous arguments (165), he turns to tackle the third problem (Maimonides's assignment of the problem of happiness to politics proper) through a consideration of Maimonides's division of the sciences, that is, his two different divisions of the sciences. This section of Strauss's piece gives an account of Maimonides's most obvious division of the sciences into seven. Here, the reader is left with the misleading initial impression that ethics has the central place among the seven. This misleading impression provides Strauss the opportunity to explore the disjunction between "common-sense morality" and the "theoretical understanding of morality," which distinguishes between the "requirements of society" and the "requirements of man's final perfection" (167). His main point is that ethics lacks centrality precisely because it does not focus on "the study of man's end" since that is one of the jobs of politics proper (166). A key implication: politics proper must not be confused with what Strauss referred to on page 159 as "the most practical part of the political teaching of the philosophers." On the contrary, politics proper is nothing if it is not, or at least does not include, the "theoretical understanding of morality" (167).[33]

Maimonides's apparent division of science into seven sciences leads one to other important problems—problems brought to the fore by Maimonides's playful use of numerology. Although here the modern reader is very remote indeed from the methods considered acceptable by twentieth-century positivistic political science, it is also evident that Maimonides does indeed employ numerology, even if playfully, to set forth hints in his *Guide*. Strauss need only inventory the number of chapters in the *Logic* (7 x 2) and the number of terms explained in the work (7 x 25) to muster evidence that the number seven—into which Maimonides has also divided the sciences—plays some role in that work. Perhaps most interesting of all, Strauss goes on to show that this elaborate use of the number seven is only part of the surface teaching regarding the division of the sciences. As we will see, Maimonides's more profound division is in fact into eleven! Before proceeding any further, however, it is worth highlighting one of the most striking insights of Strauss's foray into numerology here. Ultimately in the deeper second division, Strauss will uncover Maimonides's own critique of numerology. The latter will distance himself from serious numerology, as practiced by ancient Presocratic philosophers, namely, the Pythagoreans (168n23)—and in doing so also call into question his own link to the mysticism of the Talmudic Sages (169). In this substantive footnote, Strauss directs the attentive reader to not only a radically new interpretation of Maimonides but also to what appears to be a significant revision of Strauss's own way of reading the medieval Jewish and Islamic political philosophy.

Let us begin at the beginning, however (165–66). The number seven stands for the pure (forms or) intelligences, among which are included the traditional angels of Jewish lore as the subordinate unmoved movers of the Aristotelian tradition.[34] The number fourteen stands for man as the composite of matter and form, as Maimonides confirms when much later he discusses human procreation (among other crucial things about man) in *Guide*, 1.7, and Adam as man in *Guide*, 1.14. Strauss notes that the number fourteen recurs repeatedly in Maimonides's works, especially in his three different divisions of the Law. He follows up this connection between law and man in the number fourteen through a consideration of Maimonides's palace simile of *Guide*, 3.51. Maimonides interprets the simile twice. In the first iteration, the fourth level of the palatial hierarchy is occupied by the practitioners of *fiqh*, or the legalistic science of the Law; in the second iteration, the same level is occupied by students of logic.[35] Interestingly, Strauss does not mention that Maimonides includes in the latter group students of mathematics as well as logic—an omission that may be of interest when interpreting Strauss's key note on numerology. By the striking parallel between law and logic, Strauss is led to wonder whether Maimonides is inferring a proportion of the following sort: man's matter : man's form :: law : logic. This strange conjecture is confirmed by Maimonides's shocking contrast between the goods of the body and the goods of the soul in *Guide*, 3.27–28. From seven and fourteen, Strauss turns eventually to the number seventeen (the number referring to nature, cf. *Guide*, 1.17, on natural science) and the observation that though the whole of the *Guide* is divided into seven sections, only one section consists of seven chapters: the Account of the Chariot in 3.1–7.[36] Although that chapter is shrouded in mystery, it is surrounded by what are likely the two most important sections of the *Guide*, 2.32–48 (on prophetology) and 3.8–24 (on providence), both of which happen to consist of seventeen chapters.[37]

E. The Deeper Impression Left by Maimonides's Division of the Sciences (167–69)

According to Strauss, the more profound division of the sciences, the division into eleven sciences, "leads directly into the center of the fundamental problem." In this division, rather than ethics, the central position is occupied by "God and the angels," leading us to "wonder whether 'the account of the chariot' is identical with the science of God and the angels" (168). Of course, this question of identity is the central conceit of Maimonides's *Guide*, that is, whether the two greatest mysteries of Judaism are identical with the two most important theoretical sciences in ancient philosophy (*Guide*, pt. 1, introd., 6). Strauss goes on to raise the question whether the Talmudic Sages were "men of science or not" (169)—implying the same question that the central conceit of the *Guide* raises. Although Strauss gives many hints as to how to resolve this central conceit, our clearest hint is contained in the obvious connection between Maimonides's use of numerology and the traditional mystical use of it. To address this central conceit, we return to the elusive key footnote concerning numerology (168n23).

In note 23 Strauss argues that in the second division of the sciences into eleven, theoretical science itself was divided into seven parts with music in the center (arithmetic, geometry, astronomy, music, physics, speech about God and the angels, metaphysics). According to Strauss, placing music in the center of the philosophical sciences is reminiscent of the "ancient" or Presocratic or Pythagorean view of music as the center of theoretical science and theoretical science as the center of philosophy. Only when seen in light of all eleven of the sciences (including the four practical sciences: "ethics, economics, governance of the city, governance of the great nation or of the nations" [167]) and the centrality of the problem of God and the angels does the true center of philosophy come into view. That center is the theologico-political problem. The older view, which privileges numbers or mathematics, is oddly dogged by the accusation of mysticism—as Pythagoreanism came to be. Only at this most remote distance from what Strauss elsewhere refers to as the "monistic positivism of the nineteenth and twentieth centuries" (182) do we see that the opposites mathematics and mysticism possess a peculiar affinity to each other. We are reminded once again of the strange similarities between the hostility toward political science that Maimonides faced and the hostility Strauss faces in the form of contemporary historicism—which historicism, though it appears to be the polar opposite of monistic positivism, is merely the other side of the coin of contemporary philosophy.

Something even more curious than all these affinities between Presocratic, medieval, and late modern excesses is that Strauss diagnoses the problem by means not only of Maimonides's *Logic* but also of Alfarabi's *Philosophy of Plato*. The primary excess of Pythagoreanism was an overstated confidence not only in the centrality of music and number but also in the view that "only the theoretical sciences are philosophic" (168n23). Now Strauss himself, in his much discussed "Farabi's *Plato*" (1945), came dangerously close to the view that only the theoretical sciences are philosophic (*FP*, 365, 381). After all, in that article he insinuated that Alfarabi's view is that political philosophy is little more than the exoteric face of theoretical philosophy. *What Is Political Philosophy?* as a whole is a crucial document in understanding the crisis in Strauss's thought, which he refers to as his "shipwreck" (1946).[38] Note 23, strange and off the beaten path though it seems to be, is one of the most telling confrontations with the central problem of philosophy. Following the shipwreck, Strauss seems to have come to appreciate more deeply the theoretical significance of political philosophy.

As I argued at the beginning of this chapter, the secretive alliance of philosophy and princes so central to the Averroistic tradition, of which Maimonides is a part, is radically transformed in the hands of Machiavelli—especially by his blasphemous ire as expressed in propaganda (45–46). Yet the ambition for universal rule (exemplified in monotheism), which gave rise to this secrecy in the first place, has endured and at times only intensified throughout the history of Western political thought, even as, perhaps in part because, Machiavelli's antireligious propaganda heaped success upon success. For Maimonides, monotheism poses a novel challenge to political science: the former insinuates the latter is obsolete. Yet classical political philosophy has answers to monotheism's universal ambitions, as Strauss's humble "Statement on Political Science" begins to show.[39] If classical political philosophy possesses such resources, there is little reason to accept the argument of Kojève that the universalistic ambitions of his own brand of Hegelianism can be realized by means of the unprecedented resources of the biblical tradition. The "improbable" cities of the classics are in a sense more "possible" than are the fantastic promises of Kojève's Hegelianism to provide "the actual satisfaction of all human beings" (131–32).[40]

PART FOUR

Political Philosophy as First Philosophy

CHAPTER NINE

Theoretical Philosophy, Political Philosophy, and Happiness

As so many of my reflections on Strauss, Alfarabi, and Maimonides, the impetus for this chapter first came from reflections on Shlomo Pines's 1979 "Limitations."[1] Over the past three decades, much has been written contesting Pines's insinuation that, according to Maimonides, the only happiness for human beings is political happiness. I have myself added my voice to the chorus of consternation because it seemed to me Pines anachronistically assimilates Maimonides (as well as Alfarabi and Ibn Bajja) to Kant.[2]

Pines's piece has led in two opposing directions: on the one hand, political happiness is the only happiness, a view one finds sometimes being voiced by some "Straussians," and, on the other hand, since the highest theoretical knowledge is impossible, revelation must be our guide in human affairs. Both arguments place a great deal of weight on human things but one is resolutely rationalistic and the other resolutely religious.[3] Both also seem, much as Pines's piece seemed, like a caricature of a moment in Leo Strauss's early interpretation of Maimonides. The moment to which I refer is in Strauss's (1935) *Philosophy and Law*, in which, on the one hand, he highlights the centrality of divine law as a political phenomenon in the *Guide*, and, on the other hand, he highlights Maimonides's insinuations that the prophet is superior to the philosopher(-king) because he is the recipient of supernatural insight, beyond the access of human reason (90–91). As Daniel Tanguay has noted, Strauss never appeals to supernatural insight (or the limits of knowledge that seem to demand such an appeal) after *Philosophy and Law*.[4] Thus, a caricature of this particular moment in Strauss's oeuvre would be misleading about his own most considered views.[5] For now, I want to consider what was missing from both Strauss's early account as well as Pines's very late account. The main thing missing was what Strauss would later call "political philosophy broadly understood" (*CM*, 20)—in other words, reflection on politics in its relation to the whole and human knowledge of the whole, which is quite different from so-called political happiness.

Although it has been argued in recent years that politics for Maimonides is a matter of the imagination much as it is for Spinoza, I, along with other scholars, have contested this view of Maimonides.[6] Obviously, if politics were purely the product of the imagination, Maimonides would have little interest in the possibility that politics could have anything to do with happiness—so low is his estimation of imagination. Those who insist that imagination drives all politics, even good politics in the *Guide*, do so on the basis of misreadings of 1.2 and 2.37—or readings of them in isolation from the development of what Maimonides refers to most explicitly in 1.72 as the noblest of human faculties, namely, that unpronounceable term for him in the *Guide*, prudence.[7] Since I do not accept the view that he means to suggest by these cryptic references to this ruling faculty that political happiness is the only happiness known to human beings, what am I arguing? Precisely because Maimonides does conceive of prudence as integral to good politics, he does consider politics important, but prudence is so directly involved in the strain of actual politics that it cannot yield individual happiness. (Here, I abstract completely from whether the notion of communal happiness holds any water—something that those who so stress "political happiness" seem to take for granted.) As Aristotle stresses in *Nicomachean Ethics*, book 10, prudence, like politics itself, is not itself pleasurable. The pleasure we derive from it results primarily or in the highest instance from retrospective contemplation (*theoria*) of virtuous action (1169b30–1170a5)—so much for the very possibility of so-called political happiness.

Though politics itself is filled with strain, perhaps knowledge of politics might play some role in happiness. It is widely accepted that for Aristotle, and one would therefore assume for so-called Islamic Aristotelians and Maimonides, there are two (actually three, including mathematics) theoretical inquiries: physics and metaphysics.[8] Of course, on the basis of *Nicomachean Ethics*, book 10, it is usually assumed that the highest form of happiness for Aristotle is only one of these theoretical activities, namely, (what Aristotle calls) first philosophy or theology or (what came to be called) metaphysics. And on the basis of Aristotle's insistence early on in that his present ethical, that is, political inquiry, is not for the sake of *theoria* but for the sake of becoming good, it is often assumed that the lines between theoretical science and practical science are hard and fast: *theoria* concerns truth; practical science concerns goodness in human affairs.[9] (Here, of course, one can hardly keep oneself from thinking of *Guide*, 1.2, and the impression it leaves that the true and the good are worlds apart. Compare Pines's overstatement of the novelty of *Guide*, 1.2, in his piece on Maimonides and Spinoza on good and evil.)[10] Returning to Aristotle, because a work of practical science like *Nicomachean Ethics* is for the sake of becoming good, it does not contribute anything to *theoria*. This interpretation seems sensible until, among other things, one questions the hard and fast line between theoretical and practical science—a line made hard and fast at least to some extent because Christian Scholasticism saw great utility in maintaining and deepening this divide.[11]

Enter Alfarabi. It is not much of an exaggeration to say that Alfarabi obscures Aristotle's divide between theoretical and practical science in nearly all of his writings. He does so most strikingly in some of his accounts of political science, or in what he calls "virtuous kingly craft" in the *Enumeration*, the *Book of Religion*, and the *Attainment of Happiness*. In the *Enumeration* and the *Book of Religion*, Alfarabi obscures this divide by starting with an account of politics (PS 1) reminiscent of Aristotle's, which abstracts from theoretical science altogether, that he then follows up with an account of politics (PS 2) more reminiscent of Plato's—that is, one that more or less explicitly appeals to the possibility of the philosopher-king and the complete combination of theory and practice or, more precisely, of prudence together with the possession of all the sciences both theoretical and practical. In his early writings Strauss highlighted repeatedly the striking fact that the so-called Islamic Aristotelians, in matters political, sided with Plato. Some of Strauss's students (directly or indirectly), Muhsin Mahdi, Charles E. Butterworth, and I, have all mused about what exactly this tendency to revert to Plato signifies. It has something to do with the monotheistic setting in which Alfarabi wrote. In such settings theological opinions come to possess an unprecedented centrality in political life. This is even more the case for monotheistic faiths that are divine laws (Islam and Judaism rather than Christianity). The phenomenon of divine law is totalistic: it does not easily separate the theoretical from the practical or the theological from the political.[12]

Our first question then is, Will this reversion to Plato go along with a different estimate of the possible theoretical significance of knowledge of political or human things than the one normally ascribed to Aristotle? Our two additional questions are, What is the evidence for such a different estimate in Alfarabi? And is there any evidence for it in Maimonides? Our consideration of the evidence from Alfarabi also enables us to at least begin to answer the first question about the possible theoretical significance of knowledge of human things.

In the *Attainment of Happiness* Alfarabi engages in a broad sketch of the limits of certainty in the sciences—one addressed to an audience that seems to presuppose from the beginning that certainty has already been attained. Early on he underlines the extent to which demonstration in the strictest sense is elusive except in mathematics, but lesser forms of knowledge are possible the higher one ascends toward knowledge of the highest things. Alfarabi's path through the sciences, which at first appears only to be an ascent, turns out to be quite complicated and hard to follow. It is made so, at least in part, because his account of the sciences is rooted from the start in the four kinds of human things that make possible the attainment of happiness in this life and the next, namely, theoretical virtues, deliberative virtues, moral virtues, and practical arts. In other words, the account is oriented from the start toward the attainment of happiness—it is, as it were, anthropocentric. This is not a neutral or objective or impartial account of science but an account of the sciences with an eye to human happiness—and one that focuses on science or knowledge as perhaps the highest form of human virtue or excellence. In other words, Alfarabi allows the presumption of his audience that they already know what human happiness is (as it were always already given with great authority in monotheistic communities) to shape the course of the inquiry into the sciences.[13]

The main complication is that the ascent from math through natural science to inquiry into the soul (partly physical and partly metaphysical) seems to lead directly to human or political science (secs. 10–18), but that first political science is somehow not sufficient. Consequently, Alfarabi steps back and sees the necessity to inquire into metaphysical beings along the lines of his inquiry into natural beings, which seems to culminate in knowledge of the ultimate causes of the beings as well as knowledge of the divinity, him or itself. (And this confidence regarding metaphysical knowledge is undercut by the closing of the *Philosophy of Aristotle*.) Yet for some unstated reason, Alfarabi renews his inquiry into political science. In this political science, he highlights the likeness between hierarchical ordering in the city and in the nation, on the one hand, and the world as a whole, on the other, a theological mainstay of many of Alfarabi's writings—and a crucial theme in the third subdivision of the *Attainment of Happiness*. Immediately after outlining this political science, Alfarabi announces that this constitutes "theoretical perfection" (*al-kamāl al-naẓarī*). Although he reinvokes the four things contributing to human happiness as also comprising this theoretical perfection, neither one of these (political science along with physics and metaphysics or these four things) would in any usual Aristotelian setting comprise theoretical perfection.

One thing is clear: the *Attainment*'s visiting and revisiting of political science is highly reminiscent of PS 1 and PS 2 from the *Enumeration* and the *Book of Religion*. In other words, the second account is a return to the Platonic approach to the relation between theory and practice. It is less clear, at least initially, what role political science plays in "theoretical perfection." So far Alfarabi, through his second characterization of political science, has led us to suspect that at least one of the reasons that theoretical perfection involves political science has something to do with the putative likeness of the city to the cosmos, a kinship often invoked by medievals when they are broaching matters of providence. The character of PS 2, namely, that it includes the drawing of likenesses between the human things and the whole, is testified to not only by the *Attainment* but also by all of Alfarabi's "political writings." The nearly constant presence of quasi-theological descriptions of the order of the whole has led readers of Alfarabi to identify him as a Neoplatonist—apparently intoxicated with strange resonances between the microcosm and the macrocosm.

We have already challenged this reading of Alfarabi as well as Maimonides.[14] It is usually argued that Alfarabi reads his political teaching off of an inherited Neoplatonic cosmology. One of the main pieces of evidence against this reading is that the hierarchy is less consistent than appears at first glance. Although the Neoplatonic reading seems reasonable as long as orderly relations prevail between high and low, theoretical and practical, matters appear otherwise when such hierarchy is interrupted. Upon closer examination, Alfarabi's writings reveal a consistent pattern of disorder amid apparent hierarchy, in both the city and the cosmos. This is especially clear in his *Political Regime*, in the themes of the asp or viper in the first half and the weeds in the second half. Neoplatonism would lead us to expect that all the disorder in the whole is due to the infiltration of elements of carnality or materiality. In contrast, Alfarabi shows that the whole is shot through with such disorder even up to the top and perhaps most notably in the political realm in the case of the most interesting weed, the potential philosopher. In other words, the world lacks the kind of providential ordering first promised by the Neoplatonic hierarchy. This helps to explain why the theme of the solitary takes on such centrality not only among the Islamic Aristotelians but also in Maimonides.

Maimonides picks up the theme of the solitary (and all that it implies about prudence and providence) quite subtly in *Guide*, 1.72, in his allusions to prudence and his account of particular providence or the lack thereof; less subtly in *Guide*, 1.34 (75), in his references to the unique individual who does not need the guidance of authority; and most boldly in 3.34, in his opposition between the aim of the Law and the well-being of the unique individual, and in 3.51 (620), in his repudiation of the value of mere belief on the basis of the authority of another.[15]

Although Strauss in *Philosophy and Law* (1935), like Pines in his later writings, may have tended toward Pines's conflicting stresses on supernatural aid and divine law as a political theme, shortly after *Philosophy and Law*, in "Some Remarks on the Political Science of Maimonides and Farabi" (1936) and "The Place of the Doctrine of Providence according to Maimonides" (1937), Strauss identified the grounding of the *Guide*'s prophetology (2.32–48) and account of particular providence (3.8–24) in political science. As I have already brought out in chapter 6, Strauss shows that particular providence falls within political philosophy in the *Guide*—rather than purely theoretical inquiry. Of course for Strauss, the fate of the philosopher was a central theme in what he came to call "political philosophy." As for Strauss so for Alfarabi and Maimonides, the fate of the solitary is the highest expression of the disorder evident in not only the city but also the world.[16]

"Theoretical perfection" includes political science because the city is the part of the whole that reveals most directly the nature of the whole.[17] The whole that political philosophy ("broadly understood [as] . . . first philosophy"; *CM*, 20) reveals is not as orderly as more metaphysical readings of Alfarabi and Maimonides might lead one to expect. The latter readings blend together Neoplatonic confidence in hierarchy with revealed confidence in divine particular providence—as opposed to merely human prudence. Such Neoplatonic readings not only overstate the orderliness of the whole but also fail to take sufficiently literally or seriously the single greatest emblem of that disorder, the philosophic solitary and his ironic doppelganger, the philosopher-king. The highest happiness and purest pleasures derive from contemplation of the whole in its order and *dis*order—unless one wants to posit in advance that the truth must always be beautiful. After all, the highest happiness derives less from the unalloyed beauty of the object of contemplation than from our sense of our own progress in knowledge. Yet such a sense of progress cannot be had without ongoing awareness of the limitedness of our own knowledge so far.[18] Such awareness is far, indeed, from late modern notions of the limits of metaphysical knowledge.

CHAPTER TEN

Maimonides's *Guide* as a Work of Political Philosophy

Usually, it isn't difficult to say what discipline or science a book belongs to. Such is not the case for Maimonides's *Guide of the Perplexed*. This problem, however, is not limited to the *Guide*. Part of the difficulty comes from the side of the discipline in question, political philosophy. Although contemporary political science, even political theory, is generally confident (even overly confident) about what it is, political philosophy is less so.

What Strauss means by "political philosophy" by the time of his mature writings of the 1950s is quite different from what he means by "political science" in his interpretations of Alfarabi and Maimonides in his early writings of the 1930s (*Philosophy and Law*, "Some Remarks on the Political Science of Maimonides and Farabi," and perhaps most openly in "The Place of the Doctrine of Providence according to Maimonides"). The former (later) conception is a far more comprehensive term in the spirit of the reference to "political philosophy broadly understood is the core of philosophy or 'the first philosophy'" in *City and Man* (delivered 1962, published 1964); the latter (earlier) conception is much closer to the traditional view of political science as merely one of the sciences or as a part of science or philosophy. As Strauss explains in *City and Man*, "Not Socrates or Plato but Aristotle is truly the founder of political science: as one discipline, and by no means the most fundamental or the highest discipline, among a number of disciplines" (21). In this book, we've seen that the tendency to treat political science as a discipline was surely intensified by the medieval Christian tendency to deepen the divide between theoretical and practical science. The early Strauss, though he recognized the important influence of Plato in the political science of Alfarabi and Maimonides, did not yet fully appreciate the comprehensiveness of their Platonic political philosophy. His initial lack of understanding of the comprehensiveness of political philosophy in these thinkers may have contributed to his exaggeration of the importance of a pure form of theoretical science in Aristotle's sense. Thus, Maimonides is presented as freed up from having to do the real work of political science in *Philosophy and Law* because the Torah is the realization of the ideal state of the ancients—leaving Maimonides free to "aristotelize" (*PL*, 133). And Alfarabi is interpreted in "Farabi's *Plato*" as viewing political philosophy as merely the exoteric face of philosophy, so little is political philosophy able to partake of the esoteric. Although Strauss never argues again after the late 1930s that the *Guide* is a work of political science, I've tried to show that what he glimpsed then as merely a part of philosophy or the last part of philosophy proves ultimately to be much more than merely a part of the *Guide*. It becomes the underlying core of truth that is evident only in the surface of things.

It is not by chance that the true status of political philosophy began to take its shape only at the moment that Strauss turned to greater attention to the surface of the *Guide*, that is, in "Literary Character" (1941). Even though he would continue to overstate the merely exoteric character of "political philosophy" into the middle of the 1940s (FB, 1945), it took his intense focus on the surface of the *Guide* as "enlightened *kalām*" to begin to truly come to terms with its esoteric core.

As we have noted before, Strauss contrasts "enlightened" with "vulgar *kalām*." Alfarabi, Maimonides's esteemed predecessor in the development of enlightened kalām, describes vulgar kalām in his *Enumeration of the Sciences*, chapter 5, as Strauss notes (*PAW*, 40n9).[1] In keeping with what on this occasion we can call, speaking loosely, Alfarabi's "religious neutrality," he is not direct about which religion is defending itself or against whom (though he does allude vaguely to a religion using kalām against another religion). In *Guide*, 1.71, precisely because Maimonides is openly defending Judaism, he is more forthcoming than Alfarabi about which religion first took this up, namely, Christianity, especially Greek and Syrian Christians, and against whom, namely, the philosophers! When he goes on to trace the development of kalām, he attacks both Christian and Muslim dialectical theologians for defending religion by violating "the nature of existence" (178). He implies that he will defend Judaism in the *Guide*, however, without violating the nature of existence. But who studies the nature of existence? Of course, the philosophers study it. In effect, what Strauss means when he speaks of enlightened kalām is a kalām that does not take philosophers as its target—a very strange form of kalām, indeed. Rather than attack the philosophers, Maimonides's main vituperation is vented on the vulgar kalām (see *Guide*, 1.73–76)! Furthermore, his strategy throughout the rest of the *Guide*, and perhaps more stunningly in his juridical works such as his code of Law, the *Mishneh Torah*, is to defend God's existence, unity, and incorporeality by adopting the philosophical claim that the world is eternal (182).

Of course, Maimonides says more than once that he does not agree with the philosophic view. Nevertheless, he eschews the vulgar kalām tradition's way of defending the createdness of the world, namely, by using arguments and premises that violate the "nature of existence" or being. Although his defense of creation in part 2 (especially 2.19) relies on a type of argument readily used by the *mutakallimūn*, the particularization argument, Maimonides's version of this argument doesn't rely on any physical or metaphysical premises as do theirs. Rather, it takes advantage of the lack of an adequate astronomical explanation for (despite the existence of a perfectly adequate mathematical description of) the apparent disorder of the motions of the heavenly bodies and the dubious insistence on the apparent disorder in the placement of the stars, to insist that a God with a particularizing will must somehow be responsible for the apparent disorder.

Leaving aside the problematic, if elaborate, arguments for creation, Maimonides claims that either position (eternity or creation) must be assumed and cannot be proven. And he prefers eternity as the basis of proving God's existence, unity, and incorporeality, at least in part, because something actually needs to be and can be proven on the basis of that assumption. Not so in the case of creation: the omnipotent God's existence is always already tacitly assumed when creation is assumed (181).

Leaving the surface aside for now, what indications are there that the depth of the *Guide* is political science or philosophy? Maimonides identifies the subject matter of the *Guide* as "the true science of the Law" (pt. 1, introd., 5). He contrasts it with jurisprudence, one of the three sciences or arts identified by Alfarabi in *Enumeration* 5—the other two being kalām and political science. Since the surface is enlightened kalām, and Maimonides opposes the true science of the Law to mere jurisprudence, there is reason to suspect that he means political science or philosophy when he speaks of the true science of the Law. In spite of the "practically complete agreement" (*PAW*, 44) among contemporary scholars that the *Guide* is not a work of political philosophy, it is quite natural to assume that it is.

Why then the consensus against the obvious? There are two main reasons: the enlightened kalām surface of the *Guide* is far more obvious than any other feature of the *Guide*. Most interpreters see nothing more than the defense of Judaism—though, again, they call it "Jewish philosophy" and thereby indicate their failure to understand the character of that defense. And Maimonides seems to imply in the *Logic* as well as *Guide*, 2.39, that the giving of the Torah has made political science unnecessary. We need not repeat what was already argued in chapter 6 regarding the *Logic*, except to say that it is misread when it is taken to exclude political science from Maimonides's ken. Maimonides implies that if human beings receive divine revelation of the Law, only then is political philosophy unnecessary for the giving of such a law. As we've already seen in our brief consideration of *Guide*, 1.71, evidence abounds that he does not think that the Jewish people have no need for philosophy, if not political philosophy, in these times.

Generally, the meaning of Maimonides's true science of the Law is misinterpreted because it is conflated with or even confused with the enlightened kalām surface of the *Guide*. There are two basic ways of interpreting this true science: either it is the study of the fundamental beliefs or opinions that are thought to be the foundation of the Law or it is the political scientific study of the aims of the Law as law. In other words, it is either (largely theoretical) opinions or the ends of the Law.[2] The former view is the "Jewish philosophy" interpretation, which holds that Maimonides's task in the *Guide* is less to defend (many scholars studying Maimonides are oblivious of the character of kalām in the medieval Muslim and Jewish communities) than to explore the roots of Judaism, much as Maimonides sets them forth in his thirteen roots, or articles of faith, in *Pereq Ḥeleq*, Sanhedrin 10 of his *Commentary on the Mishnah*.[3] Maimonides leaves a clue that this interpretation is mistaken: perhaps the most theoretically contentious issue in the *Guide*, namely, whether the world is created or eternal, is not among the beliefs he requires of the Jew in his thirteen articles. That is, he does not require that the Jew believe in the world's createdness. Perhaps the main theoretical bone of contention in the *Guide* is missing from the beliefs Maimonides requires. The *Guide* then is not primarily concerned with exploring the thirteen roots that every Jew should believe.

What evidence is there that the main focus of the *Guide* is the political philosophic study of the aims of the Law? In *Guide*, 2.39, Maimonides attacks the nomoi of all other communities including Islam, Christianity, and those of the pagan Greeks (one of the most polemical moments of the *Guide*). This is the moment in the *Guide* that most resembles the argument of the *Logic* about how revelation displaces all such nomoi and is at odds with the philosophic study of them. But the very next moment, *Guide*, 2.40—at the center of the *Guide*'s center, the prophetology (running from 2.32 to 2.48)—most clearly illuminates the meaning of the true science of the Law.[4] Maimonides opens with an epitome of ancient political philosophy. He follows that epitome with an account of what makes a divine law truly divine: it is that the Law should cultivate the intellect, not merely care for the well-being of the body. The simplicity of this account is deceptive. Two problems contained within it unfold throughout the rest of the *Guide*: what does it mean to cultivate the intellect in view of the fact that Maimonides claims that belief or mere opinion (even true opinion, apparently) falls far short of the intellectual perfection he envisions (3.51, 620)? (In other words, Maimonides's view of belief is very remote from more familiar Christian notions that belief on the basis of faith saves.)

The other problem is, what distinguishes beliefs that exist for the sake of the body from beliefs that exist for the sake of the soul or knowledge for its own sake (3.27–28)? (In other words, some beliefs exist for the sake of communal well-being, which Maimonides treats as a form of or in the service of bodily well-being. It is unclear whether any of the beliefs in the Torah, regarding, for example, God's attributes and particular providence, are believed in for their own sake, as opposed to their beneficial communal consequences.) These two problems coalesce into a central theme of political philosophy, especially medieval Jewish and Islamic political philosophy, the theme of the solitary.

Guide, 2.40, identifies intellectual perfection as the aim of divine law, but *Guide*, 3.34, announces that the aim of the Law is the well-being of the majority, not the unique individual (Ar., *wāḥid*; cf. Gr., *idiotēs*; Plato, *Republic*, 620c; and Aristotle, *Nicomachean Ethics*, 1179a8) or solitary. This contradiction between 2.40 and 3.34 is ultimately as, or perhaps more, important than the closely related and more dramatic perplexity regarding whether the order of the heavenly bodies is rationally explicable or provided for by a particularly providential, omnipotent God (*Guide*, 2.24). Indeed, the disjunction between the individual and the city bears witness to an answer to the question of particular providence. As Strauss shows in "Place of Providence," Maimonides extracts the issue of particular providence from its usual position in Jewish dialectical theology as a part of God's justice and attaches it to the *Guide*'s prophetology, which is firmly rooted in the political science of 2.40 (PPr, 542). Even though 2.40 appears to make individual perfection the aim of Mosaic law, closer examination reveals that only a philosophically revised divine law combines these dissonant ends—the well-being of the city and the highest well-being of the individual.

Strauss seems to have changed his mind somewhat regarding what is central in the *Guide*. In *Philosophy and Law* (1935), he seems to argue that though political science plays an important, if not central, role, revelation somehow made it possible for Jews like Maimonides to "aristotelize" (133). This view that purely theoretical philosophy is primary for Maimonides in the *Guide*, as well as in Alfarabi, is very much in evidence at least through Strauss's "Farabi's *Plato*" (1945). As we have argued in chapter 7, by the end of the 1940s and at least the early 1950s (in "Maimonides' Statement on Political Science"), Strauss seems to have developed an even deeper appreciation of the centrality of political science or philosophy in the *Guide*. Indeed, I would go so far as to say that the *Guide* came to exemplify in Strauss's mind what he refers to later in the *City and Man* (1964) as "political philosophy broadly understood" (20)—which is the "first philosophy" (a term normally reserved for metaphysics). In other words, he went from the view that political philosophy is merely the exoteric face of philosophy ("Farabi's *Plato*") to the more considered view that political philosophy might have some theoretical significance of its own ("Maimonides' Statement on Political Science").[5] Although Strauss already saw in "Place of Providence" (1937) that prophetology and particular providence were both treated within political science, he did not yet understand fully what this means for the proper understanding of the relation between human being, city, and cosmos. It would take another fifteen to twenty years to see more fully that political philosophy has theoretical meaning.

CHAPTER ELEVEN

Da capo

An Introduction to the *Guide*

Most Jews have heard the adage from late modernity, "From Moses to Moses [Maimonides] there was no one like Moses." In a tradition in which divine law is central and Moses is believed to be the recipient of divine revelation, these are strong words about Maimonides, indeed. There is general agreement among Jews of all stripes today that Maimonides was the greatest Jewish thinker of the medieval period and perhaps of all time. For someone so highly esteemed, it may come as a surprise that some of Maimonides's books were burned at the behest of rabbis in his own time. From what we now know, it appears that his code of law, the *Mishneh Torah* (Repetition of the Law, cf. the meaning of "Deuteronomy"), was burned in part because it challenged the centrality of the Talmud in Jewish life by producing a greatly abbreviated version of it—making it less necessary for pious Jews to devote their entire lives to its study. Indeed, as he implies in his introduction to his code, one may study it together with the Bible and do without the Talmud![1] But there is another reason that the code was burned: if one need no longer devote all of one's study to the Talmud, what then should one study in its stead? Maimonides subtly implies in his code that at least some Jews should study the central mysteries of Judaism, the Account of the Beginning and the Account of the Chariot.[2] Traditionally, these two were identified with mystical teachings of some kind, but, in the introduction to part one of his *Guide of the Perplexed*, Maimonides identifies them with physics and metaphysics (6). In other words, he seems to have codified Jewish law so that at least some Jews could study philosophy.

Although this may not appear shocking to the contemporary reader, one starts to appreciate how shocking it is when one considers the status that philosophy had in Judaism prior to Maimonides. For the most part, it was identified with heresy. The typical heretic was referred to as an *epikoros*, that is, a follower of the *philosopher* Epicurus. In other words, it was widely accepted that Judaism and philosophy were at loggerheads. Consequently, Maimonides identifies responding to or somehow handling apparent contradictions between the Law and philosophy as the central task of the *Guide* (5). When two things are in apparent contradiction with each other, there are not many alternatives: one could argue that (1) the contradiction is merely apparent, (2) the two elements are true in different realms, (3) only one or the other of the elements is true, or (4) human beings cannot resolve the contradiction. For now, we will leave aside the fourth option and argue as if the contradiction can in some sense be handled or resolved. Among the most obvious contradictions between philosophy and Law are the following: the philosophic view that the world is eternal and the revealed view that God created the world; the philosophic view that God is merely generally provident and the revealed view that he is particularly provident.

That so many scholars and readers remain perplexed about what Maimonides's own resolution of these contradictions might be is an indicator itself of two things: either he was himself confused, or he knows and indicates what the proper resolution is in a highly elusive manner. Although some scholars have argued that some of the more egregious contradictions in the *Guide* are merely oversights, they do so in express contradiction of Maimonides's own assertions in the introduction to the first part to the contrary: "For the diction of this Treatise has not been chosen at haphazard, but with great exactness and exceeding precision, and with care to avoid failing to explain any obscure point. And nothing has been mentioned out of its place, save with a view to explaining some matter in its proper place" (15).[3] Subsequently, in the same introduction, he elaborates the seven causes of "contradictory or contrary statements . . . in any book or compilation" (17). Eventually, he recapitulates the kinds of causes of contradiction, taking note of which books display which kinds. Of all the kinds, the most egregious is the sixth, when an author affirms two premises whose contradiction becomes apparent only "after many premises" or "after many [intervening] syllogisms." When the author has "simply forgotten the first when writing down the second in another part of his compilation, this is a very great weakness." It is precisely this kind of contradiction that would be required for Maimonides to fall prey to "confusion." Not surprisingly, the most interesting of the causes of contradiction, the seventh cause, is effectively the opposite of the sixth cause. Here contradictory premises are used intentionally, but the contradiction between the premises is concealed by, for example, the distance between the conclusions drawn from them. And "the vulgar must in no way be aware of the contradiction; the author accordingly uses some device to conceal it by all means" (18). Subsequently, Maimonides argues that he employs the seventh type of contradiction (as well as the fifth, which is less interesting for our purposes now). Through the opposition of the sixth and seventh causes, he makes it evident that he does not think of himself as falling prey to the sixth type. Although contemporary scholars might find such assertions about one's own attention to argumentation merely arrogant, a brief consideration of Maimonides's achievements suggests that one ought at least entertain the idea that he is aware of the contradictions in his book but is intentionally elusive—after all, that is what the most literal interpretation of his introduction seems to suggest. That Maimonides wrote in a way that is intentionally elusive or esoteric has become more and more widely recognized among scholars.

One cannot but wonder what Maimonides knew that could continue to spark such controversy down to this day, all the while that he has achieved unparalleled legal authority. The man who challenged the establishment has become a central figure in the Jewish establishment. Even if his code has not displaced the study of the Talmud, it has come to be thought of as an indispensable guide to the meaning of the Talmud and the model for nearly all subsequent codifications of it. Maimonides would likely have been famous had he not even written the *Mishneh Torah* or the *Guide of the Perplexed*. Before he codified the Talmud, he wrote an important commentary on the central text of the Talmud, the Mishnah. From an early age he had come to be recognized for the brilliance of his legal mind. Most scholars agree that he was born in 1137 or 1138 in Cordova. His family was driven from Spain under the impact of a new brand of Islam, the Almohads, guided by Ibn Tumert. His family moved to Fez in what is today Morocco, visited the Holy Land, and eventually settled in Fustat, the former center of Cairo. As a young man, he studied not only the Law but also the philosophical sciences. When exactly he began to study medicine is unclear, though it was very common for those who studied philosophy, including physics, to become well versed in the medicine of the day—especially well-educated Jewish scholars. When his brother, a merchant, died at sea, Maimonides appears to have been deeply affected, as well as to have been compelled to devote more and more time to medicine to make ends meet. All the while, as an increasingly important jurisprudent, he was sent legal questions by pious Jews from around the Mediterranean and at least as far afield as Provence and Yemen, which he answered in responsa that are still studied today. At the same time, in Cairo, he became the Head of the Jews—a position that appears to have been both religious and political, to the extent Jews were the masters of their own political life under Muslim rule. Rabbi, jurisprudent, doctor, philosopher-scientist, ruler of sorts: Maimonides was truly a renaissance man. Most scholars agree that he died in Cairo in 1204.[4]

Let us return to the real or apparent contradictions between philosophy and the Law. At first glance, it appears that though contradictions between philosophy and Law may exist, Maimonides makes it amply evident that when push comes to shove, he must side with the Law. In doing so, he demonstrates his colors as a not wholly impartial defender of Judaism. To see him at work as a defender of Judaism, let us consider the most obvious case of the contradiction between philosophy and Law, that between eternity and creation. Although Maimonides mounts arguments proving that God exists, is one, and is incorporeal on the philosophic assumption of the eternity of the world (cf. *Guide*, 1.71, with pt. 2, introd., through chap. 2 and the opening of the *Mishneh Torah*), he insists that he believes in creation. At the same time, he adds that the perplexity among philosophers about how to explain the motions of the heavenly bodies can be used as evidence of some sort for the existence of a particularly providential Creator (2.19). Perhaps the greatest weakness of this argument is that although philosophers have been unable to explain the causes of the motions of the heavenly bodies, they can discover patterns of regularity behind the apparent disorder in their motions. The very regularity of motion, even without an available causal explanation, speaks against this perplexity as evidence for a particularly provident God. We are not surprised to see, then, that Maimonides concludes his long and winding argument regarding eternity and creation, in which he mounts as strong a defense of creation as he is able, by asserting that since neither can be proven, one should assume creation (2.25). His expressed reason for assuming creation is indeed telling: if one assumes eternity as Aristotle conceives of it, it "destroys the Law in its principle" (328). The principle to which he refers is not merely creation but what creation entails, namely, miracles or, as he goes on to argue on the next page, God's particular providence for the people of Israel as expressed in a particular time and place. In other words, the reason for assuming creation is that without it particular providence is impossible. This justification for upholding creation reveals starkly the role that Maimonides plays here. Far from being a neutral umpire between philosophy and Law, here at least, he is playing the role of the defender of Judaism or the Law.

    He prepared the reader for this role long before he embarked on his proofs for God's existence, unity, and incorporeality, that is, in 1.71. There he warned that though he sympathized with the efforts of the dialectical theologians first in Christianity, then in Islam, and finally in Judaism to defend their respective faiths, he would embark on a defense of Judaism that differed from all previous ones within Judaism by making arguments in accordance with the "nature of existence." He displays at great length in 1.73–76 what it means to defend one's faith in a manner that is at odds with the nature of existence. Traditional dialectical theologians made arguments in which whatever could be imagined was, as they say, "admissible." According to Maimonides, these dialectical theologians are incorrect: not everything that can be imagined is possible (1.73, tenth premise). In what capacity then does Maimonides argue in 2.25 that we must affirm the creation of the world lest we undermine the principle that God is particularly provident? Here, he seems to speak in his capacity as a defender of the faith or dialectical theologian. The question remains, however, whether his answer is wholly compatible with the nature of existence.

Now that we have some experience with the kinds of disputes between philosophy and Law that Maimonides seeks to negotiate, we can revisit the issue of what options are open to us in confronting such contradictions. Few, if any, interpreters have maintained that Maimonides adopts (2) a two-realm account akin, say, to Kant's claims regarding the deterministic character of things as phenomena and the freedom of human beings as participants in a noumenal realm. In 1979, some sixteen years after finishing his *Guide* translation, Shlomo Pines, however, adopted an element of Kant's teaching as a way of negotiating Maimonides's contradictions: he argued that regarding such conundrums as the eternity or creation of the world, (4) Maimonides was ultimately agnostic.[5] He took this approach to Maimonides's contradictions to a surprising extreme by insinuating that Maimonides deemed theoretical philosophy inaccessible to human beings. He concluded that, if this were Maimonides's view, then his only real area of concern would be practical philosophy.

In recent times Kenneth Seeskin has championed a version of this view. Eschewing Pines's conclusion, he has embraced the idea that Maimonides was agnostic about the highest matters and chose on faith to embrace the view of revelation. Although Pines's "Limitations" article spawned a large number of scholarly responses, his view has not been widely accepted. The two most widely accepted views are the two remaining: (1) the contradiction between philosophy and Law is merely apparent or (3) he indicates subtly his preference for one view over the other. The latter view seems to be Strauss's; the former view covers a wide swath of interpretations. To oversimplify for the purposes of clarity, the former view—perhaps the most widely held view—amounts to the suggestion that Maimonides presents a harmonization of the views of philosophy and revelation. It has taken on a variety of forms but amounts, for example, to the suggestion that Maimonides has found a way to harmonize eternity with creation. If this were his view ultimately, one wonders why he would have drawn so much attention to contradictions in his introduction. Why not simply offer the harmonization rather than offering so many contradictory arguments?

For now, let us leave aside the variety of options for resolving Maimonides's contradictions. We turn now to the question, where does Maimonides locate his own inquiry among the sciences or genres of inquiry? The *Guide* is among the most difficult works in the history of the West to locate with respect to genre. Aside from observing that he is writing to respond to the perplexity of those who have been exposed to both philosophy and Law, he underlines that the *Guide* is not a work of jurisprudence like most of his other writings. Rather he claims that it is concerned with the "science of the Law in the true sense" (5). We have already touched on the other religious science in Judaism most closely related to jurisprudence, namely, dialectical theology. We have also seen that he looks down on traditional dialectical theology in Judaism and that he indicates his intention in 1.71 to defend Judaism, while arguing in accordance with the "nature of existence." Is some form of dialectical theology then what he means by the "science of the Law in the true sense"? One other possible significance remains as a serious contender, though—namely, the philosophic study of the Law, or political philosophy. By the end of this introduction, we will try to make the case that Maimonides intends both of these meanings (defense of Judaism and political philosophy) in his ambiguous phrase. For now, though, it is worth noticing that there are two main interpretations of the genre of the *Guide*. Some, probably most, interpreters argue that it is a metaphysical inquiry into the fundamental beliefs enshrined in the Law (cf. dialectical theology compatible with the "nature of existence"); others argue that it is a political philosophical inquiry into the ends of the Law. The interpretation that we offer leaves some room for both of these main lines of interpretation.

In the meantime, we need to confront some challenges to the minority view that the *Guide* is at least in part a work of political philosophy. The most obvious challenge is Maimonides's shocking denigration of action. Beginning in 1.2 and ending in the final chapter (3.54, 635), he mounts a rhetorical attack on action so fierce that some have concluded that he is a conventionalist. Many interpreters then have, if they have even considered the possibility that the *Guide* is a work of political philosophy, thought that surely no thinker who so attacks action could be seriously concerned with political philosophy. Before accepting this view, let us consider why Maimonides might have so attacked action. Although belief in God had always been important, Judaism allowed action to be the center of Jewish life. The philosophic concern with theoretical matters that Maimonides gives every indication of trying to bolster in the *Guide* was hardly a natural fit for Judaism. Perhaps Maimonides attacks action so fiercely to provide a toehold for philosophy or speculation. Another related observation lends some credence to this view: other works in the history of political philosophy have come close to engaging in so strong an attack on action—perhaps the most famous of all, Plato's *Republic*, is similar in at least this respect.

Another challenge to the minority view that the *Guide* is at least in part a work of political philosophy seems to come from two passages in Maimonides's oeuvre: in *Guide*, 2.39, and chapter 14 of his *Logic*. In the *Logic* Maimonides seems to assert that now that we have received revelation we have no need for political philosophy. While defining and elaborating upon the meaning of political science, he says,

> The learned men of the past religious communities used to formulate, each of them according to his perfection, regimens and rules through which their princes governed the subjects; they called them nomoi [laws]; and the nations used to be governed by those nomoi. On all these things, the philosophers have many books that have been translated into Arabic, and the ones that have not been translated are perhaps even more numerous. In these times, all this—I mean the regimes and the nomoi—has been dispensed with, and men are being commanded by divine commands.[6]

Although Maimonides here does not go quite so far as to say that political science or philosophy is unnecessary, he does come close to insinuating as much. After all, what need have we of political philosophy if we are able to receive the Law from God? In the *Guide* Maimonides's defense of Judaism reaches a peak similar to the end of the *Logic* in 2.39: shortly after impugning the nomoi of Christians and Muslims, he denigrates the "nomoi of the Greeks" by associating them with what he calls the "ravings of the Sabians" (2.39, 381). He opens the next chapter, however, with a brief epitome of political science, marked at the beginning and end by two apparent quotations from Aristotle's two most important works of political science: "It has been explained with utmost clarity that man is political by nature and that it is his nature to live in society. . . . Therefore, I say that the Law, although it is not natural, enters into what is natural."[7] In brief, although Maimonides is consistent in criticizing the nomoi of Greek communities, he never states explicitly that he rejects political philosophy.[8] This epitome of political science, however, is buried in the middle of the *Guide*'s extended inquiry into prophecy, or prophetology (2.32–48), which at times seems highly theoretical. Many interpreters have focused on the theoretical complications in the psychology of the prophet, yet 2.40 underlines that what makes the Law divine is that it aims at human perfection. And what is human perfection, according to Maimonides, but the intellectual perfection made so famous by philosophers like Plato and Aristotle? In brief, what appears at first glance to be a highly theoretical treatment of prophecy proves ultimately to be an exploration of the character of human intellectual perfection and its relation to law, a central theme of political philosophy not only in Maimonides but in such works as Plato's *Laws*.

Having lent some credence to the idea that the *Guide* is not only a metaphysical or theological work, let us consider what is known about Maimonides's sources. Based on correspondence especially with his students, it is widely accepted that he considered Aristotle to be the most dependable teacher at least with respect to logic, terrestrial physics, and ethics (also cf. *Guide*, 2.22, 319; 2.24, 326). He encourages the study of Aristotle with the guidance of various Greek commentators, especially Alexander of Aphrodisias and Themistius. Alexander can be described as little touched if at all by Neoplatonism—since he seems to have preceded Plotinus by some years. This means that his commentaries tend to be more literal and closer to Aristotle than subsequent commentaries.[9] Like Alfarabi, who will be discussed later, Maimonides is often described as blending Aristotle and Neoplatonism in a manner characteristic of much of the commentary tradition. It is noteworthy, however, that the commentator he most highlights, Alexander, is one who seems not to have so blended Neoplatonism with Aristotle. About Themistius far less is known today except that he lived well after Plotinus and had a penchant for harmonizing Plato and Aristotle. The Neoplatonism of Plotinus has a deeply ascetic strain, which Maimonides echoes at times but which at other times he seems to argue against (see 1.46, 3.8, and 10).

Although Maimonides did not speak favorably of Plato's writings, his own writing style is oddly reminiscent of Plato's dialogues, with its striking use of the conceit that the *Guide* is a series of letters to his ambitious student Joseph ben Judah. More important, Maimonides embraces certain tropes central to the dialogues—most obviously, the identification of the legislating prophet as philosopher-king. There is little evidence that he knew Platonic writings directly, but there is ample evidence that he imbibed these tropes through the thought of Alfarabi, especially his logical writings but also his so-called *Principle of Beings*, that is, *Political Regime*. In that work and many others, Alfarabi adapts Plato's arguments that, on the one hand, the best regime is ruled by philosopher-kings, and, on the other, that if men were gods then philosopher-kings would be plausible, but because men are not—in their place the second best arrangement is for the laws to rule.[10] Alfarabi subtly blends the best and second-best regimes to suit the context of divine law: since the best regime was said to be the rule of philosopher-kings, it is best to argue that the prophet is the philosopher-king. And since the most important event in Judaism, as in Islam, was the giving of the Law by the most important prophet, the legislating prophet comes to be identified with the philosopher-king.[11] Maimonides makes this amply evident in his analysis of the psychology of prophecy. In 2.36, he sets forth his standard account of the divine overflow from God by way of the Active Intellect to the human intellect and then to the imagination of the perfect prophet. At the end of that chapter he announces surprisingly that Moses is unique in receiving overflow to his intellect alone. In 2.37 he explains the significance of the inclusion of both the intellect and the imagination in the standard account by noting that when the overflow is to the intellect alone, one has reached the rank of the theoretical types, and when the overflow is to the imagination alone, one has reached the rank of mere political actors, including not only legislators but also such unsavory types as soothsayers. Subsequently, he recapitulates the standard account underlining the superiority of combining overflow to the intellect and then the imagination—in other words, combining the virtues of the philosopher with the most virtuous political actor, namely, the king. Repeatedly, he insists on Moses's superiority to all other prophets, despite the odd fact that, according to Maimonides's own account, Moses is somehow lacking in imagination. Leaving aside the oddities of Maimonides's account of Moses, we can at least underline the extent to which Maimonides, in his standard account of prophecy, is recapitulating Alfarabi's blending of the legislator of Plato's *Laws* with the philosopher-king of his *Republic*. Although details in his account are reminiscent of Avicenna (esp. in 2.38), Maimonides's debt to Alfarabi regarding the legislating prophet as philosopher-king is readily apparent—and gives shape and impetus to the rest of his approach to the relation between prophecy and Law.

Some contemporary interpreters of Maimonides have resisted acknowledging links between Maimonides and Alfarabi, which is often linked to resistance to the notion that political philosophy plays a significant role in the *Guide*. In addition, there are links between these two resistances and an insistence on the more purely Jewish character of the *Guide*. A key difficulty for the merely Jewish provenance of the *Guide*, however, is Maimonides's own silence in it about towering Jewish figures such as Saadya Gaon and Judah Halevi. What little Maimonides does say about Saadya is negative.[12] More important, comparison of the *Guide* with Saadya's *Book of Doctrines and Beliefs* reveals, despite some important similarities, ultimately more interesting differences. Saadya follows more closely the Muʿtazilite dialectical theologians in dividing his work neatly into a first part on God's unity (treatises 1 and 2) and a second part on God's justice (treatises 3 through 10).[13] His account of God's particular providence is central to his account of God's justice. In contrast, Maimonides discusses particular providence as a part of his discussions of law and prophecy. In other words, he includes an account of particular providence through the lens of political philosophy rather than through the lens of revealed theology, as we expect him to.[14]

With this, we may turn to a concluding effort to offer an overarching, and therefore necessarily very rough, interpretation of the *Guide*. Earlier our inquiry into the contradictions between philosophy and Law led us to two basic interpretive options: (1) the contradiction between philosophy and Law is merely apparent, or (3) Maimonides indicates subtly his preference for one view over the other. Perhaps the most widely held view is the former. In this interpretation, the contradictions in the foreground of the *Guide* are supposed to dissolve. They dissolve because Maimonides offers an approach to said contradictions that yields a "Jewish philosophy" or a "metaphysics" or "Jewish theology" that harmonizes reason and revelation. The pattern for this approach to Maimonides was established by following the pattern foremost in the interpretation of Christian Scholasticism. Although this approach is quite fitting in the case of Christianity, there is reason to doubt its applicability to Judaism. Christianity, as a religion focused on belief or faith more than action, had from its inception found itself at odds with philosophy's search for knowledge or true opinion—and, as a result, at significant pains to establish a reconciliation of reason and faith. The most typical reconciliation was for reason to forgo the relative independence it had acquired in the philosophic way of life and subordinate itself to the service of the faith, conceding its role as an inferior beholden to revealed theology. There was far less impetus to such an arrangement in Judaism.

Here it is worth recalling the oddity of Maimonides's approach to philosophy. Because Judaism so stresses the primacy of action, he was at pains to denigrate action as a means of providing a foothold for speculative inquiry— a challenge never confronted in Christianity because of its stress on theology from early in its development. Because Judaism placed such stress on action, theology developed in Judaism after it developed in Christianity and Islam! Philosophy, then, was even more foreign than theology to the Law. One should not expect to find a harmonization of reason with faith in Judaism, in which reason easily subordinates itself to faith. Instead, philosophy and Law confront each other as more contradictory in Judaism. Although this can appear disheartening at first because no easy resolution in the relation between reason and faith is readily at hand in Judaism, the independence that reason maintains in the Jewish fold may mean that philosophy as a way of life continues in the Jewish setting in ways that it did not in Christendom.[15]

If this portrait is accurate, then perhaps (3) that Maimonides indicates his preference for philosophy or Law, not a harmonization of the two, may be the more plausible interpretation. At first it seems readily apparent that the greatest medieval Jewish authority, Moses Maimonides, should embrace the Law at the expense of philosophy, until we recall that Maimonides, though he embraced the endeavor of the dialectical theologians of Christianity, Islam, and Judaism for defending their faiths, rejected their willingness to eschew the "nature of existence." What is the aim of philosophy if not the discovery of the nature of existence—by which is meant not only human existence but of the existence of the whole of what is? That Maimonides offers a defense of Judaism in the *Guide* is a truth too often lost on contemporary interpreters, perhaps especially those who suppose that the *Guide* is "Jewish philosophy." This label leaves one complacent about where the truth lies. By allowing it to hover between the Law and philosophy, we fail to take sufficiently seriously the contradictions with which the *Guide* confronts us. That Maimonides here defends Judaism is undeniable, but is that all that he does? Might he mean by "the science of the Law in the true sense" not only a form of dialectical theology but also a philosophic exploration of the aims of the Law, that is, a political philosophy? One thing is generally agreed on by scholars who have devoted significant time to the study of the *Guide*: Maimonides's inquiry into the Law constitutes an exploration of the grounds of Judaism with few if any match in the Jewish tradition. What might be even more surprising to attentive readers, Jewish or not, is that there may be no more profound exploration of the relation between human being, city, and cosmos than the *Guide of the Perplexed*.

APPENDIX

A Critique of Pines's "Limitations" Article

Shortly after publishing the definitive English translation of the *Guide of the Perplexed* in 1963, Shlomo Pines, in 1968, entered on a new avenue of research on Maimonides.[1] He began a series of articles stressing deep similarities between Maimonides and his Muslim predecessor, Alfarabi, on the one hand, and various modern authors such as Spinoza and Kant, on the other. He thereby contributed mightily to a gradual process of effacing the line between medieval or premodern and modern thought in contemporary scholarship. Pines's new approach was most evident in the thesis of his most renowned article, published in 1979, "The Limitations of Human Knowledge according to al-Fārābī, Ibn Bājja, and Maimonides."[2] His thesis is that Alfarabi and Maimonides maintain a view of the limitations of human knowledge highly similar to Kant's.

Pines's articles have had the cumulative effect not only of effacing the distinction between medieval and modern but also of modernizing Alfarabi and especially Maimonides. Leaving aside the bad effects this has on our historical understanding, it impedes our ability to read and benefit from these medieval thinkers. This effect has been formidable. Indeed, Pines's 1979 article may be the most influential article on Maimonides written in the last quarter of the twentieth century. As a result, many leading Maimonides scholars have defended their views on Maimonides.[3] Although few have embraced the claim that Maimonides was as close to Kant as Pines seemed to argue, his article has contributed profoundly to the impression that there are deeper affinities between Maimonides and modern thought generally than has been recognized heretofore.[4] Despite reservations about Pines's specific formulation about Maimonides and Kant, the general trend toward the drawing of parallels between Maimonides and various modern thinkers has grown rapidly since Pines's article.[5] These parallels, though they may raise provocative questions of influence, are, I believe, more misleading than helpful. I offer criticisms of Pines's assimilation of Alfarabi and Maimonides to Kant. I hope thereby to clarify not only Alfarabi and Maimonides's relation to Kant and of premodern to modern thought in general but also the relation between politics and metaphysics in each of these thinkers.

My disagreement with Pines is not merely about the evidence or its proper interpretation but also about his method of reading. For lack of a better term I refer to his method as one focused on "influence." This is the stock and trade of the modern historian of philosophy. Of course, Pines had already applied the tools of his trade with impressive results in the translator's introduction to the *Guide of the Perplexed*. Yet in that case, he focused most of his efforts on authors whom Maimonides himself identified as worthy authors, his ancient and medieval predecessors. The case is different for both Kant and Spinoza. Of course, in the case of Kant there is little or no evidence of an influence of Maimonides on Kant. Now, Pines does not claim influence here. Nevertheless, his training in the tracing of influence leads him to draw connections between similar-looking arguments even when he is not claiming a connection of influence. Matters are different with Spinoza; he indicates his familiarity with Maimonides. Despite this difference in Maimonides's relation to Spinoza and Kant, respectively, Pines feels no qualms in drawing parallels between similar-looking arguments in Maimonides and each of them. Unfortunately, many modern historians of philosophy look favorably on abstracting particular arguments from their context and comparing them to similar arguments made by other authors in wholly different contexts.

Leo Strauss has already provided us with the basis for deciphering why the modern historian of philosophy is predisposed to abstract from argumentative context. Ironically, he traces this method to Spinoza. Modern history of philosophy takes its lead from the hermeneutical principle Spinoza devised for the interpretation of the Bible. As is well known, Spinoza interprets the Bible on the model of natural science (*PAW*, 184). According to that model, it is appropriate to collect statements in a text (as from nature) and to arrange them lucidly (145). The need for such an arrangement (or rearrangement) is dictated by the unintelligibility of the original text (148). Because the original is unintelligible and the reorganization is lucid, there is inevitably a disjunction between the two (146). Because Spinoza views his own works as intelligible, he would look askance at efforts to apply the method he himself employs in reading the Bible to his own writings (149). Although Strauss qualifies this initial contrast (150–51) and develops complicated hermeneutic principles for the contemporary reading of Spinoza (154, 161), none of these principles warrants the tendency one sees in Pines to abstract specific arguments from their argumentative context. This tendency again flows from the historians of philosophy's conviction that when interpreting an old text they are within their rights to rearrange that text for the sake of greater lucidity or relevance.

The difficulties with Pines's method of interpreting Maimonides came to the fore at first in 1968, just five years after the publication of his translation of the *Guide*.[6] Despite extensive qualifications of the parallels he was to draw between Maimonides and Spinoza, Pines did engage in this article in the picking and choosing of what seemed to be parallel arguments in Spinoza and Maimonides. Indeed, he made the broad claim that Spinoza adopted the conceptual framework of Maimonides, primarily on the basis of an accumulation of parallel arguments between them, as do those who follow him.[7] Ironically, Pines cites Strauss and Strauss alone on Spinoza and dedicates his article to him. Although Pines is no doubt aware of Strauss's rejection of the idea that Spinoza is the last medieval philosopher, he does not seem to be aware of the connection Strauss draws between the prevalence of modern methods in the history of philosophy and that mistaken conclusion (*PAW*, 158–59).

Pines's "Limitations of Human Knowledge" (1979)

I turn now to the difficulties posed by Pines's own method of historical scholarship in the "Limitations" article. Although I agree with Warren Zev Harvey that Pines has overstated Maimonides's understanding of the limits of knowledge, I believe this not only because of internal evidence within the Maimonidean corpus, but also because Pines's method of scholarship has led him to misrepresent Alfarabi and his possible influence on Maimonides.[8] This is important for both Maimonides and Alfarabi scholarship. Pines's interpretation of Alfarabi has come to be taken for granted by Maimonides scholars and has, because of the sheer size of Maimonides scholarship, come to be reproduced without reflection. His main claim about Alfarabi is that in his lost commentary on the *Nicomachean Ethics* he embraces the view that the only happiness is political happiness (*al-saʿāda al-madaniyya*). Pines infers this primarily from a reported statement in an unnamed text from Ibn Bajja.[9] Pines infers that Maimonides, as a follower of Alfarabi, was also likely to have held that all metaphysical knowledge is impossible. In effect, Maimonides adopts the Kantian view that ethics or politics or the life of action is the best or highest aspect of human life. The problems with Pines's method of analysis in this 1979 article become apparent only in a later 1990 article meant, at least in part, to shore up this thesis, however.[10]

Before turning to that 1990 article, I should at least give more than the thumbnail sketch of Ibn Bajja's report of Alfarabi. According to Pines's translation, Alfarabi is reported to have remarked that "after death and demise there is no afterlife, that there is no happiness except political happiness, and that there is no existence except that which is perceived by the senses and that that through which it is said another existence than the one which [has just been mentioned comes about] is nothing but old wives' tales."[11] Ibn Bajja's main concern about these purported Alfarabian claims is the denial of the afterlife, as is that of Ibn Tufayl in *Hayy the Son of Yaqzan* in his report of the same passage.[12] Pines's focus is quite different from that of Alfarabi's medieval contemporaries. He treats this passage as a decisive declaration by Alfarabi that all metaphysical knowledge is impossible. Pines is not the first to have made this mistake in interpreting Alfarabi. As I have argued elsewhere, at least in his earlier writings, Strauss similarly conflates the problems of metaphysical knowledge and immortality of the soul. In his "Farabi's *Plato*" he combines Plato's silence on the Ideas and on immortality as at least implying the possibility that Alfarabi denies both (376, 392). Although Alfarabi might deny by omission the existence of *separate* Ideas, this cannot be taken as evidence that he denied all metaphysical knowledge. Unfortunately for us, in medieval philosophy, proofs of the immortality of the soul are so blended with metaphysical inquiry that a denial of one seems tantamount to the wholesale dismissal of the other. Indeed, it may be the case that the medieval philosophers argued at length about conjunction and the various intellects, less out of a concern for these intellects than with an eye to maintaining belief in the immortality of the soul. This blending of the two issues is unfortunate for us because, although the immortality of the soul is a less pressing matter than it once was, the wholesale dismissal of metaphysics as beyond human ken is not.

To claim that Alfarabi denies not only immortality but also all metaphysical knowledge, as Pines does, is tantamount to the admission that he was agnostic on the createdness versus eternity of the world.[13] Herein lies the attractiveness of Pines's interpretation of Maimonides. It seems to confirm the most widely accepted interpretation of Maimonides that, although he may have followed Aristotle regarding earthly physics, Aristotle's account of the heavens is so rife with doubt that he defers to revelation in all matters "above the sphere of the moon."[14] I believe that this is a false inference drawn by Pines with an eye to maintaining his thesis about Maimonides (like Alfarabi) as a Kantian avant la lettre. In the *Guide* (2.15)—as Pines, as its translator, is no doubt well aware— Maimonides even takes Alfarabi to task for holding that Aristotle believed he could demonstrate the eternity of the world.[15] In other words, Maimonides censures Alfarabi for excessive confidence about the eternity of the world—a central metaphysical issue or question about what is above the sphere of the moon. To get around the obvious tension between such Alfarabian claims about eternity and the reputed wholesale denial of metaphysical knowledge, Pines offers, albeit with many a qualification, the development thesis, one of the weakest ways of accounting for contradictory claims within the corpus of a philosopher.[16] This is a favorite thesis among modern historians of philosophy. Pines views the development of Alfarabi's thought at work as follows. The claim that political happiness is true happiness is Alfarabi's mature view. Claims to the contrary are earlier views.[17]

Pines's "Truth and Falsehood" (1990): A Key Insight into the Lost Commentary on the Ethics Overlooked

Let us turn now to Pines's "Truth and Falsehood" article in an effort to show that his claim that Alfarabi and Maimonides are Kantians avant la lettre is made possible only by having abstracted the claim about "political happiness" from its argumentative context.[18] The shocking fact is that in his 1990 article Pines offers us all the evidence we need to make the case against his radical interpretation of Alfarabi and Maimonides in his 1979 article. According to Pines in 1990, the claim that political happiness is the only happiness "according to Ibn Bajja, occurs in al-Farabi's lost commentary in [*sic*] the *Nicomachean Ethics*, apparently *not far from the beginning* [my emphasis]."[19] Now Pines himself adds that this claim about political happiness is "consonant with the general tenor of the first book of Aristotle's *Ethics*." Alfarabi, far from being a radical antitheoretical thinker, is arguing in a tone consonant with the tone of the opening of the *Ethics*! Already one begins to wonder whether Alfarabi's comment was such a radical denial of all metaphysical knowledge. Perhaps this radical part of the lost commentary reflected the radical privileging of the power (*dunamis*) or science (*epistēmē*) of politics in the opening of the *Ethics*.

Unfortunately for the thesis of "Limitations," Pines confirms our suspicion. In a footnote to the very same passage, he claims that there is a "flagrant contradiction" in the *Ethics* between the tenor of book 1 and the tenor of book 10. This comes as no surprise to the attentive reader of Aristotle. What follows however comes as a surprise to the reader of the "Limitations" article: "This may account fo[r] the fact that, according to Ibn Bajja's report, one or several passages which apparently occur in the last part of his Commentary seem, if compared to those found in the first part, to reflect a somewhat modified position."[20] In other words, Alfarabi's radical opening remarks elaborate on the radical opening of the *Ethics* and later passages qualify the early silence on all nonpolitical knowledge. When one puts together all of Ibn Bajja's reports, rather than the partial ones we received in "Limitations," a fuller picture begins to emerge. Alfarabi's lost commentary on the *Ethics*, shocking as its opening might have been in denying immortality, cannot be taken as tantamount to

Alfarabi's announcement that all metaphysical knowledge is beyond human beings in the Kantian spirit. Rather, we may suppose that the opening elaborates on a possible radical implication of Aristotle's antimetaphysical opening to the *Ethics*. We are no longer in a position to assume that Alfarabi's "mature position" was that political happiness is the only happiness.

Ironically, Pines does not make anything out of the tension between Alfarabi's accounts of books 1 and 10 of the *Ethics*. The irony only grows in the following pages. There Pines underlines—admittedly as part of his divergent pursuit of the genealogy of philosophic views on the relation between true and false versus good and evil—his view that Maimonides (and Alfarabi) could not have been aware of the tension between metaphysics and ethics in the thought of Aristotle. Furthermore, they could not have been aware of the possibility that metaphysics could be thought to integrate certain aspects of the inquiry into the good in ethics into metaphysics.[21] Pines makes this broad claim for two reasons. In his view, Maimonides establishes an unprecedented rift between truth and falsehood as the object of intellect and good and evil as the object of the imagination in *Guide*, 1.2. According to Pines, Maimonides's view of good and evil is a profound departure from the Aristotelian distinction of good and evil as the object of practical intellect or prudence or the science of politics from truth and falsehood.[22]

Maimonides establishes such a rift because he, like Alfarabi, was unaware that Aristotle used the good not only in ethics but also in metaphysics. The great surprise is not that Pines might arrive at such interpretations because Maimonides is surprisingly quiet about prudence in the *Guide* (though not so in the *Eight Chapters*) and adopts a restrained reading of Aristotelian teleology. Rather, the great surprise is his justification for these interpretations of Maimonides in relation to Aristotle. Again, he offers a rationale often found in the pages of modern historians of philosophy for apparent divergences between authors. Alfarabi and Maimonides appear to diverge from Aristotle because they lacked the appropriate texts. Because the first book of the *Metaphysics* was not available to Alfarabi and Maimonides, they could not have been aware that Aristotle set up a tension between the ruling (or *architektonikē*) function of politics or political science in the opening of the *Ethics* (1094a27) and the ruling (or most elevated! or *archikōtatē*) function of metaphysics in the opening of the *Metaphysics* (982b4). And without that first book, they could not have been aware of the way Aristotle integrated an extended sense of the good into his metaphysics as part of a bridging of this rift between metaphysics and ethics. This contradicts quite flatly the evidence Pines has already brought forward from the lost commentary on the *Ethics*. We have every reason to suspect that Alfarabi (and therefore Maimonides) was aware of the tension between ethics (bk. 1) and metaphysics (bk. 10, and even 6) within the *NE* itself.[23]

Furthermore, the closing lines of *NE* 6, which we have every reason to assume Alfarabi (and Maimonides) was aware of, offer the same basic resolution alluded to in *Metaphysics* 1, namely, politics or political science rules for the sake of, but not over, its superior, metaphysics. Politics can only "rule" metaphysics in the appropriate fashion once it has moved from a wholly worldly preference for political happiness (bk. 1) to an appropriate deference to the superiority of the theoretical life (bks. 6–10). Would metaphysics or first philosophy be worthy of such deference if it were wholly devoid of content? Indeed, if the *bios praktikos* were really the highest way of life, then why would Alfarabi and Maimonides both be so critical of the imaginary or erroneous goods desired by strictly political human beings?[24] Far from being incompatible with Aristotle's own view, I take this to be the interpretation of Aristotle adopted by both Alfarabi and Maimonides.

Why All Metaphysical Questions Are Not Created Equal

Perhaps the greatest difficulty with the main thesis of the "Limitations" (1979) article, that political happiness is the sole happiness, is the manner in which Pines subsequently lumps all metaphysical knowledge together and excludes it from human ken.[25] Although Kant is intent on excluding all of what was traditionally understood as "transcendental philosophy," namely, the *metaphysica specialis* of the later Scholastics, from human ken, there is little evidence that Alfarabi and Maimonides so excluded it. Most Maimonides scholars who have criticized Pines's "Limitations" article have focused on showing that Maimonides is convinced that we, or some human beings, can, indeed, attain conjunction with the Active Intellect.[26] The warrant for focusing on conjunction is both that Pines devotes much attention to Ibn Bajja's various treatments of it in "Limitations" and that such an enormous quantity of ink was spilled on this subject by the medieval philosophers in general, if not Maimonides in particular.

Maimonides's views on conjunction are important for giving an account of the psychology of prophecy, but I believe the main significance of conjunction is for distinguishing the kinds of human types: statesman, philosopher, and prophet. Indeed, these human types and the psychology of prophecy can be understood without certainty about Maimonides's own views on conjunction. It is sufficient to clarify his views on the relative roles of the powers or faculties of the soul to grasp his views on human types and prophecy. Conjunction is also so intimately connected with the problem of immortality that I believe we will be hard put to determine what Maimonides's real views on conjunction are. All medieval philosophers felt it incumbent upon themselves to preserve belief in some form of immortality. For this very reason, it is a topic filled with hyperbole and overstatement. Of course, when we turn from conjunction to a more relevant metaphysical issue, eternity versus creation, we would seem to be stymied by Maimonides's notorious ambiguity on this topic. Here, Maimonides (not to mention Alfarabi) was not likely to have taken a Kantian approach to the eternity versus creation dilemma. In other words, I cannot accept Pines's inference that just as Alfarabi and Maimonides were uncertain about the essence of metaphysical beings (and the possibility of conjunction with them) so they were uncertain about eternity versus creation.[27]

Maimonides claims that Aristotle is "indubitably correct" about sublunar physics (*Guide*, 2.22). Pines focuses on Maimonides's proclaimed reservations about superlunary physics and metaphysics, although he acknowledges in passing Maimonides's declaration of human knowledge of the sublunar.[28] He pays little attention to the latter claim at the peril of his own argument. How can Aristotelian physics apply in the sublunar realm without eternity?[29] Of course, we have Maimonides's compromise in the final chapter of the *Eight Chapters* that after six days of creation nature is fixed or all miracles emerge in a predetermined fashion.[30] And we have a similar version of that compromise in *Guide*, 2.29. Yet Maimonides's arguments that seem to permit miracles effectively must deny miracles in the true sense. Although God has the power to change natures at will, he in fact changes nothing but the "particulars" of a given nature (2.29, 346). Here, we recall his claim that Aristotle's account of the sublunar realm is correct. Unless we assume that he is deceiving us about that, we must conclude that either Maimonides is not to be included in the "we" who hold this view about miracles or what Maimonides means by a "miraculous" change in the particulars of a given nature is not a true change of nature. The Aristotelian account of the sublunar realm is incompatible with any true changes or miracles in nature. The only way to exculpate Maimonides from this association with the belief in eternity is to show that he believed creation is compatible with nature, form, or essence.[31] It is not by chance that Kant, who turns away from such metaphysical arguments as regards the eternity or beginning of the cosmos, also turns away from all reflection on natures. He has no room in his thought for formal causes. This is a decisive metaphysical difference between Maimonides (and Alfarabi), on the one hand, and Kant, on the other. Maimonides's ignorance about the details regarding conjunction, separate intellects, or even the essence of God have fewer repercussions than ignorance about form and nature and its correlate eternity would.

The Theologico-Political Divergence between Kant and the Medievals

Leaving aside all details about intellects, conjunction, and the immortality of the soul, Maimonides and Alfarabi have not jettisoned metaphysics in the manner of Kant. Maimonides, following Alfarabi, expresses his views about eternity versus creation most frankly in his earliest presentation of the opposition between the philosophers and the *mutakallimūn*. He sides with the philosophers. The *mutakallimūn* "did not conform in their premises to the appearance of that which exists" (1.71, 178). They did so with an eye to preserving belief in creation (178, 181). Maimonides excoriates them repeatedly for abolishing the "nature (*ṭabīʿa*) of existence" (182–83). Of course, Alfarabi makes the same argument earlier in the closing chapter of the *Enumeration of the Sciences*.

Maimonides's excoriation of the *mutakallimūn* follows immediately after he admits that in the *Guide* he will adopt the procedure he adopts in his "books of *fiqh*," to demonstrate everything based on the Aristotelian assumption of eternity.[32] In the immediate context he claims that he does this because to prove God's existence on the assumption of creation is to assume what one must prove (181). Even so, the pressing question remains what one has done to shore up the belief in creation by demonstrations based on the assumption of eternity. Although Maimonides might reassure us that we must trust his assurances that he chooses the assumption of creation over eternity because of prophecy (2.16), we must also remember his exhortation to take into account not the number but the greatness of the things doubted in connection with each opinion (2.23). Whether Maimonides's views on prophecy are consonant with creation or eternity would be decisive. For the present I merely leave the matter at noting the amazing proximity of his views to those of the philosophers (2.32).

The Maimonidean and Alfarabian affirmation of nature is incompatible with the Kantian exclusion of knowledge about cosmological questions. Their affirmation of nature flows from a Platonic-Aristotelian tradition of trust (*pistis*) in perceptibles.[33] I will not rehearse the history of the modern attack on natures or forms in any detail. Despite the continuing use of the word form or essence in thinkers as diverse as Descartes and Spinoza, forms had become a liability not only to thought but also to society. That liability was a theologico-political one. In the cauldron that was Europe in the wake of the Reformation, thinkers thought it better to avoid argument about formal or divine or ghostly causes. Of course, I refer here not only to God but also to the immortality of the soul. After all, arguments over such issues not only put thinkers at risk of losing their lives but also put society at the risk of incessant sectarian conflict. Our contemporary attitude toward the question of the immortality of the soul flows from the early modern avoidance of formal causes. Despite a long history of philosophic reservations about the immortality of the soul, its compatibility with the search for the nature, form, or essence of the beings was such that ancient and especially medieval thinkers continued to argue at great length and with great verve about the former issue. Let me be clear. I am not calling for a revival of thought about the immortality of soul. I merely intend to question the notion that Alfarabi and Maimonides were so convinced of the limits of human knowledge that they sought to discourage inquiry into the nature of the beings.

It is frequently suggested that modernity is rooted in the scientific pursuit of efficient causes. The question "What are they leaving out and why?" is often neglected. Why do they ignore formal causes? The usual answer is that they discovered what could be done with efficient causes. Their predecessors had ignored them. In short, a few experiments convinced early modern thinkers of the great secrets modern science could unlock. Yet this ignores the self-conscious choice for causes that unlock the power of nature. The power of nature is preferred to knowledge of the forms of beings because the pursuit and distribution of power is determined to be less problematic and more desirable than the old search for knowledge.

Despite the attacks of Bacon, Descartes, Spinoza, and Hobbes on formal causes and the attack on final causes most clearly enunciated by Spinoza and Hobbes, it was not until Hume that doubts were raised even about efficient causes. When Kant comes along like a knight in shining armor to save "metaphysics" from Hume's reservations even about efficient causality, it is easy to fail to see how precious little Kant restores. One thing is certain, Kant does not restore forms or essences. After all, for Kant, the substance of any thing in itself is beyond human access. At best, substance is the relation of representations synthesized by apperception. Not only can human beings not know the details about God, they cannot know whether the world is infinite or finite because neither claim is true within the limits of human experience. The world whose eternity or createdness we seek is the world in itself, but that world we cannot know. Most shocking of all, not only can't we know whether our souls are immortal, but also our selves, as things in themselves, are properly speaking also unknown. If substance is nothing but a relation, there is no substance to substance.[34] Consequently, form is off where it belongs with God and the immortal soul in a noumenal realm about which human beings can possess nothing more than subjectively valid knowledge.[35] Of course, Kant could not have set out to withdraw the divine into a subjective, private realm without establishing an ethic that avoids appeals to heteronomous supports such as the good or God.

The subjective character of our knowledge of God, the soul, and the cosmos in Kant reinforces the leading theologico-political objective of modernity, namely, to withdraw the explosive questions at the root of both persecution of heterodox thought and religious warfare from the public realm to the harmless realm of not only private but also subjective reflection. Although earlier thinkers had sought to guarantee the privacy of philosophic reflection, they had never attacked thought about forms, natures, or essences as merely subjective. Indeed, the leading theologico-political objective of both Alfarabi and Maimonides was to protect private reflection about the natures of things by promoting some rudiments of belief about the divine in the public realm. Furthermore, Maimonides did not have any qualms about appealing to something as heteronomous as (fear of) the God of the Bible for the sake of morality or public order or the well-being of the body. Such appeals may tend to fall on deaf ears in a society that avoids ghostly formal causes, as our does.[36] Indeed, we tend to view all such appeals as a crude use of intellectual power to subject the ignorant to ghostly powers.

Whatever Maimonides's views on eternity versus creation might be, he, unlike Kant, saw value in highlighting tension between the two positions. He does not show any evidence of attempting to exile such metaphysical questions to a noumenal realm. Modern scholars have spilled so much ink on Maimonides's real views on the dilemma between eternity and creation that it should be evident that he sought to promote rather than stifle continued reflection on these alternatives. How different is Kant's view that these alternatives are part of an antinomy, both elements of which are false! Although Kant is confident that some human beings may continue to be so recalcitrant as to continue to reflect on such matters, he had hoped to establish a permanent pale within which "serious" thinkers could avoid the pursuit of such mere "speculation."[37]

True, Kant embraces the limits of knowledge to make room for faith. Although it is tempting to suppose that Maimonides is doing the same thing, he offers little or no evidence that "faith" is important to his argument regarding the Law. That he feels it incumbent upon himself to defend the Law is undeniable, but that he is motivated to offer such a defense because he is moved by faith also does not seem evident. Above all, the vague acknowledgment of the limits of knowledge in Alfarabi and Maimonides regarding metaphysics do not indicate that theoretical truth is wholly uninteresting to them; on the contrary, it indicates that theoretical truth, the knowledge of eternal things, is not limited to an inquiry into the heavenly bodies. Political philosophy can be first philosophy only if inquiry into the divine has its basis in the inquiry into human things.

NOTES

Introduction

1. Leo Strauss, Preface to *Hobbes' Politische Wissenschaft*, in Leo Strauss, *Jewish Philosophy and the Crisis of Modernity: Essays and Lectures in Modern Jewish Thought*, ed. Kenneth Hart Green (Albany: SUNY Press, 1997), 453–56, esp. 453.
2. Leo Strauss, *Spinoza's Critique of Religion*, trans. E. M. Sinclair (New York: Schocken, 1965), 3 (hereafter cited as *SCR*). The 1965 preface to *SCR* is often referred to as "the autobiographical preface to the Spinoza book."
3. Preface to *Hobbes' Politische Wissenschaft*, in Strauss, *Jewish Philosophy*, 453.
4. All references to the *Guide of the Perplexed* (hereafter cited as *Guide*) are by part and chapter number. When page numbers are included they follow a comma and refer to Shlomo Pines's translation (Chicago: University of Chicago Press, 1963).
5. Leo Strauss, *Persecution and the Art of Writing* (Chicago: University of Chicago Press, 1988), 41 (hereafter cited as *PAW*). Although *Persecution* was first published in 1952, it included chapters previously published as early as 1941. The Arabic word *kalām* is typically translated as "dialectical theology." As we will see, it refers to a highly apologetic form of theology.
6. Leo Strauss, *Philosophy and Law* (Albany: SUNY Press, 1995) (hereafter cited as *PL*).
7. *Treatise on the Art of Logic*, chap. 14, trans. Muhsin Mahdi, in *Medieval Political Philosophy*, ed. Joshua Parens and Joseph C. Macfarland, 2nd ed. (Ithaca, NY: Cornell University Press, 2011), 180–82 (hereafter cited as *Logic*).
8. Leo Strauss, "Farabi's *Plato*," in *Louis Ginzberg*, Jubilee volume, ed. Alexander Marx, Saul Lieberman, Shalom Spiegel, and Solomon Zeitlin (New York: American Academy for Jewish Research, 1945), 357–93 (hereafter cited as FP).
9. Strauss's strongest claims about the purely speculative character of philosophy here are based on an analysis of the relation between the ways of life of Socrates, Timaeus, Thrasymachus, and Plato in Alfarabi's *Philosophy of Plato*. These strongest claims should be contrasted with the more ambiguous analysis of the same passages in "How Fārābī Read Plato's *Laws*," in *What Is Political Philosophy?* (Chicago: University of Chicago Press, 1988), 153 (hereafter cited as *WIPP*). Among the most striking effects of the different interpretations of the same passages is that Socrates in the earlier work appears to be a mere "moralist" while in the later work he appears to be a purely speculative man. What this might mean about the way of Plato is a profound question.

10. Perhaps Strauss's continued stress on contemplation was part of his own scholarly probity regarding the importance of his discovery rather than an indicator of his mature views on the matter. In the 1930s and 1940s, Strauss seems to have wanted to avoid assuming that because the theologico-political problem was his central concern, that it was central in human thought.
11. Leo Strauss, *Thoughts on Machiavelli* (Chicago: University of Chicago Press, 1984); Strauss, *The City and Man* (Chicago: University of Chicago Press, 1978) (hereafter cited as *CM*).
12. *WIPP*, 38–40. As Strauss's student Seth Benardete has clarified, Strauss is referring to the dualism of the two Platonic dialogues the *Sophist* and the *Statesman*, which are inquiries undertaken in the pursuit of the knowledge of what is the philosopher. See *The Argument of the Action*, ed. Ronna Burger and Michael Davis (Chicago: University of Chicago Press, 2000), 303.
13. On the role of "abstraction" in Platonic political philosophy, see *CM*, 50–138, esp. 62, 79, 109, 110–12, 116–17, 133–34, 138.

Chapter One

1. I do not mean to suggest that this Aristotelian kind of separation of sciences and powers (not to mention Christianity's inherent tendency to distinguish between ecclesiastical and secular) was a (were) sufficient condition(s) for the modern emergence of the separation of religion from politics. It would seem that the limited success of Aquinas, Dante, and Marsilius to establish some durable relation between these two powers show the limits of what could be achieved by following the Aristotelian model. Subsequently, Machiavelli (1469–1527) not only separated religion from politics but also radically demoted religion in comparison with these medievals.
2. My claim that this separation was avoided in Islamic and Jewish philosophical circles should not be confused with a description of the facts on the ground in Islamic lands—not to mention among Jews amid their state of political dependence in the medieval period. Very often secular power and ecclesiastical power were divided in reality, even if philosophers tended to undercut this as a division of the sciences.
3. For further elaboration of this point, see chapter 6 of this text.
4. See also chapter 4 of this text.
5. See also parts 3 and 4 of this text.
6. Maimonides wrote the *Guide* (indeed, most of his works, with the exception of his massive Jewish code of law, the *Mishneh Torah*) in Arabic and is obviously deeply indebted to the Muslim tradition, especially the other author I consider, here, Alfarabi.
7. Maimonides describes the historical background of kalām in *Guide*, 1.71, showing how it entered Judaism by way of Islam. If space allowed, I would attempt

8. For evidence that the Law's aim is both practical and theoretical, see *Guide*, 2.40 and 3.27–28. For a discussion of the intimate relation between the aims or purposes of divine laws and the roots of law, see my *Metaphysics as Rhetoric: Alfarabi's "Summary of Plato's 'Laws'"* (Albany: State University of New York Press, 1995), 13–15. See also Alfarabi, *Book of Religion*, trans. Charles E. Butterworth, in Parens and Macfarland, *Medieval Political Philosophy*, 24–35, esp. secs. 2–5 (hereafter cited as *BR*).
9. It should be admitted that within a page or so Maimonides claims that the *Guide* touches on the two mysteries of Judaism, the Account of the Beginning and the Account of the Chariot, and especially their identity with natural science (physics) and divine science (metaphysics). At other times, he states explicitly that the *Guide* is not devoted to providing epitomes of physics and metaphysics (see 2.2, preface).
10. Of course, this is "put very roughly" since we have just seen that the "true science of the Law" is, at least according to Maimonides, somehow superior to jurisprudence.
11. Majid Fakhry, *A History of Islamic Philosophy*, 3rd ed. (New York: Columbia University Press, 2004).
12. We return to this in greater depth in chapter 3.
13. Alfarabi, *Al-Farabi on the Perfect State*, trans. Richard Walzer (Oxford: Clarendon, 1985). Alfarabi was the most important Muslim logician in the medieval period. Surely he knew how far short of rigorous theological argumentation his cosmological descriptions fell.
14. The only exception with which I'm familiar is Alfarabi's *Enumeration of the Sciences*, which presents the Islamic sciences and the philosophic sciences in isolation. Chapter 4 contains philosophic theology; chapter 5 contains Islamic kalām. This was not Alfarabi's final conception of their relation but an account of how they appeared as he arrived on the scene—at odds.
15. Alfarabi, *Philosophy of Aristotle*, sec. 99, 133.1–2. The trilogy consists of the *Attainment of Happiness* (hereafter cited as *AH*), the *Philosophy of Plato*, and the *Philosophy of Aristotle*. The trilogy appears in English as *Alfarabi: Philosophy of Plato and Aristotle*, trans. Muhsin Mahdi (Ithaca, NY: Cornell University Press, 2001).
16. In his *Politics*, Aristotle engages in a long and sophisticated critique of the rule of the philosopher-wise man in Plato's *Republic*. That critique is complemented in his *Nicomachean Ethics* by the cultivation of a distinctively practical or political form of rational virtue, prudence (*phronēsis*). In these ways and in his separation of practical from theoretical science, Aristotle seems intent upon criticizing the most literal reading of the *Republic*, namely, that Socrates is very much in earnest when he says in *Republic*, book 5: Until philosophers become kings there will be "no rest from ills for the cities" (473d). Aristotle establishes the separation of theoretical from practical to consolidate the view that politics need not be run by philosophers to be decent. I (along with many others) have argued, in spite of

appearances to the contrary, that, ultimately, that view is also Socrates's own view in the *Republic*. See my *An Islamic Philosophy of Virtuous Religions: Introducing Alfarabi* (Albany: State University of New York Press, 2006), chap. 2. Socrates's argument for philosopher-kings is less a realistic plan than a defense of the philosophic life before the legal bar of the city.

Chapter Two

1. Leo Strauss, *Philosophie und Gesetz: Beiträge zum Verständnis Maimunis und Seiner Vorläufer* (Berlin: Schocken Verlag, 1935); translated in *PL*, 21.
2. Leo Strauss, *Studies in Platonic Political Philosophy* (Chicago: University of Chicago Press, 1983).
3. *PL*, 29–31. See also his autobiographical preface to the English translation of *SCR*, 28–29.
4. Leo Strauss, "Progress or Return?" *Modern Judaism* 1 (1981): 17–45.
5. Although it cannot be denied that because of its intense concern with the conscience of the believer, Christianity contributed mightily to the need for privacy of conscience, championed by early modern political philosophers; one should never confuse our stress on privacy of conscience with the only possible approach to interior life.
6. According to Joseph Cropsey in the foreword, Strauss completed this manuscript in 1971 (Leo Strauss, *The Argument and Action of Plato's "Laws"* [Chicago: University of Chicago Press, 1975], vii). Strauss died in 1973. For his final work, see Strauss, *Platonic Political Philosophy*, which was published even later than *Argument and Action*.
7. Contrast Strauss's use of "ideal state" throughout *Philosophy and Law* with "Some Remarks on the Political Science of Maimonides and Farabi," trans. Robert Bartlett, *Interpretation* 18, no. 1 (1990): 3–30, esp. 10–12 (hereafter cited as SRMF). See also chapter 6 of this text.
8. Friedrich Nietzsche, *Beyond Good and Evil*, trans. Walter Kaufman (New York: Random House, 1966), aphor. 30.
9. The Mu'tazilite kalām is the more rationalistic of the two schools of kalām in Islam.
10. See Parens and Macfarland, introd. to Jewish part, in Parens and Macfarland, *Medieval Political Philosophy*, 149–50.
11. Parens and Macfarland, *Medieval Political Philosophy*, 36, 53–55, 73, and introd. to the first part of Maimonides's *Guide*.
12. See Alfarabi, *Abū Naṣr al- Fārābī, Kitāb al-Milla wa Nuṣūṣ Ukhrā*, ed. Muhsin Mahdi (Beirut: Dar al-Mashriq, 1968). In FP, 358, Strauss seems to make reference to the *Book of Religion*, when he argues that the full understanding of the *Political Regime* requires the understanding of two works he describes as "parallel works," which he refers to as "*The principles of the opinions of the virtuous city*

and *The virtuous religious community*, the second of which has not been edited at all." It is unclear to me whether Strauss had substantive knowledge of the *Book of Religion*. If he had, it would have confirmed his reading of Maimonides in relation to the *Enumeration of the Sciences*. Although Strauss refers to *the virtuous religious community* in "Farabi's *Plato*"; in his revision of it in his introduction to *Persecution* (14), he does so only to claim that in it Alfarabi "pronounces more or less orthodox views." And in "Literary Character," also in *Persecution*, where one might expect him to take advantage of the potentially fruitful comparison of the *Enumeration of the Sciences* with the *Book of Religion*, he draws no such comparison (cf. *PAW*, 40n9). It is because of the lack of any such comparison that I previously insinuated that Strauss was wholly unaware of the *Book of Religion* in an earlier version of chapter 7. See Martin D. Yaffe and Richard S. Ruderman, eds., *Reorientation: Strauss in the 1930s* (Palgrave Macmillan, 2014), 169n33.

13. For a more elaborate discussion of dialectic and rhetoric in the *Book of Religion*, see chapter 6 of this text.
14. In brief, the thirteen roots are (1) God exists; (2) he is one; (3) he is incorporeal; (4) he is eternal; (5) he alone is to be worshiped; (6) prophecy is a reality; (7) Moses is unique among prophets; (8) the Torah is from God; (9) the Torah is authentic; (10) God knows all human actions; (11) God rewards and punishes; (12) the Messiah or Anointed King will come; and (13) the dead will be resurrected in the Messianic age.
15. In numerical or numerological terms, the center with respect to chapters is 2.13 (creation versus eternity) (the 89th chapter out of 178 chapters), but since there are three main theological themes in the *Guide* (creation [esp. 2.13, 2.25], prophecy [2.32–48], and providence [3.8–24]) prophecy is the thematic center of the *Guide*. Of course, 3.1–7 is the most mysterious section of the *Guide*—a discussion of the biblical Account of the Chariot—but it is surrounded by the two most important sections of the *Guide* (the prophetology and the account of particular providence), which Strauss has shown are both parts of Maimonides's political science. See Leo Strauss, "The Place of the Doctrine of Providence according to Maimonides," trans. Gabriel Bartlett and Svetozar Minkov, *Review of Metaphysics* 57 (2004): 537–49 (hereafter cited as PPr). Maimonides indicates the centrality of these chapters by making each set seventeen chapters long. Nasser Behnegar has shown that Strauss identifies seventeen as the numerological equivalent of "nature" for Maimonides and others. See Rafael Major, ed., *Defense of the Philosophic Life: Reading "What Is Political Philosophy?"* (Chicago: University of Chicago Press, 2012), 41n5.
16. See PPr, 542, and chapters 7 and 11 of this text.

Chapter Three

1. As Robert C. Bartlett and Susan S. Collins, whose translation of the *Nicomachean Ethics* (Chicago: University of Chicago Press, 2011) is here quoted with

minor changes, indicate, they have adopted Bywater's emendation, which drops "political" from the readings of the manuscripts (3n10).

2. Those who are troubled about this last issue are most emphatic that "political" referred to in note 1 must be restored—contrary to Bywater's emendation. I thank Edward Macierowski for insisting on the importance of contravening Bywater's emendation at an NEH Summer Institute that Douglas Kries, Joseph C. Macfarland, and I codirected at Gonzaga University in the summer of 2014. Yet the third sentence seems to argue against dropping Bywater's emendation.

3. Sachs has "most ruling" (cf. *-krate*) and Ross-Barnes has "most authoritative" (cf. *kurios*). Cf. *architektonikē* with *archikōtatē*: The former term denotes a master craft; the later, though there might be some connotation of the rule of the *archon*, does not refer unambiguously to rule. It's the superlative of what is first in rank. We leave aside here the formidable problem of reconciling this apparent reversion to some universal good or best being, which has already been repudiated in Aristotle's *Nicomachean Ethics*, 1.6. This moment in the *Metaphysics*, after all, is a survey of *endoxa*.

4. It should also be noted, however, that Alfarabi includes a relatively extensive discussion of vicious regimes in *Virtuous City*; or, *Principles of the Opinions of the Inhabitants of the Virtuous City*, in *Al-Farabi on the Perfect State*.

5. "Weeds" become a leitmotif of subsequent Islamic medieval political philosophy, especially that of Ibn Bajja and Ibn Tufayl—though the meaning of "weed" is not always identical to Alfarabi's sense.

6. I have my doubts that he adheres to anything like the teleology Aristotle offers in *Politics* 1.8 (what I take Seth Benardete to mean when he speaks of "teleological physics," in contrast to Socrates's forms," in his preface to *Socrates' Second Sailing* [Chicago: University of Chicago Press, 1989]), where all living things are said to find their fulfillment in subordination to the human. Indeed, I doubt that even Aristotle means this seriously as a theoretical claim. After all, the claim is made in his most political or practical work.

7. See Parens, *Islamic Philosophy*.

8. See note 2 of this chapter.

Chapter Four

1. For a far more extensive and wider ranging study of the interest and contribution of nineteenth- and twentieth-century Jewish scholars to the study of Islam, see Martin Kramer, *The Jewish Discovery of Islam* (Syracuse: Syracuse University Press, 1999). I thank Ronna Burger for drawing my attention to this book.

2. I have decided to use Strauss's rather awkward phrasing "Islamic and Jewish medieval philosophy" and "Islamic medieval philosophy" and "Jewish medieval philosophy—rather than the more widely used "medieval Jewish and Islamic philosophy"—because this nontypical phrasing reminds the reader to question the very notion of "Jewish philosophy" and "Islamic philosophy."

3. Over the course of this chapter, I refer to "opponents of Strauss" and "anti-Straussian" interpreters. I do this for lack of less confrontational shorthand with which to refer to those with whom Strauss disagrees. As far as I know, Strauss had relatively good rapport with his contemporaries. E. I. J. Rosenthal in particular frequently cites Strauss, as does Strauss cite E. I. J. Rosenthal. And Strauss certainly cites Wolfson.
4. Harry Austryn Wolfson, *Philo: Foundations of Religious Philosophy in Judaism, Christianity, and Islam* (Cambridge, MA: Harvard University Press, 1968); and Wolfson, *The Philosophy of Spinoza* (Cambridge, MA: Harvard University Press, 1934).
5. At the risk of making this account too nuanced, too quickly, however, I need to acknowledge that Strauss does not argue that this divide between Christianity and Judaism/Islam is rigid. Ultimately, he argues that there are Christians who follow the Farabian model, often referred to as "Averroism" (for example, Marsilius of Padua) and Jews and Muslims who follow the "Scholastic" model (for example, Saadya Gaon, Judah Halevi, and the Muʻtazilite dialectical theologians). See *PAW*, 10–11, 96–97. Nevertheless, he does argue that the prevailing approach in Christianity, on the one hand, and Judaism and Islam, on the other, follows this pattern.
6. See Daniel H. Frank, "What Is Jewish Philosophy?," in *History of Jewish Philosophy*, edited by Daniel Frank and Oliver Leaman (London: Routledge, 1997), 1–10.
7. See *PAW*, 19, 43.
8. See note 5 of this chapter.
9. According to Strauss, attempted syntheses, like these in the medieval period, result in the victory of one pole of the opposition between reason and revelation over the other, because philosophy and revelation constituted total "ways of life." In the modern period, philosophy has ceased to have such a character. That change in philosophy makes the tension between reason and revelation more difficult to grasp for contemporary readers, not to mention the insistence of some believers that their religious faith includes and perfects reason.
10. I want to reiterate the point I made earlier: Strauss's characterization of Scholasticism here refers only to the prevailing approach in Christendom to the relation between reason and revelation. Cf. note 5 and the text preceding note 9.

 Although E. I. J. Rosenthal recognizes many of the special affinities of Islam and Judaism mentioned in the previous paragraph (see "Maimonides' Conception of State and Society," in *Moses Maimonides*, ed. I. Epstein [London: Soncino, 1935], 191–206, esp. 192–94), he does not draw the key inference that Strauss does, that these features led medieval philosophers within Islam and Judaism to avoid the synthesis of reason and revelation so prevalent in Christianity (193, 200).
11. At times, disagreements that I refer to as thematic appear also to be methodological. This distinction is not precise.

12. E. I. J. Rosenthal, "The Place of Politics in the Philosophy of Ibn Bājja," in *Studia Semitica*, vol. 2, *Islamic Themes* (Cambridge: Cambridge University Press, 1971), 35–59, esp. 44–45; E. Rosenthal, "The Place of Politics in the Philosophy of Al-Farabi," *Islamic Culture* 29 (1955): 157–78, esp. 158, 159, 160, 178; E. Rosenthal, "Some Aspects of Islamic Political Thought," *Islamic Culture* 22 (1948): 1–17, esp. 6, 10; E. Rosenthal, "Maimonides' Conception," 193, 202–3, 203–4; Richard Walzer, "On the Legacy of the Classics in the Islamic World," in *Greek into Arabic* (Cambridge, MA: Harvard University Press, 1962), 29–37, esp. 36; in Walzer's introduction to Alfarabi, *Al-Farabi on the Perfect State*, 9; Richard Walzer, "Arabic Transmission of Greek Thought to Medieval Europe," *Bulletin of the John Rylands Library* 29 (1945–46): 160–83, esp. 178; Walzer, "The Rise of Islamic Philosophy," *Oriens* 3 (1950): 1–19, esp. 9 (al-Kindi), 12, 14.
13. See also Alfarabi's frank description of the mercenary character of much of dialectical theology in the concluding section of the *Enumeration of the Sciences*, 21–23.
14. Thomas Aquinas, *Summa theologiae*, 1a.1.1.
15. See *Guide*, 1.73, tenth premise, 206–12, esp. 211; and Maimonides, *Eight Chapters*, chap. 1. Cf. Aristotle, *Metaphysics*, 5.5, 12.
16. Contrast Maimonides's approach to the "nature of existence" with Thomas Aquinas's wholesale revision of the Aristotelian approach to being in *De ente et essentia*. Although it can be argued that Maimonides adopts certain revisions of the Aristotelian conception of being established by some of his Islamic predecessors such as Avicenna, none of those revisions is comparable to Aquinas's radical demotion of form and essence, as well as his elevation of "existence" (*esse*) as the individual being of beings. Those revisions make it possible to argue that God knows and has direct causal influence over particulars or individuals. Maimonides never goes so far in his revisions of Aristotle.
17. I use the term "Neoplatonism" (a modern invention) to distinguish Plato proper from the authors that the Church Fathers such as Augustine referred to loosely as "Platonism." The mainstay of the Neoplatonists was the assertion in Plato's *Republic*, book 6, that the good is beyond being (509b), which led to an intensification of Socratic dualism—and eventually to an antipolitical animus among thinkers such as Plotinus and Proclus. This antipolitical animus, which Alfarabi and Maimonides reject, fits well with the otherworldly focus of the Church Fathers. Cf. chapter 3 and note 32 for further discussion of Neoplatonism.
18. E. Rosenthal, "Philosophy of Al-Farabi," 158; and E. Rosenthal, "Maimonides' Conception," 193. See also Franz Rosenthal, "On the Knowledge of Plato's Philosophy in the Islamic World," *Islamic Culture* 14 (1940): 387–422, esp. 411–12.
19. E. I. J. Rosenthal refers to it as the *Agreement* rather than the *Harmonization*. For a complete English translation and introduction, see Butterworth's translation in *Alfarabi: The Political Writings: "Selected Aphorisms" and Other Texts*, trans. Charles E. Butterworth (Ithaca, NY: Cornell University Press, 2001), 115–67.

For the Arabic (and a French translation), see *L'Harmonie entre les opinions de Platon et d'Aristote*, ed. Fawzi M. Najjar and Dominique Mallet (Damascus: Institut Français de Damas, 1999).

20. Although Strauss has led the way in relating Alfarabi's use of the *Theology* to his *Philosophy of Plato and Aristotle* (*PAW*, 11–12, 17–18, esp. 18), some of what follows is an elaboration on and extrapolation from Strauss's insights, in part because he refers only indirectly to the *Harmonization* in the introduction to *PAW* (18).

21. See also *WIPP*, 127. The reason for specifying Socratic political philosophy is both that it can include Plato and Aristotle and that it rightly stresses the primacy of Plato and Socrates in Islamic and Jewish medieval philosophy. As E. I. J. Rosenthal acknowledges ("Maimonides' Conception," 194, 204nn4–5, and 205), Strauss was responsible for recovering the centrality of Plato, especially his *Laws*, for the ethics and politics of Alfarabi, Averroës, and Maimonides.

22. See Marwan Rashed, "On the Authorship of the Treatise *On the Harmonization of the Opinions of the Two Sages* Attributed to al-Fārābī," *Arabic Sciences and Philosophy* 19, no. 1 (2009): 43–82.

23. E. Rosenthal, "Philosophy of Al-Farabi," 158.

24. E. Rosenthal, "Maimonides' Conception," 203; Parens and Macfarland, *Medieval Political Philosophy*, 36.

25. For an example of such large differences resulting from relatively subtle differences of detail, consider the presence of what Alfarabi calls "determination" in the opening lines of the *Book of Religion* as it is manifested in a work like the *Virtuous City*, as compared with the *Book of Religion*, from which determination is nearly absent. Determination is the sign of religion, and lack of it is the sign of philosophy. See Parens, "Prudence, Imagination, and Determination of Law in Alfarabi and Maimonides," in *Enlightening Revolutions: Essays in Honor of Ralph Lerner*, ed. Svetozar Minkov and Stéphane Douard (Lanham, MD: Lexington Books, 2006), 31–55. Also consider that the *Book of Religion* ends with a survey of the order of the whole, but the *Virtuous City* begins with such a survey. The first detail suggests that the *Book of Religion* is ultimately a less popular and more philosophic work than the *Virtuous City*. The second detail suggests that such a physical and metaphysical survey is not the ground of the account of human life from the more philosophic point of view. For evidence that Alfarabi was highly attuned to the different ways in which one can write to conceal one's intentions from readers, see his comparison of the different modes of concealment employed by Plato and Aristotle in the selection from Alfarabi's *Summary of Plato's Laws*, in Parens and Macfarland, *Medieval Political Philosophy*, 72–73.

26. E. Rosenthal, "Philosophy of Al-Farabi," 158; Walzer, "Rise of Islamic Philosophy," 16 (cf. citation of *Attainment of Happiness* passage on 14–15); Walzer, "Arabic Transmission," 172–74; introductionWalzer's to Alfarabi, *Al-Farabi on the Perfect State*, section 4, 9–13. Cf. Muhsin Mahdi's extensive critique of Walzer's ongoing hypothesizing of Neoplatonic or Middle Platonist predecessors, in

spite of many years of failed searching, in Muhsin Mahdi's review of *Al-Farabi on the Perfect State*, trans. Richard Walzer, *Journal of the American Oriental Society* 110, no. 4 (1990): 691–726.

27. E. Rosenthal, "Philosophy of Al-Farabi," 158; Walzer, "Arabic Transmission," 177, 182–83; Walzer, "Rise of Islamic Philosophy," 10–11, 15–16; F. Rosenthal, "Knowledge of Plato," 410–12.

One must be careful to distinguish meaningful originality from the superficial sort that has come into favor in recent times. Alfarabi's originality is evident in his ability to break free from the excessive focus on the otherworldly concerns of the Neoplatonism of his time. Strauss has argued that Alfarabi did for Islam, and Maimonides did for Judaism, what Plato did for his community (*WIPP*, 126–27). The similarities of Alfarabi and Maimonides to Plato should not be confused with lack of originality. Cf. Menachem Kellner, who confuses the recognition of similarities between Alfarabi and Maimonides with Richard Walzer's denial of any originality to Alfarabi (*Maimonides on Human Perfection* [Atlanta: Scholars, 1990], 50n10). In the case of Walzer, lack of originality rises to the level of requiring that Alfarabi should be copying a Middle Platonist predecessor. Compare my criticisms of Dimitri Gutas and Richard Walzer in Parens, *Metaphysics as Rhetoric*, xxxi–xxxiv, 21–24.

28. E. Rosenthal, "Philosophy of Al-Farabi," 158.
29. For example, see Walzer's introduction to Alfarabi, *Al-Farabi on the Perfect State*, 8; and Walzer, "Platonism in Islamic Philosophy," in *Greek into Arabic*, 236–52, esp. 246. And see Plato, *Timaeus*, 29b–c.
30. In Alfarabi, this imagery is quite prevalent. See esp. *Political Regime*, trans. Charles E. Butterworth, in Parens and Macfarland, *Medieval Political Philosophy*, 36–55; *Virtuous City*; and *Book of Religion*. In Maimonides, see *Guide*, 1.72 and 2.10; cf. in Maimonides, *Mishneh Torah*, vol. 1, The *Book of Knowledge*, ed. Moses Hyamson (Jerusalem: Feldheim, 1981), the opening four chapters of the entire work, which contain a thumbnail sketch of the Account of the Chariot (divine science or theology or metaphysics) and the Account of the Beginning (natural science).
31. See chapter 7 and part 4 of this text.
32. I do not mean to imply that Neoplatonists deny the existence of evil. Rather, they link evil to materiality alone. This leads to accusations on the part of thinkers such as Augustine that Neoplatonism is prone to some of the same pitfalls as Manicheanism. For the Neoplatonist, the result of this view of materiality is that everything metaphysical displays untroubled hierarchy. As we will see shortly, Alfarabi in contrast, like Aristotle, acknowledges that the deficiencies of human life involve human thought—not merely the human body. (Cf. the connection between evil and privation in Maimonides and Aristotle [*Guide*, 3.10; *Physics*, 1.9, and *Metaphysics*, 9.9].)
33. There are many classes of these weeds, *al-nawābit*. For evidence that Alfarabi intends to allude not only to sophists but also to Socrates with this metaphor, see

this account of the weeds in Butterworth's translation in Parens and Macfarland, *Medieval Political Philosophy*, 53–55, with Alfarabi's account of Socrates in *Philosophy of Plato*, sec. 30.

34. For further evidence that Maimonides has profound reservations about the perfect orderliness of the whole of being, consider his account of Aristotelian teleology in *Guide*, 3.13. There he claims that Aristotle affirms "first finality," by which he means that the end of each being is the form exemplified by its species, but he denies that Aristotle thought he knew the "ultimate finality" of each kind of being, by which he means the ways in which each species serves others higher than it (449–50). This amazingly un-Scholastic version of Aristotle is perfectly in keeping with Alfarabi's disorderly vipers and weeds.
35. Ibid., 1.72, 190.
36. See Parens, *Maimonides and Spinoza: Their Conflicting Views of Human Nature* (Chicago: University of Chicago Press, 2012), chap. 6.
37. See ibid.
38. Aristotle, *Nicomachean Ethics*, 1144a23–30, 1150a8. Cf. Maimonides's reference to the "infinity of desire" in *Guide*, 3.12, 445.
39. For further confirmation that privation rather than matter is the problem, also consider *Guide*, 3.11, which argues that the crucial source of evil in human life is ignorance or the privation of knowledge. For arguments against the view that Maimonides's outspoken denigration of the sense of touch in the *Guide* expresses his own views, see Joshua Parens, "Maimonidean Ethics Revisited," *Journal of Jewish Thought and Philosophy* 12, no. 3 (2003): 33–62, and *PAW*, 75–76.
40. I have argued elsewhere at great length that the philosopher-king, though an indispensable part of both Alfarabi's and Maimonides's teaching on prophecy, is not a serious proposal at least in the unalloyed form in which Socrates presents it in the *Republic*. See my *Islamic Philosophy*, chap. 2.
41. Cf. the usual way in which Alfarabi's philosophy is interpreted, namely, as starting by setting forth a metaphysics or cosmology from which actions are then inferred. Just such rapid settling on the order of things seems to be characteristic of religion.
42. *PAW*, 114. See also Aristotle, *Nicomachean Ethics*, 5.1129b12–1130a4.
43. Cf. note 5, where I warn the reader that Strauss's account of the synthesis/non-synthesis (or privileging of revelation/reason) divide is more complicated than it first appears.
44. See the opening of the *Mishneh Torah* in the *Book of Knowledge*, which itself begins with the Account of the Chariot or metaphysics, with the opening of the Mishnah in Berakhot as well as the claim in the closing paragraph of the *Book of Knowledge* that we can love God only to the extent that we know Him; and see *Guide*, 1.2, 1.34 (76), 2.40, 3.27–28, 3.51 (esp. 620, 627), and 3.54 (635).
45. I thank Greg Stern of the University of Massachusetts, Amherst, for making me aware that many readers, in the early days of the reception of the *Guide*, viewed the "moral" focus of these four chapters as a radical departure from the rest of the

Guide. Note, however, that in the previous note I have cited moments of shocking denigration of morality, even in these chapters.

46. Review chapter 2, final section, and see parts 3 and 4 of this text.
47. I argue this in full awareness of those moments in the *Guide* (2.39, end, 381) and the *Logic* (chapter 14, end) when Maimonides seems to doubt the need for political science or philosophy in his times. See chapter 8 of this text.
48. Walzer, "Arabic Transmission," 178–81; Walzer, "Rise of Islamic Philosophy," 17.
49. Walzer, "Rise of Islamic Philosophy," 10, 17; 14, 18.
50. We recall here, again, that Alfarabi never wrote a work called "The Perfect State" nor even "The Virtuous City." *Virtuous City* is more accurately *The Principles of the Opinions of the Inhabitants of the Virtuous City* (*Mabādi' ārā' ahl al-madīna al-fāḍila*). Furthermore, it is worth remembering what has already been observed in passing about the *Political Regime*, namely, the philosopher appears among the weeds even in the "virtuous city"!
51. Rosenthal distinguishes Alfarabi and Averroës from Ibn Bajja based on the claim that the former two require this state and the latter one has little if any need for it, as a condition of philosophic perfection. See E. Rosenthal, "Philosophy of Ibn Bājja," 39, 44, 45, 50n53, 52–53, 58–59; E. Rosenthal, "Islamic Political Thought," 6; E. Rosenthal, "Philosophy of Al-Farabi," 162, 171; E. Rosenthal, "Maimonides' Conception," 196. See also Walzer, "Rise of Islamic Philosophy," 12, 13. Like many readers of the *Republic*, Rosenthal seems to have missed the irony of such plans for what is called in the *Republic*, *kallipolis* (beautiful city). Is it truly plausible to suggest, as Rosenthal does, that Alfarabi and Averroës hold that the "ideal state" is a precondition of philosophic perfection? (Cf. the final sentence of the previous note! Also consider that Alfarabi states more than once that even if the true philosopher never rules, he is the true ruler [*AH*, sec. 62, and *Alfarabi, Selected Aphorisms*, aphor. 32]; he implies thereby that actual rule would not perfect the philosopher as philosopher.) Didn't Alfarabi and Averroës, along with Plato and Aristotle, bring philosophy to a high degree of perfection, while living in far from ideal regimes? For further evidence that Alfarabi does not really require the realization of such a perfect political life as a condition of philosophic "perfection," see chapter 2 of my *Islamic Philosophy*. In brief, neither Alfarabi nor Averroës held that an ideal political life is required for philosophic perfection. Furthermore, the difference between Ibn Bajja (1085–1138 CE) and these other two philosophers is *not* that he abandons ideal politics as a precondition of philosophic perfection; rather, the difference is that, living in times under the relatively direct influence of Alghazali (1058–1111 CE), Ibn Bajja was especially concerned to draw the indelible image of Alghazali's mystical solitary back toward philosophy. He could not have done so effectively by continuing to extol, however ironically, the identity of philosophy with public-spirited rule.
52. See chapter 7 of this text for evidence that Strauss himself did not realize until late in the 1930s how important it was to avoid the use of "state" (or *staat*) to render *madīna*.

53. Of course, other things such as the great differences between our contemporary views of writing and publicity from premodern views of the same contribute greatly to our obliviousness to the possibility of esotericism. The belief in intellectual and moral progress of the Enlightenment and subsequent developments in what Nietzsche calls the "historical sense" played their role in the development of that great difference, as Strauss explains in *PAW* and *WIPP*, especially in the latter work and in the Spinoza essay in the former. See chapter 5 of this text.
54. See note 41 of this chapter.

Chapter Five

1. That subtitle is the following: "containing some Dissertations by which it is shown not only that the Freedom of Philosophizing can be Granted in keeping with Piety and the Peace of the Republic, but that it cannot be Removed unless along with that very Piety and Peace of the Republic." Spinoza, *Theologico-Political Treatise*, trans. Martin D. Yaffe (Newburyport, MA: Focus, 2004).
2. *PAW*, 33n12; Kant, *Critique of Pure Reason*, B370.
3. Of course, this view of superiority to the past was already somewhat evident in the push for liberal democracy of thinkers such as Spinoza and Locke. Cf. this view of the relation between the arts and morals with Aristotle, *Politics*, 2.8.
4. One of Nietzsche's most prominent pronouncements on esotericism is "our highest insights must—and should—sound like follies and sometimes like crimes when they are heard without permission by those who are not predisposed and predestined for them. The difference between the exoteric and the esoteric, formerly known to philosophers—among the Indians as among the Greeks, Persians, and Muslims, in short, wherever one believed in an order or rank and *not* in equality and equal rights" (Nietzsche, *Beyond Good and Evil*, aphor. 30). For Strauss's interest in Nietzsche during his twenties, see his letter to Löwith as cited in Strauss, *Jewish Philosophy*, 62–63n30.
5. Strauss, "A Giving of Accounts," in Strauss, *Jewish Philosophy*, 457–66, esp. 460. Since he first read Plato in his late teens, it would appear that his dalliance with Nietzsche in his twenties (see previous note) led Strauss to revisit the Greeks as well as the "Muslims."
6. It should be underlined that for Strauss not only were Avicenna and especially Averroës deeply indebted to Alfarabi, but also that it was Avicenna's observation in the *On the Division of the Rational Sciences* (in Parens and Macfarland, *Medieval Political Philosophy*, 74–76) that awakened Strauss to the debt of Maimonides and all these *falāsifa* to Plato: "the treatment of prophecy and the Law (*sharīʿa*) is contained in [Plato's and Aristotle's] books on the laws" (epigraph to Strauss, *Argument and Action*, 1).

7. Long before Hegel characterized this disjunction as the rift between universal (philosophy or science) and (human) individual, Christian theology taught that the appearance of God as man made it possible for the believers of the Church to be one in the body of the Christ. At least in principle, Christianity proposed itself as the overcoming of the conflict between philosopher and city, such as one finds it in the comedy of Plato's *Republic*.
8. Joep Lameer, *Al-Farabi and Aristotelian Syllogistics: Greek Theory and Islamic Practice* (Leiden, NY: Brill, 1994); and Rashed, "On the Authorship."
9. Miriam Galston, "A Re-examination of al-Fārābī's Neoplatonism," *Journal of the History of Philosophy* 25, no. 1 (1977): 13–32.
10. Cf. this with the strange resonances of Pythagoreanism with Heidegger in chapter 8 of this text.
11. See the next note regarding this moment. Some have argued, based on this passage and on Strauss's characterization of Spinoza's decision in favor of unbelief as against belief (*SCR*, preface, 29–30), that Strauss holds that whether one leads the life of philosophy or of religious belief is as such and always a matter of decision. This seems to me to confuse Spinoza's modus operandi with that of all philosophers, including premoderns like Alfarabi and Maimonides—which does not seem to square with Strauss's view of the matter or with his late, relatively undivided attention to Plato and Xenophon.
12. Strauss doubts the possibility of a philosopher becoming a believing Jew (*PAW*, 105) but then observes that Halevi seems to have been tempted to philosophy: "we prefer to think for a very short time" and then reverted to Judaism (109). From these observations and from Halevi's evident refusal to present a profound and ongoing dispute between a believer and a philosopher in the *Kuzari* (108), one could infer that Halevi is a philosopher. I believe that this is a misreading of the significance of page 109. Reversion to the faith of one's fathers is one thing; embracing monotheism having never been a monotheist and having been a philosopher is quite another.

Chapter Six

1. E. Rosenthal, "Philosophy of Al-Farabi," esp. 158. Cf. chap. 4.
2. Fakhry, *Islamic Philosophy*, 121, previously cited by me in *Metaphysics as Rhetoric*, 19n8.
3. Mahdi's edition (*Kitāb al-Milla wa Nuṣūṣ Ukhrā*) appeared in 1968.
4. Thomas Aquinas, *Summa contra gentiles*, trans. Anton Pegis (Notre Dame, IN: University of Notre Dame Press, 1975), bk. 1, p. 42.
5. Aquinas, *Summa theologiae*, 1a.1.4.
6. Aristotle, *Nicomachean Ethics*, 1095b; *Phys.*, 1.1.
7. See Étienne Gilson, *History of Christian Philosophy in the Middle Ages* (New York: Random House, 1955), 229n38, as cited in Pegis's translation of Aquinas, *Summa contra gentiles*, bk. 1, 68n2.

8. Cf. *AH*, sec. 55, with *BR*, secs. 4–5; see also Alfarabi, *Book of Letters*, ed. Muhsin Mahdi (Beirut: Dar al-Mashriq, 1969), secs. 109–10, 147–58.
9. *Guide*, 2.32–48, esp. 36; and review note 7 of this chapter. Among the most important reasons for revelation is what Alfarabi refers to as "determination" (*BR*, sec. 1), which is, of course, characteristic of things imagined. Philosophy as philosophy, that is, as inquiry into universals is incapable of providing determination. See also *Guide*, 2.25, on the crucial reason to side with creation, despite certain advantages of Plato over Aristotle regarding miracles.
10. Compare this usage to what appears to be the first use of the *theo-logia* (lit., speeches about the gods) in the West by Socrates in *Republic*, book 2. See Allan Bloom's translation of 379a4 and the endnote to this passage. *The Republic of Plato* (New York: Basic Books, 1968).
11. To be more precise, sophistic is sometimes ranged between dialectic and rhetoric. See, for example, *AH*, sec. 4, and Alfarabi, *Philosophy of Aristotle*, secs. 13–16. For the inclusion of rhetoric and poetics in the so-called Alexandrian approach to Aristotle's Organon, see Muhsin Mahdi, "Science, Philosophy, and Religion in Alfarabi's *Enumeration of the Sciences*," in *The Cultural Context of Medieval Learning*, ed. J. E. Murdoch and E. D. Sylla (Dordrecht, Holland: Reidel, 1975), 146–47.
12. Aristotle, *Nicomachean Ethics*, 5.10. See also *Guide*, 3.26, and Maimonides, *Eight Chapters*, chap. 6, both in Parens and Macfarland, *Medieval Political Philosophy*.
13. See Parens, "Determination of Law"; my review of *Alfarabi and the Foundation of Islamic Political Philosophy*, by Muhsin Mahdi, *American Political Science Review* 96, no. 2 (2002): 410–11; and chapter 6 of Parens, *Maimonides and Spinoza*.
14. The most obvious emblem of this in Plato is Glaucon's casual positing of the difference between erotic and geometric necessity (*Republic*, 458d4), which Socrates then develops into the basis of the comically implausible use of geometric or mathematical necessity to regulate erotic necessity in the nuptial number (460a, 546b–547a) and the calculation of the superiority of the kingly, virtuous life and soul over the tyrannical, vicious life and soul (587c–e).
15. The first challenge in understanding prudence derives, in the first instance, from the fact that it reasons about particulars. Debate rages about what role the syllogism, especially the practical syllogism, might play in such reasoning. Such debate is deepened by the fact that prudence is permeated by intuition in a manner that theoretical science is not, which, though it begins in intuition and ends in intuition, is constituted in the middle, so to speak, as discursive reasoning. When one adds to this that prudence is not limited to personal or political prudence but extends to legislative prudence, one is confronted by the challenge of reasoning about universals, not merely particulars, whose relation to scientific knowledge is complex and elusive.
16. Aquinas, *Summa theologiae*, 1a.1.5.
17. See the appendix of this text.
18. I say "at the cusp of metaphysics" for two reasons: because astronomy is technically a part of mathematics for Alfarabi, and medieval Jewish and Islamic

thinkers generally, and because the Active Intellect represents the lowest separate intellect, which straddles the border between physics and metaphysics, that is, between the sublunar and the superlunary.

19. See Alfarabi, *Book of Letters*; English translation forthcoming by Charles E. Butterworth; and Alfarabi's brief summary of Aristotle's *Metaphysics*, which Avicenna says had such influence on him, presented in Dimitri Gutas, *Avicenna and the Aristotelian Tradition* (Leiden: Brill, 1988).

20. To be more precise, in the first account, political science is divorced from that faculty, prudence, which would make virtuous rule possible—though the possibility of their unification is exemplified by what Alfarabi calls "virtuous kingly craft." Political science here is concerned solely with the universals of political life. And virtuous kingly craft seems to be limited to a combination of political science with the experiential faculty (Alfarabi's equivalent to cleverness). In the second account, virtuous kingly craft takes the lead and extends its reach to cover, not only political science but all practical and theoretical sciences. That extension of virtuous kingly craft to include theoretical science cannot but remind one of the Platonic philosopher-king—especially once it becomes clear that again the sciences are complemented by the experiential faculty or prudence. The addition of theoretical science to the quiver of the practitioner of virtuous kingly craft and the step back from Aristotle to Plato appears to be due to the fact of the rise of monotheistic religion. In a sense, political science remains the same throughout; however, what Alfarabi refers to as virtuous kingly craft encompasses more from the account of PS 1 to PS 2. Ultimately, it is virtuous kingly craft more than bare political science that reaches to what Strauss means by "political philosophy."

21. See "An Epilogue," in Strauss, *Liberalism Ancient and Modern* (New York: Basic Books, 1968), 206. But cf. *CM*, 25, with 21, 27, 28. At *CM*, 25, Strauss states more boldly than almost anywhere else (see also *On Tyranny*, rev. and exp. ed. Victor Gourevitch and Michael S. Roth [New York: Free Press, 1991), 277, Strauss to Kojeve, May 28, 1957) that Aristotle thought that "theoretical wisdom . . . is available." This interpretation of Aristotle should be compared not only with the other pages cited earlier but also with Alfarabi's concluding remarks regarding metaphysics in the *Philosophy of Aristotle*, quoted earlier. Many rightly influential students of Strauss have over time developed an ever more Platonic view of Aristotle.

Chapter Seven

1. Daniel Tanguay, *Leo Strauss: An Intellectual Biography*, trans. Christopher Nadon (New Haven: Yale University Press, 2007), 80.
2. *Philosophy and Law* was originally published as Strauss, *Philosophie und Gesetz*; "Some Remarks" was originally published as "Quelques remarques sur la science

politique de Maïmonide et Farabi," *Revue des Études Juives* 100 (1936): 1–37, translated by Robert Bartlett for *Interpretation* 18, no. 1 (1990): 3–30; "Place of Providence" was originally published as "Der Ort der Vorsehungslehre nach der Ansicht Maimunis," *Monatschrift für Geschichte und Wissenschaft des Judentums* 81, no. 1 (1937): 93–105, translated by Gabriel Bartlett and Svetozar Minkov for the *Review of Metaphysics* 57 (2004): 537–49.

3. Tanguay, *Leo Strauss*, cf. 55, 57, and 61 with 65, 66, 67, and 97.
4. "Literary Character" was originally published in *Essays on Maimonides*, 37–91, ed. Salo Baron (New York: Columbia University Press, 1941); it was eventually included in *PAW*, 38–94.
5. See chapter 8 of this text.
6. As Tanguay argues (*Leo Strauss*, 84), Alfarabi is the thinker who made Strauss aware of a different, more political and less metaphysical understanding of Plato. All the while that Maimonides's debt to Alfarabi became more apparent to Strauss, however, he seems to have grown increasingly uneasy about underlining the political character of Maimonides's teaching.
7. See Tanguay, *Leo Strauss*, 56, and chapter 4 of this text.
8. Why do we call these "central chapters"? (After all, the numerically central chapter in Maimonides's *Guide* is 2.13, the first of two crucial chapters on eternity versus creation.) First, these chapters surround what Maimonides seems to be setting up as the holy of holies, 3.1–7. Second, the prophetology is of the essence of the theme of the *Guide*, the true science of the (divine) Law. Third, these two sections identified by Strauss consist of seventeen chapters each. As Nasser Behnegar has noted, according to Strauss, the number 17 stands numerologically for "nature"—in a sense, the true center of all philosophizing (qtd. in Major, *Philosophic Life*, 41n5).
9. In the Aristotelian tradition to which Maimonides adheres at least in this, psychology is a theoretical science containing elements of natural science and divine science. Cf. Aristotle, *On the Soul*, 402a5–7, 403a3–403b18.
10. Julius Guttman, *Philosophies of Judaism* (New York: Schocken, 1973).
11. This stress on supernaturalism and the limits of human knowledge should be compared with the approach to Maimonides developed by Shlomo Pines and his students after Pines published his "Limits" article. See chapter 9 and appendix. Cf. Parens, *Maimonides and Spinoza*, chap. 1, for evidence that Maimonides's arguments regarding the limits of knowledge are anything but straightforward, or, as Strauss states, immediately before this quotation from *Philosophy and Law*, "beyond doubt."
12. Averroës, or Ibn Rushd (1126–98 CE), *Decisive Treatise*, trans. Charles E. Butterworth, in Parens and Macfarland, *Medieval Political Philosophy*, 162–79. Gersonides, or Levi ben Gershom (1288–344 CE), *The Wars of the Lord*, trans. Seymour Feldman, 3 vols. (Philadelphia: Jewish Publication Society, 1984).
13. Cf. Parens, *Maimonides and Spinoza*, 112–15, on withholding and whether it is natural or supernatural.

14. And this, despite Strauss's insistence that the Islamic Aristotelians did not possess the *Politics*. Cf. Shlomo Pines, "Aristotle's *Politics* in Arabic Philosophy," *Israel Oriental Studies* 5 (1975): 150–60.
15. Avicenna, *Healing: Metaphysics* 10 and *Division of the Rational Sciences*, in Parens and Macfarland, *Medieval Political Philosophy*, 77–88, 74–76; Alfarabi, *Virtuous City*.
16. Cf. chapter 8 of this text.
17. See Warren Zev Harvey, "Why Maimonides Was Not a Mutakallim," in *Perspectives on Maimonides*, ed. Joel L. Kraemer (Oxford: Oxford University Press, 1991), 105–14, cited in Sarah Stroumsa, *Maimonides in His World: Portrait of a Mediterranean Thinker* (Princeton: Princeton University Press, 2009), 37n47.
18. See Heinrich Meier, *Leo Strauss and the Theologico-Political Problem* (New York: Cambridge University Press, 2006).
19. See Haggai Ben Shammai, "Kalam in Medieval Jewish Philosophy," in Frank and Oliver Leaman, *History of Jewish Philosophy*, 127–32.
20. See Alfarabi, *Enumeration of the Sciences*, 21–23.
21. I believe that Strauss's scholarly understanding of political science or political philosophy in Maimonides developed in the direction of what he would refer to in the Platonic context as "political philosophy broadly understood" (*CM*, 20). The view that political science or political philosophy is a mere discipline, still expressed here in "Place of Providence," is due in part to the continued influence of medieval Christian views of the division of the sciences on Strauss. I say that despite Strauss's evidently growing awareness of the divide between Maimonides and the Islamic *falāsifa*, on the one hand, and medieval Christian thought of the Thomistic school, on the other (e.g., PPr, 541, 543n18; *PL*, 73n25). For more on medieval Christian views on the status of political science, see chapter 1, part 2 as a whole, and the following discussion of Abravanel.
22. See esp. PPr, 542–43n17. It appears that in "Some Remarks" Strauss did not understand fully that the political center of the *Guide* was in the prophetology. In SRMF, 12, he linked the articles or principles of faith that Maimonides enumerates in *Commentary on the Mishnah*, *Pereq Ḥeleq*, with *Guide*, 3.25–50, rather than with 2.39–40. He did so by referring to 3.25–50 as Maimonides's discussion of the "divine law." In other words, in "Some Remarks" he had not fully grasped that the prophetology was the very heart of Maimonides's analysis of divine law. This might help to explain the extent of Strauss's focus on the psychology of prophecy in *Philosophy and Law*. (Then there's the problem of when these three pieces were actually written. Though they came out in 1935, 1936, and 1937, it was not necessarily the case that SRMF was not written before *PL*.) Perhaps not until "Place of Providence" did Strauss come to understand fully the extent to which the core of the true science of the (divine) Law, the prophetology, was part of political philosophy.
23. Strauss, "On Abravanel's Philosophical Tendency and Political Teaching," in *Isaac Abravanel: Six Lectures*, ed. J. B. Trend and H. Loewe (Cambridge: Cambridge University Press, 1937), 95–129.

24. Strauss, "On Abravanel's Philosophical Tendency, in Trend and Loewe, *Isaac Abravanel*, 104, 128.
25. Readers who have read widely in Strauss's thought will recognize here a phrasing that Strauss used again, nearly verbatim, to describe the position of Martin Heidegger in "Philosophy as Rigorous Science and Political Philosophy," in Strauss, *Platonic Political Philosophy*, 30. See also chapter 8, note 6, and the closing pages of chapter 8 of this text.
26. See the general introduction to Parens and Macfarland, *Medieval Political Philosophy*, 12–17; and chapter 4 of this text.
27. See "Zu Abravanels Kritik des Königtums," in *Gesammelte Schriften*, vol 2, *Philosophie und Gesetz—Frühe Schriften*, ed. Heinrich Meier (Stuttgart: Metzler, 1997), 233–34; translated into English as "On Abravanel's Critique of Monarchy" (1937), as appendix E in Yaffe and Ruderman, *Reorientation*. In that piece, Strauss took H. Finkelscherer to task for arguing in a journal essay in *Monatsschrift für Geschichte und Wissenschaft des Judentums* (1937) that Ibn Kaspi (1297–1340 CE) already maintained the kind of hostility toward kingship expressed by Abravanel. (In "On Abravanel's Philosophical Tendency," in Trend and Loewe, *Isaac Abravanel*, 101n1, Strauss merely alludes to the divide between Abravanel and Ibn Kaspi.) In "Abravanel's Critique of Monarchy" Strauss notes that Ibn Kaspi likens monarchy to sacrifices. Finkelscherer didn't think through the significance of this reference to sacrifices, which are paradigmatic in Maimonides's *Guide*, 3.32, of legislation that expresses the second rather than the first intention of the legislator. They are merely conditionally rather than absolutely good. This kind of goodness is a far cry from Abravanel's rejection of monarchy as bad.
28. See *PAW*, 40n9—and the *Book of Religion*, a book that Strauss had little, if any, access to.
29. "Lost Writing of Farabi's" was originally published as "Eine vermisste Schrift Farābīs," in *Monatsschrift für Geschichte und Wissenschaft des Judentums* 80 (1936): 96–106. The translation appears as appendix D, in Yaffe and Ruderman, *Reorientation*.
30. As we saw in chapter 2, Strauss seems to have had, at best, limited access to the *Book of Religion*.
31. *CM*, 20. See Strauss's observation in "Lost Writing" that Ibn al-Qifti was wrong in thinking that the missing metaphysics at the end of the *Philosophy of Aristotle* was due to textual corruption (Yaffe and Ruderman, *Reorientation*, app. D, 260–62).

Chapter Eight

1. Strauss, "Maimonides' Statement on Political Science" (originally published in 1953, in *Proceedings of the American Academy for Jewish Research*) is here cited in *WIPP*, 155–69 (hereafter cited as MSPS).

2. The PAAJR was a setting in which so conjectural a paper would not appear completely out of place.
3. Lawrence V. Berman, "A Reexamination of Maimonides' 'Statement on Political Science,'" *Journal of the American Oriental Society* 89, no. 1 (1969): 106–11; Joel L. Kraemer, "Maimonides on the Philosophic Sciences in his *Treatise on the Art of Logic*," in Kraemer, *Perspectives on Maimonides*, 77–104. For complete bibliographic information on the Arabic versions and the critical edition produced by Mubahat Türker, consult the first footnote of either of these articles. For an English translation more accurate than Strauss could produce, see the selected translation of chapter 14 by Muhsin Mahdi, in Parens and Macfarland, *Medieval Political Philosophy*; see also the translation of the complete chapter 14 as well as selections from chapters 3 and 8 by Charles E. Butterworth, in *Ethical Writings of Maimonides*, ed. Raymond L. Weiss and Charles Butterworth (New York: Dover, 1983), 158–63. Finally, the interested reader should also compare Strauss's much later and even briefer piece on the Logic, titled "Note on Maimonides' *Treatise on the Art of Logic*" and published in Strauss, *Platonic Political Philosophy*, 208–9.

    Herbert Davidson attempted to raise doubts about the authorship of the *Logic* in his *Moses Maimonides: The Man and His Work* (New York: Oxford University Press, 2004), 318. He had expressed these objections in print prior to the publication of his book. Ahmad Hasnawi put these doubts to rest in his "Réflexions sur la terminologie logique de Maïmonide et son contexte farabien: Le *Guide de perplexes* et la Traité de logique," in *Maïmonide: Philosophe et Savant*, ed. Tony Lévy and Roshdi Rashed (Leuven: Peeters, 2004), 39–78. I thank Joel L. Kraemer for making me aware of this article.
4. Unless otherwise noted, all parenthetical citations in this chapter refer to page numbers in *What Is Political Philosophy?*
5. Cf. Maimonides's praise of Alfarabi, especially his *Principles of the Beings* (viz., *Political Regime*), in one of his letters to Samuel Ibn Tibbon, cited in the biographical introduction to Charles E. Butterworth's translation of Alfarabi's *Political Regime* in Parens and Macfarland, *Medieval Political Philosophy*, 36, and the related passage cited by Shlomo Pines in his translator's introduction to *Guide*, lx.
6. See also Strauss's comment: "There is no room for political philosophy in Heidegger's work, and this may well be due to the fact that the room in question is occupied by gods or the gods," in "Philosophy as Rigorous Science and Political Philosophy," in Strauss, *Platonic Political Philosophy*, 30.
7. Meier, *Theologico-Political Problem*. Regarding the connection between Machiavelli and the medievals, see especially the introduction to *PAW*, 15. Regarding Maimonides's Averroism, see the introduction to "The Law of Reason in the *Kuzari*," in *PAW*, 95–98.
8. This characterization of the relation between premodern and modern critiques of religion should be contrasted with Strauss's characterization of that relation in *PL* and in *SCR*, 37–52.

9. Modern political philosophy eschews conventional slavery; however, classical political philosophy does not develop arguments to eliminate such slavery. This is an example of the difference in the political solution of ancients and moderns, but it does not preclude the possibility that classical political philosophy offers the resources to understand why one might wish to eliminate conventional slavery. See chapter 5 of this text for further exploration of the difference between the political solutions and the other less obvious difference, namely, the relation between philosopher and city or man and city in the premodern versus modern settings.
10. *PAW*, 15, 17. For evidence that Alfarabi is the medieval founder of what Strauss refers to as "Averroism" and evidence that Maimonides (though a contemporary of Averroës rather than a student of his thought) was as a follower of Alfarabi also an "Averroist." See *PAW*, introd. and pp. 95–98.
11. See MSPS, 164–65n19, citing *Guide*, 1.31. Also cf. note 32 of this chapter.
12. Strauss does not qualify the first claim with "seems"; furthermore, he devotes significant attention to the question "for whom" their teaching is useless. The Hebrew versions warrant the use of "we"; the Arabic versions are in the passive. Kraemer, "Philosophic Sciences" takes Strauss to task at length for providing such a "fine example of how reliance on Hebrew translations of Arabic texts wreaks havoc with our understanding" (98–101). Strauss, however, offers the equivalence of the Hebrew "we" to "we Jews" as a questionable interpretation, which he entertains among other possibilities. Kraemer insists that Maimonides states clearly what is and is not relevant about classical political philosophy in this penultimate paragraph of the *Logic*, at least in the Arabic versions. I try to show that the relevant passage does insinuate a rejection of political science, as broad as Strauss claims.
13. Kraemer objects that Strauss has made Maimonides's claim to dispense with philosophy in politics far too broad (ibid., 99). Strauss is addressing the mere *appearance* that Maimonides is dispensing with political science. Kraemer attempts to argue that Maimonides does not claim to dispense with so much. Ultimately, Strauss agrees that political science remains relevant.
14. Cf. ibid., 99.
15. Ibid., 99–101.
16. Cf. Strauss's reference to these chapters of Maimonides's *Guide*, 164n17.
17. Cf. Kraemer, "Philosophic Sciences," 100–103.
18. See Mahdi's translation in Parens and Macfarland, *Medieval Political Philosophy*. Note that Strauss himself refers to this passage in the "Statement on Political Science" while confirming that Maimonides's *Guide*'s prophetology is a branch of political science (161).
19. For the difference between enlightened kalām (dialectical theology or apologetics) and traditional kalām, see "The Literary Character of the *Guide for the Perplexed*," in *PAW*, esp. 40–41. For accounts of traditional kalām, see Alfarabi, *Enumeration of the Sciences*, chap. 5; and *Guide*, 1.71.

20. See note 12 of this chapter for the acknowledgment that the Hebrew versions use "we" but the Arabic are in the passive.
21. See Kenneth H. Green's edition of MSPS, in *Leo Strauss on Maimonides: The Complete Writings* (Chicago: University of Chicago Press, 2013), 402n2, for full citations of the relevant commentaries and a translation of the relevant passage from Mendelssohn. Of course, Mendelssohn's interpretation follows the lead of Spinoza's *Theologico-Political Treatise*—despite his well-known preference for Leibniz—in claiming that with the loss of the Jewish homeland Jewish Law becomes irrelevant.
22. It is well worth comparing this determination of the audience of the *Logic* with the opening lines of Strauss's later piece on the same work: "Maimonides' *Treatise on the Art of Logic* is not a Jewish book. He wrote it in his capacity as a student of the art of logic at the request of a master of the legal (religious) sciences, as a man of high education in the Arabic tongue who wished to have explained to him as briefly as possible the meaning of the terms frequently occurring in the art of logic" (*Platonic Political Philosophy*, 208). The reference to the "master of the legal (religious) sciences" echoes his reference in MSPS to "the men who speculate about the principles or roots" (159). Furthermore, the opening sentence from the later work was already anticipated in MSPS, 162.
23. One thing is certain: one must be very careful not to confuse "the most practical part of the political teaching of the philosophers" with what was previously referred to as "politics proper." It would be more accurate to say that that practical part is more or less the same thing as what was referred to earlier as the "political solution." Indeed, "politics proper" in the "Statement" is more or less equivalent to the "theoretical understanding of revealed religion" or the "framework" of classical political philosophy.
24. In his "Philosophic Sciences," Kraemer offers an exhaustive exploration of parallel passages in his immediate antecedent, Alfarabi (90–94), as well as the possible ultimate antecedent, Aristotle, and in particular a conjectured paraphrase of Aristotle's *Politics* (94–95). In conjecturing such an ultimate antecedent, Kraemer relies on Pines, "Aristotle's *Politics*," 156–59.
25. In note 9 on page 159 of MSPS, *Siyāsāt* = *Political Regime* and *Al-madīna al-fāḍila* = *Virtuous City*.
26. Strauss's citations on 159–60nn7 and 10 of MSPS refer to Harry Austryn Wolfson, "Note on Maimonides' Classification of the Sciences" *Jewish Quarterly Review* 26 (1935–36): 369–77; Strauss mistakenly added the letter "s" to "Note," making it "Notes."
27. Cf. Strauss's interpretation of the prophetology and the *Guide* with Kraemer's in "Philosophic Sciences," 101–4. Although Kraemer argues here with great delicacy against Strauss, I think that his conclusion that the *Guide* is a dialectical, philosophic book (101–2) and a "book of political governance (just as the Torah is a book of political governance)" (103) is not an advance over Strauss's claim that it is, in the first instance, a work of enlightened kalām and, in the second

28. instance and at a much deeper level, a work of political philosophy, especially in the prophetology section (2.32–48) and in its mate the section on providence (3.8–24). (Cf. note 14 of this chapter; MSPS, 166; and Strauss's "Place of Providence.") Kraemer's account gives a far more harmonious portrait of the *Guide* than Strauss's.
28. Kraemer objects to this interpretation based on similarity between this passage in the *Logic* and one in Alfarabi's *Book of Religion* ("Philosophic Sciences," 93). For reasons I lack space to treat here, I think that he overstates the similarity—though such a similarity would not undermine the essential point—which is that these terms are not references to differences in size but in religion.
29. I have added diacritical marks (as well as English translations of the Hebrew), which were missing from Strauss's original version due to printing limitations of the time.
30. See Butterworth's translation for this rendering. The list of terms is omitted from Mahdi's translation. It should also be underlined that the term "command" or "commands" (though not *ḥukm*) appears in the *Logic*. Indeed, the phrase "divine commands" (*al-awāmir al-ilāhiyya*) is the concluding phrase of the body text (as opposed to the concluding list of terms) in chapter 14. See both Mahdi's and Butterworth's translations. Strauss's translation based on the Hebrew has "things" for "commands"—though "things" is also a plausible rendering of *awāmir* (156).
31. Of course, Strauss is correct that Maimonides contrasts individual and law in a radical, even shocking, way in the chapters of the *Guide* that Strauss then cites (3.34 and 2.40, 163n15). Nevertheless, Strauss's conjecture about "'commands' and *nomoi*" lacks textual support in the original Arabic of the *Logic*, to which he did not have access.
32. Strauss directs the interested reader in 165n19 to *Guide*, 1.17, 31; 3.29; and other passages. See especially 1.31.
33. Compare the preceding two sentences with note 23 of this chapter.
34. Cf. Ralph Lerner's translation of the opening four chapters of Maimonides's *Mishneh Torah*, in which Maimonides summarizes the Account of the Chariot (chaps. 1 and 2) and the Account of the Beginning (chaps. 3 and 4) (*Maimonides' Empire of Light* [Chicago: University of Chicago Press, 2000], 141–53, esp. 145). See also *Guide*, 2.3–12 and 3.1–7.
35. See the Pines translation of the *Guide*, 3.51, 619, pars. 4 and 6, respectively.
36. See also Nasser Behneghar's observation (in Major, *Philosophic Life*, 41n5) that Strauss traces the source of the numerological significance of the number seventeen to the existence of seventeen consonants in Greek. We are not surprised that Maimonides would rely on a Greek tradition here once we remember that the Hebrew Bible does not have any word for "nature."
37. See note 27 of this chapter.
38. Strauss, *Gesammelte Schriften*, vol. 3, *Hobbes' Politische Wissenschaft und zugehörige Schriften—Briefe*, ed. Heinrich Meier (Stuttgart: Metzler, 2001), 660. See also Meier, *Theologico-Political Problem*, 29n1.

39. Cf. Joel L. Kraemer, "Philosophic Sciences," 93n46; and his citation in footnote 46 of his "On Maimonides' Messianic Posture," in *Studies in Medieval and Jewish History and Literature*, ed. Isadore Twersky (Cambridge, MA: Harvard University Press for the Littman Library, 1984), 2:109–42, esp. 141; and Kraemer's "The *Jihād* of the *Falāsifa*," *Jerusalem Studies in Arabic and Islam* 10 (1987): 288–324 with my *Islamic Philosophy*, chap. 4, esp. 60–76.
40. Cf. ibid., chap. 2.

Chapter Nine

1. Shlomo Pines, "Limitations of Human Knowledge according to al-Fārābī, Ibn Bājja, and Maimonides," in Twersky, *Medieval Jewish History*, 82–109.
2. See the appendix of this text.
3. In arguing for a four-level esotericism, Warren Zev Harvey has attempted to reconcile these opposing tendencies in Pines's thought (also ascribing it to medieval commentators such as Ibn Kaspi and Maimonides's Hebrew translator, Samuel Ibn Tibbon), though it appears to some extent at the expense of the political happiness thesis. See Harvey's "Maimonides' Critical Epistemology and *Guide* 2:24," *Aleph* 8 (2008): 213–35.
4. Tanguay, *Leo Strauss*, cf. 55, 57, 61, with 65, 66, 67, and 97.
5. Since this chapter is not directly about the limits of knowledge, we cannot indulge here in an exploration of Maimonides's views on those limits. The interested reader should see Parens, *Maimonides and Spinoza*, chap. 1.
6. See Parens, *Maimonides and Spinoza*, chap. 6.
7. See Steven Harvey, "Aristotle's *Phronesis* in Medieval Islamic and Jewish Philosophy," paper presented at the University of Georgia, Athens, on April 25, 2012; Parens, "Determination of Law"; and Parens, *Maimonides and Spinoza*, chap. 6.
8. Cf. Aristotle's *Metaphysics*, 6.2.
9. Aristotle, *Nicomachean Ethics*, 2.2, 1103b26–30. Strauss follows this model not only in *Philosophy and Law* but also in "Farabi's *Plato*"—see chapter 8.
10. Pines, "Truth and Falsehood Versus Good and Evil: A Study in Jewish and General Philosophy in Connection with the *Guide of the Perplexed*, I, 2," in *Studies in Maimonides*, ed. Isadore Twersky, 95–157 (Cambridge: Harvard University Press, 1990). See also the appendix of this text.
11. The following are other reasons to doubt how rigid is this distinction: (1) the likelihood that at this early point in *Nicomachean Ethics*, Aristotle is bringing along his less-than-theoretically inclined gentleman (*kaloskagathos*) to pursue their ethical inquiry, which might allow for other audiences for this work, deriving different benefits from reading it (cf. Pines's overreading of the fragmentary account of Alfarabi's lost commentary on the *Ethics* in Ibn Bajja); (2) the ample evidence that in the *Metaphysics* Aristotle does not stick to a purely theoretical inquiry throughout, which is supported by Strauss's suggestion that though

Aristotle's political writings are not grounded on his theoretical writings, his theoretical writings *are* in the business of offering accounts that square with sensible politics. See the appendix of this text; and Strauss, "An Epilogue," in *Liberalism Ancient and Modern*, 203–23, esp. 205–6; and *CM*, 21, 25–26. Review chapter 1 of this text.

12. Review chapters 2 and 3 of this text.
13. Cf. Aristotle, *Politics*, 1.8, and my discussion of it in *Islamic Philosophy*, 108–9.
14. See chapter 4 and 3 of this text.
15. For *Guide*, 1.72, see chapter 4 of this text; for *Guide*, 1.34, see Parens, *Maimonides and Spinoza*, chap. 1. The choice of the thirty-fourth chapter of both parts 1 and 3 to address this human type, whatever numerological significance it might have, indicates how salient this theme of the solitary is in Maimonides's mind.
16. By stressing disorder, we do not want to lead the reader to think that our account of Maimonides resembles the Razian account that he critiques (*Guide*, 3.12). The disorder to which we refer is not tantamount to the conviction that someone or something malevolent targets individuals for suffering. As I argue in *Maimonides and Spinoza*, chapter 4, Razi's view, though it is voiced by an opponent of revelation, expresses a view of particular providence that resembles nothing so much as the view of religionists who fall prey to the view that God's omnipotence is unmitigated.
17. This obviously echoes Strauss, *WIPP*, 38–39.
18. See the section of Strauss's commentary on Xenophon's *Hiero* titled "Pleasure and Virtue," in *On Tyranny*, 92–102, cited by Laurence Lampert in *How Philosophy Became Socratic* (Chicago: University of Chicago Press, 2010), 108n133.

Chapter Ten

1. For Alfarabi's discussion of enlightened kalām, the reader should consider his account of dialectic and rhetoric in the *Book of Religion*, sec. 6, in Parens and Macfarland, *Medieval Political Philosophy*, 27.
2. See my *Metaphysics as Rhetoric*, 8–10.
3. See note 14 in chapter 2.
4. See note 15 in chapter 2.
5. See chapter 9 of this text.

Chapter Eleven

1. Introduction to the *Mishneh Torah* in Maimonides, *Book of Knowledge*, 4b.
2. Cf. in Maimonides, *Book of Knowledge*, "Laws concerning the Foundations of the Law," 4.10–13 with "Laws concerning the Study of the Torah," 1.10–12. Each of these passages can be found in the Hyamson translation on pages 39b and 58a; a

better English translation of the first passage is in Lerner, *Maimonides' Empire of Light*, 152–53.
3. Davidson, *Moses Maimonides*. Unless otherwise noted, all subsequent parenthetical numbers in this chapter refer to the Pines edition of Maimonides's *Guide*.
4. For the first critical and the best biography of Maimonides to date, see Joel L. Kraemer, *Maimonides: The Life and World of One of Civilization's Greatest Minds* (New York: Doubleday, 2008).
5. See Pines, "Limitations of Human Knowledge." It needs to be emphasized that Kant treats neither horn of this dilemma as true. To suppose that we could know such a thing presupposes a nontemporal point of view compatible with a divine, not a human, viewpoint.
6. Mahdi translation of selection from *Logic*, chap. 14, in Parens and Macfarland, *Medieval Political Philosophy*, 181–82.
7. *Politics*, 1.1253a2; Aristotle, *Nicomachean Ethics*, 2.1103a24–26.
8. See chapter 8 of this text.
9. Anyone seriously interested in these commentators should consult Richard Sorabji's pathbreaking Ancient Commentators series for Cornell University Press.
10. See Plato, *Laws* 4.713e–718a, 5.739a–e.
11. In addition to the *Political Regime*, the reader interested in the Farabian background of Maimonides's views on prophecy should also compare *Guide*, 2.32–48 with Alfarabi's *Attainment* and *Virtuous City*.
12. See, for example, Maimonides's disdainful characterization of those, such as Saadya, who speak of intellectual or rational laws as suffering from the disease of the dialectical theologians (Maimonides, *Eight Chapters*, chap. 6 in Parens and Macfarland, *Medieval Political Philosophy*, 205). And for some examples of Saadya's use of intellectual or rational law, see pages 156–61.
13. Although the Mu'tazilite dialectial theologians are usually spoken of as "rationalist," in contrast to the later and more popular Ash'arite theologians, it is not difficult to see that Maimonides resists the very "rationalism" that made them famous. In addition, his account of their position on particular providence in 3.17 gives ample evidence that it was inconsistencies in the Mu'tazilite dialectial theology that gave rise to the more consistent, if less "rational," teachings of the Ash'arites. See Parens, *Maimonides and Spinoza*, 121–24.
14. For a fuller discussion, see chapter 7 of this text.
15. See the introduction to *PAW*, 7–21, and chapter 4 of this text.

Appendix

1. Shlomo Pines, "Spinoza's *Tractatus Theologico-Politicus*, Maimonides and Kant," in *Further Studies in Philosophy*, ed. Ora Segal, Scripta Hierosolymitana 20 (Jerusalem: Magres, 1968), 20:3–54.

2. In Twersky, *Medieval Jewish History*, 82–109.
3. See Alexander Altmann, "Maimonides on the Intellect and the Scope of Metaphysics," in *Von der mittelalterlichen zur modernen Aufklärung* (Tübingen: Mohr, 1987), 2:60–129; and Herbert A. Davidson, "Maimonides on Metaphysical Knowledge," in *Maimonidean Studies*, ed. Arthur Hyman (New York: Yeshiva University Press, 1992–93), 3:49–103. Davidson counts himself among students of Pines (55).
4. See Marvin Fox, *Interpreting Maimonides* (Chicago: University of Chicago Press, 1990). Just how far Fox goes in Pines's direction is evident in the way he tries to distance himself from any reduction of Maimonides's position to Kant's on the very same page that he ascribes the method of antinomy to Maimonides (83). Fox is quite taken with Pines's stress on the limits of reason in Maimonides. Indeed, he says, "Despite the recent work of Altmann and Pines, the widespread failure to recognize Maimonides' rigorous awareness of the limits of reason continues to be one of the mysteries of the history of Jewish philosophy" (37). For a far less restrained embrace of Pines's thesis, see Kenneth Seeskin, *Searching for a Distant God* (New York: Oxford University Press, 2000), 69–70 and especially 102 for the explicit reference to Pines.
5. One of Pines's leading students, Warren Zev Harvey, has distanced himself from the Maimonides-Kant parallel. See "Political Philosophy and Halakhah in Maimonides," in *Jewish Intellectual History in the Middle Ages*, BINAH series, ed. Joseph Dan (Westport, CT: Praeger, 1994), 3:47–64, esp. 58–59. Nevertheless, Harvey has expanded elsewhere on the parallels between Maimonides and Spinoza, an insight he traces with gratitude to Pines. See Warren Zev Harvey, "A Portrait of Spinoza as a Maimonidean," *Journal of the History of Philosophy* 19, no. 2 (1981): 151–72, especially 151–53. Harvey traces the "distinctive influence" argument first and foremost to his teacher, Pines, but also to an earlier scholar, Leon Roth, as well as Arthur Hyman.
6. Pines, "Spinoza's *Tractatus Theologico-Politicus*," in Ora, *Further Studies in Philosophy*, 3–54.
7. Ibid., 6. Cf. W. Harvey, "Portrait of Spinoza," and Heidi Ravven, "Some Thoughts on What Spinoza Learned from Maimonides about the Prophetic Imagination," *Journal of the History of Philosophy* 39, no. 2 (2001): 193–214; 39, no. 3 (2001): 385–406. For an extended critique of Harvey's reading of the relation between Maimonides and Spinoza, see my *Maimonides and Spinoza*; for a critique of Ravven, see chapter 6.
8. See W. Harvey, "Halakhah in Maimonides," 58–59.
9. MS Pococke 206, Bodleian Library, University of Oxford. Strauss had already reported a similar quotation about political happiness from Ibn Tufayl in *Hayy the Son of Yaqzan*, at least as early as "Farabi's *Plato*," 372n39. Both Strauss and Pines also note the existence of reports by Averroës on this matter. See ibid. and Pines, "Limitations of Human Knowledge," 85. According to Pines, Averroës developed his doctrine of the hylic intellect in response to Alfarabi's reservations

about the possibility of human acquisition of the kind of knowledge described in Aristotle's *On the Soul*, 3.4, on the coincidence of the thinker, the thing thought, and the activity of thinking. That is, Alfarabi had reservations about whether human beings could become like Aristotle's unmoved movers in *Metaphysics*, 12.9, and thereby achieve immortality.

The Ibn Bājja text in question was published in *Rasā'il Falsafiyya li-Abī Bakr ibn Bājja*, ed. J. Alaoui (Casablanca, 1983), 197–202, cited in Davidson, "Metaphysical Knowledge," 56n26.

10. Pines, "Truth and Falsehood," in Twersky, *Studies in Maimonides*, 95–157. I say "at least in part" meant to "shore up this thesis" because a troubling contradiction soon emerges between the main focus of the 1990 (and other) article(s) (the Maimonides-Spinoza connection) and the ultimate claim of the 1979 article (the Maimonides-Kant connection). It is difficult or impossible to reconcile a Maimonides who is like Spinoza in privileging theoretical intellect and denigrating practical intellect with a Maimonides who is like Kant in privileging the practical intellect over theoretical intellect. For the Maimonides who is like Spinoza and unlike Kant, see especially Pines, "On Spinoza's Conception of Human Freedom and of Good and Evil," in *Spinoza—His Thought and Work*, ed. Nathan Rotenstreich, 147–59 (Jerusalem: Israel Academy of Sciences and Humanities, 1983), 152, which seems to be what Warren Zev Harvey cites in "Portrait of Spinoza," 151–52n4, as "A Note on Spinoza's Conception of Freedom and of Good and Evil," said to be forthcoming in a book to be published in 1983.

11. Pines, "Limitations of Human Knowledge," 82. The interested reader should see especially Ibn Bajja's interpretation of these claims (83).

12. See *Hayy the son of Yaqzan*, in Parens and Macfarland, *Medieval Political Philosophy*, 109. Again, if Pines is correct, as seems likely, that Averroës's doctrine of the hylic intellect is meant as a response to Alfarabi's lost commentary, it is readily apparent that Averroës also considered the immortality of the soul as the problem at issue.

13. Pines, "Limitations of Human Knowledge," 97. Pines assumes that with reservations about the number and essence of the separate intellects and God so come reservations about eternity versus creation. Of course, here he has the surface of the *Guide* to support him. Maimonides does seem to treat creation versus eternity as undecidable.

14. Of course, this phrase signifies more than the superlunary heavenly bodies and their intellects. It signifies divine science (*'ilm ilāhī*) or metaphysics as a whole.

15. This claim about Alfarabi has not been verified. I doubt that Alfarabi would have asserted the demonstrability of this claim. Could it be that eternity is an indemonstrable starting point? I believe that Maimonides's claim that Aristotle took this as an assumption need not imply that there is as little ground for this assumption as for the believer's assumption that the world is created. Eternity was a widely held assumption among all ancient thinkers, as is evident in Aristotle's frequent references in both the *Physics* and *Metaphysics* to the broad

consensus on the view that nothing comes from nothing. The assumption of eternity is tantamount to the assumption that the world is natural.

16. This thesis is especially problematic in interpreting the thought of a philosopher who admits so candidly the necessity of employing secretive forms of writing. See Alfarabi, introd. to his *Summary of Plato's "Laws,"* in Parens and Macfarland, *Medieval Political Philosophy*, 72–73.
17. Pines, "Truth and Falsehood," in Twersky, *Studies in Maimonides*, 116. Compare Strauss's criticism of the modern historian of philosophy's appeal to development in the Spinoza article (*PAW*, 159).
18. The sheer size of the 1990 article on "Truth and Falsehood" may be responsible in part for Pines's inattention to the problems this article poses to his earlier thesis. Its size is dictated by a view the modern historian of philosophy shares with modern science: the more exhaustive one's collection of data, the better.
19. Pines, "Truth and Falsehood," in Twersky, *Studies in Maimonides*, 110. The closest we have to such a comment in the "Limitations of Human Knowledge" article is Pines's direct translation of Ibn Bajja's excuse that the three radical theses were made based on a "first reading" of Aristotle's *Nicomachean Ethics* (82–83). Unfortunately, in "Truth and Falsehood," 110, Pines does not give a precise citation.
20. Pines, "Truth and Falsehood," in Twersky, *Studies in Maimonides*, 110n43.
21. Ibid., 113–15, esp. 114.
22. I address this theme in the second part of this chapter. See also Howard Kreisel's critique of this view as it was developed by Warren Zev Harvey and Sara Klein-Braslavy, in *Maimonides' Political Thought* (SUNY Press, 1999), chaps. 2 and 3.
23. In addition, the *Metaphysics*, especially the well-studied book 12, not to mention material in books 6, 8, and 9, is filled with the use of the good as a principle within metaphysics, not only ethics. Perhaps Maimonides believed that Aristotle at times overstated his teleology for theologico-political reasons rather than strictly theoretical reasons.
24. Alfarabi, *Political Regime*, in Parens and Macfarland, *Medieval Political Philosophy*, 46; Alfarabi, *Selected Aphorisms*, aphor. 31; *Guide*, 2.36.
25. Pines excludes all metaphysical knowledge after an unpersuasive argument that Maimonides himself seems to have reduced metaphysics to the study of God and the intellects. In other words, ignorance about these beings is tantamount to metaphysical ignorance. See Pines, "Limitations of Human Knowledge," 97–98. That this reduction of metaphysics is untenable is evident in the way that Pines already excluded knowledge of eternity versus creation on page 97. Human beings might lack a detailed knowledge of the essence of God and the intellects, perhaps even of the existence of some of them, and yet know that the world is eternal. Indeed, I believe that Maimonides achieves real insight into Aristotle's own views in questioning human knowledge of the details about the unmoved movers.
26. See Altmann, "Maimonides on the Intellect"; Davidson, "Metaphysical Knowledge"; and Barry Kogan, "'What Can We Know and When Can We Know It?'

Maimonides on the Active Intelligence and Human Cognition," in *Moses Maimonides and His Time*, ed. Eric Ormsby (Washington: Catholic University of America Press, 1989), 121–37.

27. Pines, "Limitations of Human Knowledge," 97.
28. Ibid., 93.
29. Maimonides cultivates in his inattentive reader a misleading tendency to artificially separate physics from metaphysics through his early identification of the former with the Account of the Beginning and the latter with the Account of the Chariot. Yet just as creation is said to make all miracles, especially miraculous forms of prophecy, possible (*Guide*, 2.25), so fixed sublunar natures are incompatible with such miracles.
30. Butterworth, *Ethical Writings of Maimonides*, 87.
31. To make such an argument, Thomas Aquinas felt it necessary to argue, on the one hand, for eternal creation and, on the other, that existence or *esse* is actuality; that is, God knows particular beings as well as Aristotle's God knew the forms. The latter argument in particular has had almost incalculable consequences. Maimonides does not give any evidence of having considered such an approach, as is evident, for example, in his treatment of providence.
32. Maimonides refers here to his Code of Law, or *Mishneh Torah*, and his *Commentary on the Mishnah*.
33. Contrary to the frequent citation of Socrates's doubts about the perceptible at the end of book 5 of the *Republic*, consider his identification of the third perceptible level of the divided line as the level subject to *pistis* (511d8).
34. Kant, *Prolegomena*, secs. 21, 46, 48, 52. This is implied in substance's placement under relation in the categories. It can also be argued quite easily.
35. Ibid., secs. 48, 55, 57–58.
36. Maimonides juxtaposes the connection he draws between the body and morality (*Guide*, 3.27–28, esp. 28, 514) with a stunning exploration of the role of fear of the Lord in Abraham's love of the Lord (3.24).
37. Kant, *Prolegomena*, app.

BIBLIOGRAPHY

Works by Alfarabi

Attainment of Happiness. In *Alfarabi: Philosophy of Plato and Aristotle*. Translated by Muhsin Mahdi. Rev. ed. Ithaca, NY: Cornell University Press, 2001. Selections are also in Parens and Macfarland, *Medieval Political Philosophy*, 56–71. Translated by Charles E. Butterworth. Arabic: *Taḥṣīl al-saʿāda*. Edited by Jafar al-Yasin. Beirut: al-Andaloss, 1981. See also Muhsin Mahdi's notes to the Arabic in the *Philosophy of Plato and Aristotle*.

Book of Letters. Arabic: *Kitāb al-hurūf*. Edited by Muhsin Mahdi. Beirut: Dar al-Mashriq, 1969.

Book of Religion. In *Alfarabi: The Political Writings; "Selected Aphorisms" and Other Texts*. Translated and annotated by Charles E. Butterworth. Ithaca, NY: Cornell University Press, 2001. Also in Parens and Macfarland, *Medieval Political Philosophy*, 24–35. Translated by Charles E. Butterworth. Arabic: *Abū Naṣr al-Fārābī, Kitāb al-Milla wa Nuṣūṣ Ukhrā*. Edited by Muhsin Mahdi. Beirut: Dar al-Mashriq, 1968.

Enumeration of the Sciences. In *Alfarabi: The Political Writings; "Selected Aphorisms" and Other Texts*. Translated and annotated by Charles E. Butterworth. Ithaca, NY: Cornell University Press, 2001. Chapter 5 is in Parens and Macfarland, *Medieval Political Philosophy*, 18–23. Translated by Charles E. Butterworth. Arabic: *Abū Naṣr al-Fārābī, Kitāb al-Milla wa Nuṣūṣ Ukhrā*. Edited by Muhsin Mahdi, 41–66. Beirut: Dar al-Mashriq, 1968. And for the final paragraphs of section 5, *Iḥṣāʾ al-ʿUlūm li-al-Fārābī*. Edited by ʿUthmān Amīn. 2nd ed. Cairo: Dār al-Fikr al-ʿArabī, 1949.

Harmonization of the Two Opinions of the Two Sages: Plato the Divine and Aristotle. In *Alfarabi: The Political Writings; "Selected Aphorisms" and Other Texts*. Translated and annotated by Charles E. Butterworth. Ithaca, NY: Cornell University Press, 2001. For the Arabic (and a French translation), see *L'Harmonie entre les opinions de Platon et d'Aristote*. Edited by Fawzi M. Najjar and Dominique Mallet. Damascus: Institut Français de Damas, 1999.

Philosophy of Aristotle. In *Alfarabi: Philosophy of Plato and Aristotle*. Translated by Muhsin Mahdi. Rev. ed. Ithaca, NY: Cornell University Press, 2001. Arabic: *Falsafat Aristūtālīs*. Edited by Muhsin Mahdi. Beirut: Dār Majallat Shiʾr, 1961.

Philosophy of Plato. In *Alfarabi: Philosophy of Plato and Aristotle*. Translated by Muhsin Mahdi. Rev. ed. Ithaca, NY: Cornell University Press, 2001. Arabic: *De Platonis philosophia*. Edited by Franz Rosenthal and Richard Walzer. London: Warburg Institute, 1943.

Political Regime. In *Alfarabi: The Political Writings*. Vol. 2, *"Political Regime" and "Summary of Plato's Laws."* Translated and annotated by Charles E. Butterworth. Ithaca, NY: Cornell University Press, 2015. Also in Parens and Macfarland, *Medieval Political Philosophy*, 36–55. Translated by Charles E. Butterworth. Ithaca, NY: Cornell University Press, 2011. Arabic: *al-Siyāsa al-Madaniyya*. Edited by Fauzi M. Najjar. Beirut: al-Matbaʻa al-kāthūlīkiyya, 1964.

Summary of Plato's Laws. In *Alfarabi: The Political Writings*. Vol. 2, *"Political Regime" and "Summary of Plato's Laws."* Translated and annotated by Charles E. Butterworth. Ithaca, NY: Cornell University Press, 2015. The preface is translated in Parens and Macfarland, *Medieval Political Philosophy*, 72–73. Translated by Muhsin Mahdi. Arabic: *Le Sommaire du livre des "Lois" de Platon (Jawāmiʻ kitāb al-nawāmīs li-Aflāṭūn)*. In *Bulletin d'Études Orient   ales* 50 (1998): 109–55.

Virtuous City; or, *Principles of the Opinions of the Inhabitants of the Virtuous City*. In *Al-Farabi on the Perfect State*. Translated by Richard Walzer. Oxford: Clarendon Press, 1985. Includes Arabic on facing pages.

Works by Maimonides

Eight Chapters. Translated by Charles E. Butterworth in *Ethical Writings of Maimonides*. Edited by Raymond L. Weiss and Charles Butterworth, 78–80. Reprint, New York: Dover, 1983. Chapter 6 is in Parens and Macfarland, *Medieval Political Philosophy*, 180–82. Translated by Joshua Parens. Judeo-Arabic: *Mishnah ʻim Perush Rabbeinu Mosheh ben Maimon*. Edited by Joseph Kafiḥ. Jerusalem: Mossad ha-Rav Kook, 1963–68.

The Guide of the Perplexed. Translated by Shlomo Pines. Chicago: University of Chicago Press, 1963. Judeo-Arabic: *Dalālat al-ḥāʼirin*. In *Le Guide des Égarés*. Edited by S. Munk. 3 Vols. Paris: A. Franck, 1856–66. Revised and reissued by Issachar Joel (Jerusalem: Yunovits, 1931).

Mishneh Torah. Vol. 1, *The Book of Knowledge*. Edited by Moses Hyamson. Jerusalem: Feldheim Publishers, 1981. Critical edition of the Hebrew on facing pages.

The Treatise on the Art of Logic. Chapter 14 is translated by Charles E. Butterworth in *Ethical Writings of Maimonides*. Edited by Raymond L. Weiss and Charles Butterworth, 158–61. Reprint, New York: Dover, 1983. Selections from chapter 14 are in Parens and Macfarland, *Medieval Political Philosophy*, 180–82. Translated by Muhsin Mahdi. Judeo-Arabic: *Maqāla fī ṣināʻat al-manṭiq*. Edited by Mubahat Türker. In *Ankara Üniversitesi Dil ve Tarih-Coğrafya Fakültesi Dergisi* 18 (1960): 40–64.

Works by Strauss

The Argument and Action of Plato's "Laws." Chicago: University of Chicago Press, 1975.

The City and Man. Chicago: University of Chicago Press, 1978.
"Eine vermisste Schrift Farābīs." *Monatsschrift für Geschichte und Wissenschaft des Judentums* 80 (1936): 96–106.
"Farabi's *Plato*." In *Louis Ginzberg*, Jubilee volume, edited by Alexander Marx, Saul Lieberman, Shalom Spiegel, and Solomon Zeitlin, 357–93. New York: American Academy for Jewish Research, 1945.
Gesammelte Schriften. Vol. 3, *Hobbes' Politische Wissenschaft und zugehörige Schriften—Briefe*. Edited by Heinrich Meier. Stuttgart: Metzler, 2001.
Jewish Philosophy and the Crisis of Modernity: Essays and Lectures in Modern Jewish Thought. Edited by Kenneth Hart Green. Albany: State University of New York, 1997.
Liberalism Ancient and Modern. New York: Basic Books, 1968.
"Maimonides' Statement on Political Science." In *WIPP*, 155–69.
"On Abravanel's Critique of Monarchy." 1937. Appendix E, in Yaffe and Ruderman, *Reorientation*. German: "Zu Abravanels Kritik des Königtums." In *Gesammelte Schriften*, vol 2, *Philosophie und Gesetz—Frühe Schriften*, edited by Heinrich Meier, 233–34. Stuttgart: Metzler, 1997.
"On Abravanel's Philosophical Tendency and Political Teaching." In *Isaac Abravanel: Six Lectures*, edited by J. B. Trend and H. Loewe, 95–129. Cambridge: Cambridge University Press, 1937.
On Tyranny. Revised and expanded by Victor Gourevitch and Michael S. Roth. New York: Free Press, 1991.
Persecution and the Art of Writing. Chicago: University of Chicago Press, 1988.
Philosophie und Gesetz: Beiträge zum Verständnis Maimunis und Seiner Vorläufer. Berlin: Schocken Verlag, 1935.
Philosophy and Law. Translated by Eve Adler. Albany: State University of New York Press, 1995. Originally published as *Philosophie und Gesetz: Beiträge zum Verständnis Maimunis und Seiner Vorläufer*. Berlin: Schocken Verlag, 1935.
"The Place of the Doctrine of Providence according to Maimonides." Translated by Gabriel Bartlett and Svetozar Minkov. *Review of Metaphysics* 57 (2004): 537–49. Originally published as "Der Ort der Vorsehungslehre nach der Ansicht Maimunis." *Monatschrift für Geschichte und Wissenschaft des Judentums* 81, no. 1 (1937): 93–105.
"Progress or Return?" *Modern Judaism* 1 (1981): 17–45.
"Some Remarks on the Political Science of Maimonides and Farabi." Translated by Robert Bartlett for *Interpretation* 18, no. 1 (1990): 3–30. Originally published as "Quelques remarques sur la science politique de Maïmonide et Farabi." *Revue des Études Juives* 100 (1936): 1–37.
Spinoza's Critique of Religion. Translated by E. M. Sinclair. New York: Schocken, 1965. Reprint, Chicago: University of Chicago Press, 1997. Originally published as *Die Religionkritik Spinozas als Grundlage seiner Bibelwissenschaft Untersuchungen zu Spinozas Theologisch-Politischen Traktat*. Berlin: Akademie-Verlag, 1930.
Studies in Platonic Political Philosophy. Chicago: University of Chicago Press, 1983.
Thoughts on Machiavelli. Chicago: University of Chicago Press, 1984.
What Is Political Philosophy? Chicago: University of Chicago Press, 1988.

Other Primary Literature

Abravanel, Isaac. Selections from his biblical commentaries. Translated by Robert Sacks. In Parens and Macfarland, *Medieval Political Philosophy*, 220–30.
Aquinas, Thomas. *Summa contra gentiles*. Translated by Anton Pegis. Notre Dame, IN: University of Notre Dame Press, 1975.
Aristotle. *Nicomachean Ethics*. Translated by Robert C. Bartlett and Susan D. Collins. Chicago: University of Chicago Press, 2011.
Averroës. *Decisive Treatise*. Translated by Charles E. Butterworth. In Parens and Macfarland, *Medieval Political Philosophy*, 162–79. Arabic: Averroës. *Decisive Treatise and Epistle Dedicatory*. Edited by Charles E. Butterworth. Provo, UT: Brigham Young University Press, 2001.
Avicenna. *Healing: Metaphysics* 10. In Parens and Macfarland, *Medieval Political Philosophy*, 77–88.
———. *On the Division of the Rational Sciences*. In Parens and Macfarland, *Medieval Political Philosophy*, 74–76.
Gersonides. *The Wars of the Lord*. Translated by Seymour Feldman. 3 vols. Philadelphia: Jewish Publication Society, 1984.
Halevi, Judah. *Kuzari; or, Book of Refutation and Proof on Behalf of the Despised Religion*. Selections translated by Barry Kogan. In Parens and Macfarland, *Medieval Political Philosophy*, 162–79.
Ibn Bājja. *Rasā'il Falsafiyya li-Abī Bakr ibn Bājja*. Edited by J. Alaoui. Casablanca, 1983.
Spinoza. *Theologico-Political Treatise*. Translated by Martin D. Yaffe. Newburyport, MA: Focus, 2004.

Secondary Literature

Altmann, Alexander. "Maimonides on the Intellect and the Scope of Metaphysics." In *Von der mittelalterlichen zur modernen Aufklärung*, edited by Alexander Altmann, 2:60–129. Tübingen: Mohr, 1987.
Benardete, Seth. *The Argument of the Action: Essays on Greek Poetry and Philosophy*. Edited by Ronna Burger and Michael Davis. Chicago: University of Chicago Press, 2000.
———. *Socrates' Second Sailing*. Chicago: University of Chicago Press, 1989.
Ben Shammai, Haggai. "Kalam in Medieval Jewish Philosophy." In *The History of Jewish Philosophy*, edited by Daniel H. Frank and Oliver Leaman, 127–32. London: Routledge, 1997.
Berman, Lawrence V. "A Reexamination of Maimonides' 'Statement on Political Science.'" *Journal of the American Oriental Society* 89, no. 1 (1969): 106–11.
Bloom, Allan. *The Republic of Plato*. New York: Basic Books, 1968.
Butterworth, Charles E. *Ethical Writings of Maimonides*. Edited by Raymond L. Weiss and Charles Butterworth. New York: Dover, 1983.

Davidson, Herbert A. "Maimonides on Metaphysical Knowledge." In *Maimonidean Studies*, edited by Arthur Hyman, 3:49–103. New York: Yeshiva University Press, 1992–93.

———. *Moses Maimonides: The Man and His Work*. New York: Oxford University Press, 2004.

Fakhry, Majid. *A History of Islamic Philosophy*. 3rd ed. New York: Columbia University Press, 2004.

Fox, Marvin. *Interpreting Maimonides*. Chicago: University of Chicago Press, 1990.

Frank, Daniel H. "What Is Jewish Philosophy?" In *The History of Jewish Philosophy*, edited by Daniel Frank and Oliver Leaman, 1–10. London: Routledge, 1997.

Galston, Miriam. "A Re-examination of al-Fārābī's Neoplatonism." *Journal of the History of Philosophy* 25, no. 1 (1977): 13–32.

Gilson, Étienne. *History of Christian Philosophy in the Middle Ages*. New York: Random House, 1955.

Green, Kenneth Hart. *Leo Strauss on Maimonides: The Complete Writings*. Chicago: University of Chicago Press, 2013.

———, ed. Preface to *Hobbes' Politische Wissenschaft*. In Strauss, *Jewish Philosophy*. 453–56.

Gutas, Dimitri. *Avicenna and the Aristotelian Tradition*. Leiden: Brill, 1988.

Guttmann, Julius. *Philosophies of Judaism*. New York: Schocken, 1973. Originally published as *Die Philosophie des Judentums*. Munich: Reinhardt, 1933.

Harvey, Steven. "Aristotle's *Phronesis* in Medieval Islamic and Jewish Philosophy." Paper presented at the University of Georgia, Athens, April 25, 2012.

Harvey, Warren Zev. "Maimonides' Critical Epistemology and *Guide* 2:24." *Aleph* 8 (2008): 213–35.

———. "Political Philosophy and Halakhah in Maimonides." In *Jewish Intellectual History in the Middle Ages*, edited by Joseph Dan, 3:47–64. BINAH series. Westport, CT: Praeger, 1994.

———. "A Portrait of Spinoza as a Maimonidean." *Journal of the History of Philosophy* 19, no. 2 (1981): 151–72.

———. "Why Maimonides Was Not a Mutakallim." In *Perspectives on Maimonides*, edited by Joel L. Kraemer, 105–14. Oxford: Oxford University Press, 1991.

Hasnawi, Ahmad. "Réflexions sur la terminologie logique de Maïmonide et son contexte farabien: Le *Guide de perplexes* et la Traité de logique." In *Maïmonide: Philosophe et Savant*, edited by Tony Lévy and Roshdi Rashed, 39–78. Leuven: Peeters, 2004.

Kellner, Menachem. *Maimonides on Human Perfection*. Atlanta: Scholars, 1990.

Kraemer, Joel L. "The *Jihād* of the *Falāsifa*." *Jerusalem Studies in Arabic and Islam* 10 (1987): 288–324.

———. "Maimonides on the Philosophic Sciences in His *Treatise on the Art of Logic*." In *Perspectives on Maimonides*, edited by Joel L. Kraemer, 77–104. Oxford: Oxford University Press for the Littman Library, 1991.

———. *Maimonides: The Life and World of One of Civilization's Greatest Minds.* New York: Doubleday, 2008.

———. "On Maimonides' Messianic Posture." In Twersky, *Medieval Jewish History,* 2:109–42.

Kramer, Martin. *The Jewish Discovery of Islam.* Syracuse: Syracuse University Press, 1999.

Kreisel, Howard. *Maimonides' Political Thought.* Albany: State University of New York Press, 1999.

Kogan, Barry. "'What Can We Know and When Can We Know It?' Maimonides on the Active Intelligence and Human Cognition." In *Moses Maimonides and His Time,* edited by Eric Ormsby, 121–37. Washington, DC: Catholic University of America Press, 1989.

Lameer, Joep. *Al-Farabi and Aristotelian Syllogistics: Greek Theory and Islamic Practice.* Leiden, NY: Brill, 1994.

Lampert, Laurence. *How Philosophy Became Socratic.* Chicago: University of Chicago Press, 2010.

Lerner, Ralph. *Maimonides' Empire of Light.* Chicago: University of Chicago Press, 2000.

Mahdi, Muhsin. *Alfarabi and the Foundation of Islamic Political Philosophy.* Edited by Charles E. Butterworth. Chicago: University of Chicago Press, 2001.

———. Review of *Al-Farabi on the Perfect State,* trans. Richard Walzer. *Journal of the American Oriental Society* 110, no. 4 (1990): 691–726.

———. "Science, Philosophy, and Religion in Alfarabi's *Enumeration of the Sciences.*" In *The Cultural Context of Medieval Learning,* edited by J. E. Murdoch and E. D. Sylla, 146–47. Dordrecht: Reidel, 1975.

Major, Rafael. *Leo Strauss's Defense of the Philosophic Life: Reading "What Is Political Philosophy?"* Chicago: University of Chicago Press, 2012.

Meier, Heinrich. *Leo Strauss and the Theologico-Political Problem.* New York: Cambridge University Press, 2006.

Nietzsche, Friedrich. *Beyond Good and Evil.* Translated by Walter Kaufman. New York: Random House, 1966.

Parens, Joshua. *An Islamic Philosophy of Virtuous Religions: Introducing Alfarabi.* Albany: State University of New York Press, 2006.

———. "Maimonidean Ethics Revisited." *Journal of Jewish Thought and Philosophy* 12, no. 3 (2003): 33–62.

———. *Maimonides and Spinoza: Their Conflicting Views of Human Nature.* Chicago: University of Chicago Press, 2012.

———. *Metaphysics as Rhetoric: Alfarabi's "Summary of Plato's 'Laws.'"* Albany: State University of New York Press, 1995.

———. "Prudence, Imagination, and Determination of Law in Alfarabi and Maimonides." In *Enlightening Revolutions: Essays in Honor of Ralph Lerner,* edited by Svetozar Minkov and Stéphane Douard, 31–55. Lanham, MD: Lexington Books, 2006.

———. Review of *Alfarabi and the Foundation of Islamic Political Philosophy*, by Muhsin Mahdi. *American Political Science Review* 96, no. 2 (2002): 410–11.
Parens, Joshua, and Joseph C. Macfarland. *Medieval Political Philosophy: A Sourcebook*. 2nd ed. Ithaca, NY: Cornell University Press, 2011.
Pines, Shlomo. "Aristotle's *Politics* in Arabic Philosophy." *Israel Oriental Studies* 5 (1975): 150–60.
———. "Limitations of Human Knowledge According to al-Fārābī, Ibn Bājja, and Maimonides." In Twersky, *Medieval Jewish History*, 82–109. Reprint, *Collected Works of Shlomo Pines*, edited by W. Z. Harvey and Moshe Idel, 5:404–31. Jerusalem: Magnes, 1997.
———. "On Spinoza's Conception of Human Freedom and of Good and Evil." In *Spinoza—His Thought and Work*, edited by Nathan Rotenstreich, 147–59. Jerusalem: Israel Academy of Sciences and Humanities, 1983. Reprint, *Collected Works of Shlomo Pines*, edited by W. Z. Harvey and Moshe Idel, 5:735–47. Jerusalem: Magnes, 1997.
———. "Spinoza's *Tractatus Theologico-Politicus*, Maimonides and Kant." In *Further Studies in Philosophy*, edited by Ora Segal, 20:3–54. Scripta Hierosolymitana 20. Jerusalem: Magres, 1968.
———. "Truth and Falsehood Versus Good and Evil: A Study in Jewish and General Philosophy in Connection with the *Guide of the Perplexed*, I, 2." In *Studies in Maimonides*, edited by Isadore Twersky, 95–157. Cambridge: Harvard University Press, 1990.
Rashed, Marwan. "On the Authorship of the Treatise *On the Harmonization of the Opinions of the Two Sages* Attributed to al-Fārābī." *Arabic Sciences and Philosophy* 19, no. 1 (2009): 43–82.
Ravven, Heidi. "Some Thoughts on What Spinoza Learned from Maimonides about the Prophetic Imagination." *Journal of the History of Philosophy* 39, no. 2 (2001): 193–214; and 39, no. 3 (2001): 385–406.
Rosenthal, Erwin I. J. "Maimonides' Conception of State and Society." In *Moses Maimonides*, edited by I. Epstein, 191–206. London: Soncino, 1935. Reprint, *Studia Semitica*. Vol. 2, *Islamic Themes*. Cambridge: Cambridge University Press, 1971.
———. "The Place of Politics in the Philosophy of Al-Farabi." *Islamic Culture* 29 (1955): 157–78. Reprint, *Studia Semitica*. Vol. 2, *Islamic Themes*. Cambridge: Cambridge University Press, 1971.
———. "The Place of Politics in the Philosophy of Ibn Bājja." In *Studia Semitica*. Vol. 2, *Islamic Themes*. Cambridge: Cambridge University Press, 1971.
———. "Some Aspects of Islamic Political Thought." *Islamic Culture* 22 (1948): 1–17. Also in "The Place of Politics in the Philosophy of Ibn Bājja." *Islamic Culture* 25 (1951): 187–211. Reprint, *Studia Semitica*. Vol. 2, *Islamic Themes*, 35–59. Cambridge: Cambridge University Press, 1971.
Rosenthal, Franz. "On the Knowledge of Plato's Philosophy in the Islamic World." *Islamic Culture* 14 (1940): 387–422.

Seeskin, Kenneth. *Searching for a Distant God*. New York: Oxford University Press, 2000.
Stroumsa, Sarah. *Maimonides in His World: Portrait of a Mediterranean Thinker*. Princeton: Princeton University Press, 2009.
Tanguay, Daniel. *Leo Strauss: An Intellectual Biography*. Translated by Christopher Nadon. New Haven: Yale University Press, 2007.
Twersky, Isadore, ed. *Studies in Medieval Jewish History and Literature*. Cambridge: Harvard University Press, 1979.
Walzer, Richard. "Arabic Transmission of Greek Thought to Medieval Europe." *Bulletin of the John Rylands Library* 29 (1945–46): 160–83.
———. "On the Legacy of the Classics in the Islamic World." In *Greek into Arabic*, edited by Richard Walzer, 29–37. Cambridge, MA: Harvard University Press, 1962.
———. "Platonism in Islamic Philosophy." In *Greek into Arabic*, edited by Richard Walzer, 236–52. Cambridge, MA: Harvard University Press, 1962.
———. "The Rise of Islamic Philosophy." *Oriens* 3 (1950): 1–19.
Wolfson, Harry Austryn. "Note on Maimonides' Classification of the Sciences." *Jewish Quarterly Review* 26 (1935–36): 369–77.
———. *Philo: Foundations of Religious Philosophy in Judaism, Christianity, and Islam*. Cambridge, MA: Harvard University Press, 1968.
———. *The Philosophy of Spinoza*. Cambridge, MA: Harvard University Press, 1934.
Yaffe, Martin D., and Richard S. Ruderman, eds. *Reorientation: Strauss in the 1930s*. New York: Palgrave Macmillan, 2014.

Index

Abravanel, Isaac, x, 84, 92–93
Active Intellect, 76, 85, 133, 143
Adler, Eve, 86
Alexander of Aphrodisias, 91, 132
Altman, William H. F., 63
Anawati, M.-M., 64
ancients versus moderns debate, 55, 137–38
anthropology, "architectonic," vii
Aquinas, Thomas, xi, 3–4, 11, 68, 70–71, 75, 77; Abravanel and, 92; on esotericism, 58; Alfarabi and, 24, 71, 73, 76–78; Maimonides and, 70–71; on natural law, 22, 51; Neo-Thomism and, x, 70; reason/revelation synthesis of, 42–43, 134
Aquinas, Thomas, works of: *Summa contra gentiles*, 68, 70–71; *Summa theologiae*, 68, 70, 75, 77
Argument and the Action of Plato's "Laws," The (Strauss), 20, 101
Aristophanes, 86
Aristotle, 34, 77–78, 139; cosmology of, 145; Alfarabi and, 15, 34, 43–44, 61, 76–78, 94, 108, 116, 139, 141; Latin translations of, ix, xi; Maimonides and, 43, 48, 132; Neoplatonism and, 30, 43, 44, 61, 132; Organon of, 73; on prudence, 30, 34, 74, 78, 114, 151n16; Qur'ān and, 43; on science, 28–29, 34; on theoretical/practical science, 11, 15, 20, 27–29, 34
Aristotle, works of: *Metaphysics*, 6, 27–29, 68–70, 142, 172n11; *Nicomachean Ethics*, 28–29, 70, 73, 77, 114–15, 141–43; *On the Soul*, 176n9; *Politics*, 77, 88, 151n16, 154n6
asceticism, 48–49, 132
Ash'arite theologians, 174n13
astronomy, 163n18

Attainment of Happiness (Alfarabi), 27, 44, 52, 94; certainty in, 64, 115–16; Neoplatonism of, 60; sources of, 45
Augustine of Hippo, ix–xi, 156n17
Averroës, ix, 59; Alfarabi and, xii, 64, 73; Machiavelli and, 97, 98; Maimonides and, 86–87, 97, 109; on natural law, 22; Pines on, 175n9; translations of, xi
"Averroism," 155n5, 169n10
Avicenna, x, 20, 59, 64, 101; on prophecy, 83, 88

Bacon, Francis, 146
Beginning, Account of the, 75, 85, 125, 151n9
Behnegar, Nasser, 153n15
Bellarmine, Robert, x
ben Judah, Joseph, 132
Benardete, Seth, 154n6
Bible, 75, 138; Amos, 103; Jeremiah, 51; Job, 89
Boethius, 58
Book of Religion (Alfarabi), 15, 24, 67–68, 71–77, 152n12
Burger, Ronna, 154n1
Butterworth, Charles E., xi, 24, 115

Chariot, Account of the, 75, 84–85, 91, 107, 125, 151n9
Cicero, viii–ix, xi
City and Man (Strauss), 5, 6, 55, 119, 123
contemplative life, 49–50, 61–63
cosmology, 117; of Aristotle, 145; of Alfarabi, 15, 47, 151n13; of Maimonides, 47–48, 128, 129, 144, 145, 147, 153n15
Cropsey, Joseph, 152n6

Dante Alighieri, xii, 11

187

INDEX

Davidson, Herbert, 168n3
democracy, 55–56, 96, 161n3
Descartes, René, 57, 146
divine law, 22, 25–26, 115, 122, 125; *nomoi* versus, 101; Pines on, 117; prophetology and, 18–21; *sharī'a* and, 12, 71, 101, 161n6; Strauss on, 113. *See also* Law
Drury, Shadia, 63

Enlightenment thought, xi, 55, 56, 86–88, 97, 161n53
Enumeration of the Sciences (Alfarabi), 24, 34, 72, 74, 94, 120
Epicurus, 125
esotericism, 41–42, 57, 87; Aquinas on, 58; degrees of, 44–45; Alfarabi on, 22, 59; irony and, 53–54; Maimonides on, 2, 4, 22, 24, 127; Nietzsche on, 59, 161n4; Spinoza on, 56–57, 138; Strauss on, 6, 21, 41–42, 87; Tanguay on, 83
Euclid's *Elements*, 57

faith, 19, 93, 128–29, 147; articles of, 25, 90, 122; monotheistic, 3, 39, 41, 98–99, 102–4, 109, 115; teaching of, 68–71. *See also* reason/faith problem
Fakhry, Majid, 14, 67, 78–79
falāsifa (philosophers), 49, 51; esotericism of, 59; Halevi and, 62–64; Maimonides and, 62–64, 88, 89; Neoplatonism of, 60–61, 64
Alfarabi, ix–xii, 2, 83–94; Aquinas and, 24, 71, 73, 76–78; Aristotle and, 15, 34, 43–44, 61, 76–78, 94, 108, 116, 139, 141; Averroës and, xii, 63, 73; cosmology of, 15, 47, 151n13; on divine law, 20; on divisions of politics, 102–3; esotericism of, 22, 52–54, 59; on happiness, 46, 139, 141–42; Ibn Bajja on, 139–40; on immortality, 52–53, 61, 140–42; on *kalām*, 4, 23, 71–75; on metaphysics, 15, 45–49, 67–68, 71, 72, 75–79; on natural law, 22; Neoplatonism and, 14–15, 27, 30–32, 44, 60–61, 64, 117–18; on philosopher-king, 34, 78, 132–33; Plato and, 15, 43–46, 52, 60–61, 94; on political science, 76–79, 115–18; predecessors of, 45; "religious neutrality" of, 120; Scholasticism and, 14–15, 59, 63–65; on theoretical/practical science, 14–15, 31–33, 115; translations of, xi. *See also specific works*
"Farabi's *Plato*" (Strauss), 5–6, 61, 108, 120, 123–24, 140
Finkelschere, H., 167n27
fiqh (jurisprudence), 13–14, 40–41, 71, 121, 145
first philosophy, 6, 7, 119, 123
Fortin, Ernest, xii
Fox, Marvin, 175n4

Galston, Miriam, 61
Gardet, Louis, 64
Gersonides (Levi ben Gershom), 86, 87
Great Chain of Being, 27, 31, 32, 48
Guide of the Perplexed (Maimonides), 2–4, 42–43, 113–18; asceticism in, 48–49; cosmology of, 47–48; esotericism of, 2, 4; Alfarabi's *Enumeration* and, 74–75; introduction to, 125–35; *kalām* in, 72; numerology in, 106; Pines's translation of, 138, 139, 149n4; as political philosophy, 119–24; prophetology in, 25–26, 84–85, 88, 107
Guttmann, Julius, 17, 20, 86, 87, 89–90

Halevi, Judah, x, 38, 134; critique of philosophy by, 22; *falāsifa* and, 62–64; *Kuzari* by, 21–22, 49–50; on reason/faith problem, 49–50; "Scholastic" model of, 155n5
happiness, 102; Alfarabi on, 46, 139, 141–42; Maimonides on, 99–101, 113–18; political, 113–18
Harvey, Warren Zev, 139, 172m3, 175n5
Hegel, G. W. F., 98, 109, 162n7
Heidegger, Martin, 162n10
hermeneutics, 138. *See also* esotericism
historicism, 17–18; definition of, 96; Scholasticism and, 57–59; Spinoza and, 56–57
Hobbes, Thomas, 3, 18, 57, 96–98, 146
Hobbes' Politische Wissenschaft (Strauss), 1
Hume, David, 146

INDEX 189

Ibn Bajja, 113, 139–41, 143, 160n51
Ibn Kaspi, 167n27
Ibn Khaldun, xi
Ibn Rushd. *See* Averroës
Ibn Sina. *See* Avicenna
Ibn Tibbon, Samuel, 22, 44, 94, 104
Ibn Tufayl, x, 140
Ibn Tumert, 127
immortality of soul, 52–53, 61, 140–43
Islamic Philosophy of Virtuous Religions, An (Parens), 77

jadal ("dialectic"), 72–73
Joseph ben Judah, 132
Judeo-Arabic, ix, 39

kalām ("dialectical theology"), 43, 71–75, 89–90, 128–30; atypical, 63; Christian theology and, 42, 135; definition of, 13–14, 149n5; "enlightened," 2, 4, 23–24, 63, 75, 90, 101, 120–22; *jadal* versus, 72–73; pitfalls of, 90; traditional, 23–24, 73, 90, 169n19; "vulgar," 4, 23, 75, 120–21
al-kamāl al-naẓarī ("theoretical perfection"), 116, 118
Kant, Immanuel, 57, 76, 113, 129, 137–38; metaphysics of, 143, 144–45, 147
Kojève, Alexandre, 98, 109
Kraemer, Joel L., 100–101, 169nn12–13, 170n27
Kries, Douglas, vii–xii, 154n2

Law, 2, 22, 51, 105, 117, 135; prophetology and, 18–21; revealed, 12, 15; "true science" of, 13, 14, 90, 121–22, 130–31. *See also* divine law
"Law of Reason in the *Kuzari*" (Strauss), 50–51, 62–63, 92
Lessing, Gotthold Ephraim, 17
"Literary Character of the *Guide for the Perplexed*" (Strauss), 2, 6, 23, 24, 83–84, 89–90, 93, 120
Locke, John, 56, 96–97
Lovejoy, Arthur, 27, 31

Machiavelli, Niccolò, 60, 96–99; Averroës and, 97, 98; critique of religion by, 99, 105, 150n1; Maimonides and, 97, 99, 109

Macierowski, Edward, 154n2
macrocosm/microcosm, 46–48, 117
Mahdi, Muhsin, 24, 63, 78–79, 100; career of, xi; on Alfarabi's Platonism, 115
Maimonides, Moses, ix–xi, 23–24, 143–44; Aristotle and, 43, 48, 132; Averroës and, 86–87, 97, 109; career of, 127; cosmology of, 47–48, 128, 129, 144, 145, 147, 153n15; division of sciences by, 105–9; esotericism of, 2, 4, 22, 24, 127; *falāsifa* and, 62–64, 88, 89; on *fiqh*, 13–14; on happiness, 99–101, 113–18; Machiavelli and, 97, 99, 109; Mendelssohn on, 102; on metaphysics, 14, 45–49, 75, 134, 143–44, 151n9; on miracles, 144; as *mutakallim*, 89–90; on natural law, 22; on numerology, 95, 106–8; on philosopher-king, 93, 133; political science of, 7, 100–101, 121–22, 131–32; on prudence, 114, 117, 142; rationalism of, 17; on reason/faith problem, 23, 42–43, 49, 50; on theoretical/practical science, 13–14
Maimonides, Moses, works of: *Commentary on the Mishnah*, 25, 51, 122; *Mishneh Torah*, 88, 120, 125, 127, 150n6; *Treatise on the Art of Logic*, 7, 24–25, 95, 99–109, 121–22, 131. See also *Guide of the Perplexed*
"Maimonides' Statement on Political Science" (Strauss), 95, 97
Manicheanism, 30
Marsilius of Padua, 11, 22, 51, 155n5
Meier, Heinrich, 5, 97
Mendelssohn, Moses, 102
metaphysics, 114, 116; Aristotle on, 6, 27–29, 68–70, 142, 172n11; ethics and, 142; Alfarabi on, 15, 45–49, 67–68, 71, 72, 75–79; happiness and, 114; Maimonides on, 14, 45–49, 75, 134, 143–44, 151n9; political philosophy and, 6, 33, 72, 76–79. *See also* theology
Metaphysics as Rhetoric (Parens), 67, 151n8, 158n27
microcosm/macrocosm, 46–48, 117. *See also* cosmology
modernity, 17–18, 67, 146, 147

monotheism, 3, 39, 41, 98–99; as universalistic religion, 102–4, 109, 115
Moses, 25, 93, 101, 125, 133
mutakallimūm (dialectical theologians), 43; atypical, 63; Maimonides on, 89–90, 121, 145. *See also kalām*
Mu'tazilite kalām, 22, 63, 152n9, 174n13; Guttmann on, 89–90; "Scholastic" model of, 155n5
mysticism, 92–93, 106, 108

natural law, 22, 51
Neo-Thomism, x, 70
Neoplatonism, 48; Aristotle and, 30, 43, 44, 61, 132; definition of, 156n17; Alfarabi and, 14–15, 27, 30–32, 44, 60–61, 64, 117–18; Plato and, 30, 44–46, 52, 60–61; Rosenthal on, 43; on wisdom, 28
Nietzsche, Friedrich, 1, 3, 63; on esotericism, 59, 161n4; on Platonism, 30
nomoi, 22, 100, 122, 131; commands and, 104–5; divine law versus, 101; Torah versus, 103
numerology, 95, 106–8

ordo cognoscendi/ordo essendi, 69
Owen, Joseph, 68

particularization argument, 73–74, 121
Pegis, Anton, 68
Persecution and the Art of Writing (Strauss), 39, 46, 49–51, 56–64; on esotericism, 59, 87; on immortality, 52–53; on intellectuals, 58; on Maimonides's *Guide*, 74–75; Plato in, 91–92; Spinoza in, 56–57
Philo Judaeus, 39–40
philosopher-king, 15, 115; Abravanel on, 93; as advocate of totalitarianism, 22; Alfarabi on, 34, 78, 132–33; Maimonides on, 93, 133; prophet and, 20–23, 25, 87–88, 113; Socrates as, 29–30
Philosophy and Law (Strauss), 3, 17, 55, 83–89
Philosophy of Plato and Aristotle (Alfarabi), 44–46, 52, 60–61, 76, 94, 108, 116

Pines, Shlomo, 113, 114; on divine law, 117; "Limitations of Human Knowledge" by, 129, 137–47; on Mu'tazilite kalām, 89–90; translation of *The Guide* by, 138, 139, 149n4
"Place of Providence" (Strauss), 89–92
Plato, 6, 30, 69–70, 77; Cicero and, ix; Alfarabi and, 15, 43–46, 52, 60–61, 94; Neoplatonism and, 30, 45, 52, 60–61; Nietzsche on, 30; Presocratics and, 106, 108; theoretical/practical science and, 15, 29–30, 34, 69–70
Plato, works of: *Apology*, 29–30, 86; *The Laws*, 20, 91, 101, 132; *Phaedo*, 30, 71, 86; *Phaedrus*, 30; *Republic*, 20, 30, 33, 70, 92, 131; *Sophist*, 34; *Statesman*, 34; *Timaeus*, 46. *See also* Neoplatonism
Plotinus, 43, 132
political philosophy, viii–ix, 11–15, 33–36, 113–18; Maimonides's *Guide* as, 119–24; political thought versus, vii–x; totalitarian, 20
Political Regime (Alfarabi), 15, 22, 31–33, 44, 117; Maimonides and, 94, 132; metaphysics in, 67–68, 71, 77; Socrates in, 47
political science, 119; Alfarabi on, 33–34, 75–78, 115–18; Maimonides on, 7, 33–34, 100–101, 121–22, 131–32; metaphysics and, 6, 33, 72, 76–79; prophetology as, 84–85, 88, 103; "theoretical perfection" and, 116, 118
practical science. *See* theoretical/practical science
Presocratics, 106, 108
Principles of the Beings (Alfarabi). *See Political Regime*
prophecy, 57, 76, 131–33; Avicenna on, 83, 88; philosopher-king and, 20–23, 25, 87–88, 113; politics and, 88; psychology of, 143
prophetology, 23, 122; divine law and, 18–21; in Maimonides's *Guide*, 25–26, 84–85, 88, 107; as political science, 84–85, 88, 103; providence and, 124
providence, 89, 107; doctrine of, 83–85, 117; particular, 61, 124

prudence, 73; Aristotle on, 30, 34, 74, 78, 114, 151n16; Maimonides on, 114, 117, 142
Pseudo-Dionysius the Areopagite, 70
Pythagoreanism, 30, 89, 108, 162n10

rational law, 22, 51
Reale, Giovanni, 68
reason/faith problem, 2–5, 23, 41–44, 48–52, 54, 58, 134. *See also* faith
religious consciousness, 18, 86
resurrection, bodily, 52–53
Rosenthal, Erwin I. J., 20, 39–40, 77, 160n51; on Alfarabi's sources, 45; on Alfarabi's writings, 44; on reason/revelation synthesis, 42; on *Virtuous City*, 46, 67, 78–79
Rosenthal, Franz, 20, 39–40, 45
Rousseau, Jean-Jacques, 3

Saadya Gaon, 22, 39; Maimonides on, 133–34; Muʿtazilite kalām and, 89; on natural law, 51; "Scholastic" model of, 155n5
Scholasticism, 3–5, 23–26, 39–41, 105, 134; Alfarabi and, 14–15, 59, 63–65; historicism and, 57–59; Maimonides and, 23–24; theoretical/practical science in, 115
ṣedakah (righteousness), 51
Seeskin, Kenneth, 129
sharīʿa, 12, 71, 101, 161n6. *See also* divine law
Socrates, x; death of, viii, 29–30, 47, 61, 70; political philosophy of, 6
Socratic irony, 52–54
solitary philosopher, 21–23, 26, 117–18, 123
sophists, 22, 31, 47
soul, 30, 116; immortality of, 52–53, 61, 140–43
Spinoza, Benedict de, 1–3, 55, 65, 86, 137–39; ecumenism of, 18; esotericism of, 56–57, 138; on final causes, 146; historicism and, 56–57; on politics, 114
Spinoza's Critique of Religion (Strauss), 55

spontaneous generation, 47
Syrian Christians, 72, 120

Talmud, 13, 40–41, 106, 107, 125, 127
Tanguay, Daniel, 83–84, 113
Themistius, 132
theologico-political problem, 1–7, 18, 34–36, 59–61, 97, 150n10
theology, 12, 40–41; apologetic, 71; Aquinas on, 68, 70, 75, 77; jurisprudence and, 14; philosophy and, 39–40, 49–52, 68–71, 75, 134; politics and, 45–49, 67, 105. *See also kalām*; metaphysics
"theoretical perfection" (*al-kamāl al-naẓarī*), 116, 118
theoretical/practical science, 11–15, 34, 114–15; in Aristotle, 11, 15, 20, 27–29, 34; in Alfarabi, 14–15, 31–33, 115; in Maimonides, 13–14; in Plato, 15, 29–30, 34, 69–70
theoria, 5, 114–15
Thomism, x, 70. *See also* Aquinas, Thomas
Thoughts on Machiavelli (Strauss), 5, 6, 55, 60
Torah, 26, 100–103, 119–23; Gersonides on, 87; mysteries of, 75, 85; study of, 13
totalitarianism, 20, 22
Türker, Mubahat, 168n3

virtue: Aristotle on, 28, 30, 151n16; Alfarabi on, 32, 116; Maimonides on, 50, 133; Plato on, 92
Virtuous City (Alfarabi), 15, 31, 44, 46, 67–68, 71, 77
Voegelin, Eric, 98

Walzer, Richard, 39–40; on Alfarabi's sources, 45, 52–53; on immortality, 52; on reason/revelation synthesis, 42
What Is Political Philosophy? (Strauss), 5–6, 95–98, 108
Wolfson, Harry Austryn, 20, 39–42, 103

Xenophon, 95–98

Leo Strauss is known primarily for reviving classical political philosophy. Strauss recovered that great tradition of thought largely lost to the West by beginning his study of classical thought with its teaching on politics rather than its metaphysics. What brought Strauss to this way of reading the classics, however, was a discovery he made as a young political scientist studying the obscure texts of Islamic and Jewish medieval political thought.

In this volume, Joshua Parens examines Strauss's investigations of medieval political philosophy, offering interpretations of his writings on the great thinkers of that tradition, including interpretations of his most difficult writings on Alfarabi and Maimonides. In addition Parens explicates Strauss's statements on Christian medieval thought and his argument for rejecting the Scholastic paradigm as a method for interpreting Islamic and Jewish thought. Contrasting Scholasticism with Islamic and Jewish medieval political philosophy, Parens clarifies the theme of Strauss's thought, what Strauss calls the "theologico-political problem," and reveals the significance of medieval political philosophy in the Western tradition.

Joshua Parens is professor of philosophy and politics and dean of the Braniff Graduate School at the University of Dallas.

www.ingramcontent.com/pod-product-compliance
Lightning Source LLC
Chambersburg PA
CBHW060953230426
43665CB00015B/2175